D1010775

# The Death of the American Trial

# The Death of the American Trial

ROBERT P. BURNS

THE UNIVERSITY OF CHICAGO PRESS     CHICAGO AND LONDON

ROBERT P. BURNS is professor of law at Northwestern University.

The University of Chicago Press, Chicago 60637
The University of Chicago Press, Ltd., London
© 2009 by The University of Chicago
All rights reserved. Published 2009
Printed in the United States of America

18  17  16  15  14  13  12  11  10  09      1  2  3  4  5

ISBN-13: 978-0-226-08126-7 (cloth)
ISBN-10: 0-226-08126-5 (cloth)

Library of Congress Cataloging-in-Publication Data

Burns, Robert P., 1947–
    The death of the American trial / Robert P. Burns.
        p. cm.
    Includes bibliographical references and index.
    ISBN-13: 978-0-226-08126-7 (cloth : alk. paper)
    ISBN-10: 0-226-08126-5 (cloth : alk. paper)
    1. Trials—United States. 2. Justice, Administration of—United States. I. Title.
    KF8910.B87 2009
    347.73'7—dc22                                          2008035777

# Contents

# Acknowledgments

I am grateful to Locke Bowman, Mary Burns, and Steven Lubet, each of whom brought his or her great editing gifts to this manuscript. It is a much better book for their efforts. I appreciate John Tryneski's sophisticated and learned guidance throughout the editing process. I also thank the anonymous readers at the University of Chicago Press for their keen and generous grasp of the enterprise.

Trying cases is very hard work. Lawyers who do this hard work are essential to preserving the rule of law and democratic governance. I am especially indebted to the lawyers who have contributed their services to teaching others their important craft through the National Institute for Trial Advocacy. I have learned more from them than I can tell.

I am grateful as well to my colleagues at Northwestern University School of Law and to my students. The School has generously supported my research.

Earlier versions of short sections of this book have appeared in the *California Law Review*, *American Criminal Law Review*, *DePaul Law Review*, and *Chicago-Kent Law Review*.

# Introduction

The trial as the normal way to deal with litigation, especially civil litigation, was doomed to decline, and perhaps even to vanish, and probably nothing can stop the process. If the trend can be reversed at all, it will be only slightly. We can, so to speak, keep the California condor and the whooping crane alive, but we cannot make them as common as pigeons and sparrows. —Lawrence Friedman

[If the trial dies] the cause will not be a tyrant's ax but a long and scarcely noticed process of decay. Indifference, in the long run, is deadlier than any coup, and democratic institutions are easily lost through neglect followed by decline and abandonment. —Judge William L. Dwyer

This book is an appeal, not an explanation. The American trial is one of our greatest cultural achievements. Not only does it stand in a rich tradition, but it has earned the admiration of most of the people—lawyers, judges, jurors, and social scientists—in the best position to know. Its consciously structured hybrid of languages and practices can realize a usually dormant common sense to achieve unanticipated insight into the persons and events on trial that seems not to be available any other way. Though rooted in tradition, the devices of the trial as they have evolved in response to practical challenges seem keenly calibrated to achieve what we Americans need now. That is to bring our moral and political sensibilities to bear on actual events while preserving stability and respect for the rule of law, and incrementally to adapt our basic structures to those sensibilities. The trial is one of those traditional institutions that have allowed us in the United States to escape the worst of the bureaucratized and ideo-logical cruelties of the "onslaught of modernity." To engage Friedman's analogy, we can now take the bald eagle off the endangered species list because our political will was energized to save an important symbol of our identity.

We may, however, presently be destroying it. The institution of the trial seems to be disappearing in one context after another, and this at a speed that has the sober social scientists who have chronicled it staring in disbe-lief at their own results. The percentage of federal civil cases that ended in trial declined from 11.5 percent in 1962 to an amazing 1.8 percent in 2002, *one-sixth as many*.[1] Though the absolute number of cases "disposed of"—to use a telling metaphor—has increased fivefold, even the abso-lute number of trials has declined. Similar patterns have prevailed in civil, criminal, and bankruptcy proceedings, in federal and state courts, and in both jury and bench trials. The rate of decline has rapidly accelerated in the very recent past. This implosion has occurred just as we have made simple changes in its structure that have, in my view, increasingly realized the power of the institution, its ability to do exactly what we continuously need to do. Not everyone has greeted this decline with dismay. The trial's cultured despisers—historians, economists, a few judges—have seen its demise as the more or less inevitable atrophying of a primitive vestigial organ unsuited to contemporary society. It may have been appropriate for cruder times, but not for our advanced society. This can be the expres-sion of a kind of positivist faith, often with scientistic overtones, that the trial's death is a sign of progress. It can be the expression of a faith in the impersonal workings of our economic and political systems, which are, we are to believe, benignly self-regulating. Or it can, more rarely, have almost a weary Hegelian feel: just as the institution realizes its greatest potential it must, like a ripe fruit, fall off the branch to the ground, there to slowly rot away.

Of course, very different kinds of cases are tried: white-collar and vio-lent crime, medical and (increasingly) legal and accounting malpractice claims, civil rights cases, mass tort cases, large commercial and antitrust cases. Historically, the trials afforded in these areas have been both theo-retically and practically different from each other. That remains true to-day. But the core of the trial has not changed dramatically during the past fifty years, and trials have tended to disappear in all these areas. Crimi-nal cases are plea-bargained. Civil cases are settled or subject to sum-mary dismissal without trial. The context and consequences are somewhat different, but the disappearance of the trial can helpfully be considered as a single development across all these areas. My goal is less to identify the causal mechanisms that together explain the recent catastrophic decline in the number of cases tried than to identify the significance or meaning of this decline. I will ask what this means for our legal order and what it tells us about our broader society.

I proceed in this way because, as Hannah Arendt taught, explanations are dangerous in political matters. They implicitly suggest that the shape of political practices such as the trial is a function of, is inexorably caused by, economic or social or cultural variables and that those connections are beyond political action. So our functionalist commentators are likely to be fatalist where we should be activist: acting in public to save this central mode of acting in public. As Arendt's husband, Heinrich Blücher, warned, "Pessimists are cowards and optimists are fools."[2] For us, justice must emerge from a tension of opposites: justice is strife.[3] Opposed institutions and practices can redeem each other. The more inconsistent trial methods are with our other modes of social ordering, the more necessary they may be for us.

I will argue that the trial, though in statistical decline, has a comprehensiveness among our modes of social ordering that makes it unique. It is here that political purpose, legal structure, and moral sensibility come together under "the discipline of the evidence." That is why the trial is the "central institution of law as we know it," as James Boyd White eloquently put it. It is the place whose disciplines may, in Milner Ball's subtle words, evoke from jurors and judges "a willing suspension of disbelief in their own civility" and allow them to "recognize and act on what is beyond their ordinary selves, just as constitutional law helps the citizenry as a whole to do."[4] That is why, in the more disengaged words of Friedman, a legal historian, the trial has always been central to the "ideology" of the common law.[5] Languages and practices here allow us to engage in an act of practical integration that is crucial for the health of our society. The values in play, though often incommensurable in theory, serve to illuminate the practical task and realize the lawfulness that is appropriate for us now.

I begin with an account of our contemporary trial. Without such an account, we literally do not know what we are talking about, neither when we bemoan nor when we applaud its death. This is essential because of the levels of misinformation that surround it and because the trial too often takes the rap for limitations in its surrounding institutions, both bureaucratic and market. And so I provide a compressed account of what we actually achieve at trial. This account has—indeed must have—an ideal-izing quality, in order to show how ideals are embedded in the details of what we actually do, albeit do less and less often. Here it is essential that I say to the reader, "Don't think, look!,"[6] and so it is my obligation to provide a simple descriptive account of trial practices. But I also should provide some of the layers of justification for these artificial kinds of con-versations to counteract a kind of false populism that very unpopulist crit-ics tend to bring against the trial. It is true, as critic Robert Kagan has said, that the trial combines high levels of participation with high levels of formality. I will show why this combination makes sense. And so I will show how these linguistic practices are of a piece with deeper and broader convictions, "considered judgments of justice," as Rawls likes to say.[7]

The second chapter provides some historical and institutional context. I want to show that the trial has been an important feature of our legal order in America: "Upon this point, a page of history is worth a volume of logic."[8] So, first, I supply only a very short and selective page. I hope to convince the reader that its frequency and its form have often been at the heart of historical focus and controversy and for good reason. A living tradition is always a tradition of argument. My overall argument is that it is important to identify what the death of the trial would mean for us, and, finally, that we should not let the trial "go gentle into that good night."

There are deep continuities of the form of trial as we now have it with earlier forms. Some of the most important and most significant qualities of the trial have changed little since the eighteenth century, despite dif-ferences in overall institutional and social context. Federal District Court Judge William Dwyer stressed these continuities:

> Trial by jury succeeded in part because it appealed to the same irrational val-ues that were served so well by the old methods. And it still does. Drama and catharsis are provided on a scale rivaling that of team sports. The adversary system pits one party against the other. Trial by battle lives on in the contest between hired champions called lawyers. Oath-helpers are no longer around, but character witnesses sometimes play a similar role. The requirement that the verdict be unanimous—originally adopted on the premise that the outcome must reflect the unambiguous will of God—now serves a different goal: that of making the jury listen carefully to the views of all its members.[9]

But some aspects of the trial have changed: indeed it would be impossible, as John Dewey taught, for a practice to maintain even the same qualities without changing where the general institutional context itself is changing. I will paint a very broad-brush picture of significant changes in the shape of the trial and some plausible suggestions for their appearance. Not surprisingly, especially in England, there often appeared a tension between the trial's aspiration (its "ideology") and the often grim reality of its actual functioning in a society that was, by our standards, impoverished, oppressive and deeply class-riven. Much of the significant reform in the nineteenth and twentieth centuries both in England and, to an even greater extent, in the United States involved changes that allowed us to realize the ideals that I describe in the first chapter. Further, another marker of the importance of the trial is our recognition that its characteristics are a matter of constitutional law, of *fundamental* law. Many of these details go beyond the range of legislative fiat. In my view this reflects intuitions that the institution is close to the heart of the American proposition. I survey aspects of the trial that have been recognized as fundamental in this way.

In the third chapter, I describe in a broader and less historical idiom how trials have always stood at the exact point of defining tensions within our public culture. These tensions are enduring. If "justice is conflict," then maintaining these tensions is a key aspect of achieving the only kind of justice we can aspire to. That is what is at stake in the death of the trial. Finally, I make explicit what has been implicit: that to understand the meaning of trial practices, one must emulate the hedgehogs and the foxes:[10] it is important to identify the ideals that animate the institution, often expressed by its champions, but also to see the finest of details of what takes place there.

The trial, then, has enormous normative appeal, has enjoyed a central position during the formative era of our legal order, is a creature of fundamental law, and stands astride some of the most important tensions that have defined our national character. What is the evidence that suggests that the trial is dying? In the fourth chapter, I review the empirical evidence of its decline. Marc Galanter and his colleagues have shown a rapid decline in the numbers of criminal and civil trials in the United States over the last thirty years and what can only be called a catastrophic crash over the last ten years. We are approaching the point where the word "death" is not overstatement. These declines have a self-perpetuating quality, as key actors lose the skills and dispositions necessary to try cases. Well, if the trial is such a powerful set of practices, why do the important actors, who are in a position to choose, avoid them? I survey the tentative speculations about what is fueling the decline.

I then assess what may be the most obvious explanation for the death of the trial: that it is a deeply flawed practice for achieving its human purposes. It is possible that I have painted a deceptively positive picture. The contemporary trial has not been without its critics. I survey the major criticisms and find that, where valid, they are rooted in defects of the surrounding bureaucratic and market institutions, which are candidates for reform.

Finally, I turn to the goal of this effort: to determine the significance the death of the trial would have for us. I identify the consequences for our national life of the death of this great mediating institution. In the course of answering that question, I explore some of the alternative methods of social ordering that are replacing the trial and ask what difference the differences make.

One theoretical point: I will argue here that the assumptions about the nature of the American jury trial animating at least some critics are wrong. What does it mean for an assumption about a set of public practices and institutions to be wrong? One can show that they are inconsistent with much of what we do and have done, practices that are appropriate candidates for those "considered judgments of justice," institutionalized judgments made under favorable conditions in which those who are best suited to know have a high level of confidence. The conservative insight suggests that we ought to be wary of the spirit of abstraction, an ideological temper that reduces complex and subtle practices to one or two simple ideas. (That is why I attempt a concrete picture of the trial in the first chapter.) But that is not the end of the matter. The very possibility of reform of public institutions, including those that Rawls proposes, assumes the possibility that what we actually do may be inconsistent with the ideals that should control and structure those institutions. The relationship between practices and ideals is a circular one, in which each may be refined by comparison with the other, to arrive at a position that Rawls calls "reflective equilibrium," the position in which there is at least temporary peace between practices and ideals. This calls for political judgment of a type that parallels on the level of institutions the kind of judgment that the trial itself is often able to achieve at the level of individual cases. A position on what the trial *should* be can be justified only "by the mutual support of many considerations, of everything fitting together into one coherent view."[11] After our more theoretical self-understandings are tutored by our practices, and those practices reconsidered in light of our understandings, we are in a position to give the best interpretation of the

American trial. As Clifford Geertz consistently maintained, it is by cycling between the most detailed descriptions of institutionalized practices and the broadest generalizations that we are likely to achieve real insight into both those practices and our more general ideas.[12] The task of understanding the trial is an interpretive one, "partly evaluative, since it consists in the identification of the principles which both best 'fit' or cohere with the settled law *and legal practices* of a legal system *and also provide the best moral justification for them*, thus showing the law 'in its best light'" (emphasis added).[13]

## CHAPTER ONE

# Inside the Contemporary Trial

[The jury trial] imbues all classes with a respect for the thing judged and with the notion of right. —Alexis de Tocqueville

If the American trial is in its death throes, why should we care? Many institutions and practices flourish for a while and then decline, even die. Americans who have barely heard of John Dewey naturally think that all institutions must remain in a living balance with their environments and likely to atrophy when they "lose touch" or fall "out of step" with those environments.[1] Perhaps the trial is no longer in touch with our broader social and political environment. We should expect it to atrophy and die.

Perhaps. But perhaps so much the worse for much of our social and political environment. As Judge Dwyer put it, "for us the jury is the canary in the mine shaft; if it goes, if our people lose their inherited right to do justice in court, other democratic institutions will lose breath too."[2] Of course, because both the trial and the other elements of the political environment are human creations, each is subject to revision in light of a deeper understanding of the other. There are no hard determinisms here. There are no Archimedean points from which to understand the demands of justice and democracy for our situation other than those implicit in each of the modes of social ordering, especially the trial. The world looks different when viewed from a jury box than from an elected politician's strategy session or a corporate boardroom. We will see below that the trial's critics speak from each of those perspectives. Of course, it may prove that a deeper understanding of what the trial is and has meant for us will lead us to allow it to bring larger reaches of that environment under its influence, to shape broader segments of American society in its image and likeness, the likeness of "disciplined democracy." This is, of course, what those powerful forces that are waging a war against the trial fear. They would, however, have no reason to deploy such resources against the trial unless the perspective from the jury box continued to have real power.

In this chapter, I will describe what the trial is and has been for us. First, I will provide a description of what goes on at trial. Unfortunately, there exist layers of misapprehension cooked up in a brew of television melodrama and often mocking and distorting propaganda that have to be cleared away. These portray the trial as an undisciplined reaction by hoodwinked or runaway jurors in response to purely emotional appeals. I cannot overemphasize the importance of keeping before our eyes some simple descriptive truths about the trial. Ludwig Wittgenstein told us that what is closest to us is what is hardest to see. Doctor Johnson remarked that it is more important to be reminded than to be instructed. I then try to go a bit deeper and offer an account of why so many of those who know the most about American trials hold them in such high regard. In the next chapter I step outside the trial itself to provide a condensed account of aspects of the place of the trial in the American experience, something also preliminary to determining what its loss would mean.

## Autonomy and Discipline: Direct Examination

One of the fixed points of the social-scientific study of the trial is that the juror makes his or her decision after an intense encounter with the evidence, and it is the evidence in the case, more than any other factor, that determines the outcome.[3] Unless prevented by the application of rules of evidence announced beforehand and equally applicable to both sides, each party may present any evidence that supports his or her position. He or she is not dependent, as are parties in more authoritarian regimes,[4] on the judge's choice of questions to ask and exhibits to present. The state official does not have full operational control over what is at issue, "what this case is about," as trial lawyers like to say. This independence of the parties is, of course, supported by the adversary ethos of the legal profession, whose allegiance is primarily to the client and constrained only by rules that prohibit misrepresentations. The ethical rules attempt a tense balance between energy on the client's behalf and respect for the facts, "what we cannot change; metaphorically, . . . the ground on which we stand and the sky that stretches above us."[5]

The principal method of presenting evidence at trial is the direct examination of witnesses. Some have complained that the conventions of direct examination do not allow the witness to speak spontaneously, in his or her own way and in his or her own words. Its conventions are an example of the combination of party participation and formalism that characterizes the American trial. But direct examination is simply a conversation between lawyer and witness. It is true that the rules of evidence and the conventions of trial practice make direct examination a very specific form of public conversation. This is for very specific reasons. Direct examination offers the jury a series of vignettes of past events whose order of presentation is dictated by considerations of relative importance and clarity. The rules and conventions conspire to require that each vignette be described in a rhythm between physical description, setting the scene, and chronological narrative of what the witness saw and did. Set the scene, then run the action.

Witnesses in direct examination are generally limited to testifying in response to nonleading questions and in the language of perception.[6] They may describe what they saw and what they did. This means that the witness's account must be relatively devoid of interpretations, conclusions, opinions, and most of the other things we do with words. (Witnesses may not make promises, for example not to do it again, or give advice as to how the case ought to be decided.) The trial takes facts seriously. Aristotle taught that what distinguishes a legal forum from a political one is the importance of the narrative of specific events in legal forums. We will see that there are political dimensions to American trials, but those dimensions are more or less suppressed. The conventions of direct examination suggest that judgment can come too easily: it is too tempting to seize upon a few abstract dimensions of a situation—the race or gender or nationality of the parties for example, or a very general notion of the *kind* of case it is—and remain blind to the important factual details. The trial says, in effect, "Both God and the devil are in the details, and, for every man's sake, attention is to be paid." Central to its democratic character is the fact that a group of laymen, for whom jury service is an unusual event, is more likely than a professional judge (who can too easily become a bored or overbearing bureaucrat) to pay attention. As Chesterton put it in his wonderful tribute to the jury:

> The trend of our epoch up to this time has been consistently towards specialism and professionalism.... Many legalists have declared that the untrained jury should be altogether supplanted by the trained judge.... [However,] the more a man looks at a thing, the less he can see it, and the more a man learns a thing the less he knows it.... [T]hat the man who is trained should be the man who is trusted would be absolutely unanswerable if it were really true that a man who studied a thing and practiced it every day went on seeing more and more of its significance. But he does not. He goes on seeing less and less of its significance.... Now it is a terrible business to mark a man out for the judgment of men. But it is a thing to which a man can grow accustomed, as he can to other terrible things.... And the horrible thing about all legal officials, even the best, about all judges, magistrates, barristers, detectives, and policemen, is not that they are wicked (some of them are good), not that they are stupid (several of them are quite intelligent), it is simply that they have got used to it.... Strictly they do not see the prisoner in the dock; all they see is the usual man in the usual place. They do not see the awful court of judgment; they only see their own workshop. Therefore the instinct of Christian civilization has most wisely declared that into their judgments there shall upon every occasion be infused fresh blood and fresh thoughts from the streets.[7]

Justice Fortas put the same thought in more conventional terms:

> [J]udges do become case-hardened. Judges do sometimes tend, after many years, to take a somewhat jaundiced view of defendants. Many trial judges tend to become a bit prosecution minded. That's the basic justification for a jury.[8]

In ordinary life, we do not talk the way we talk during direct examination, because most conversations are aimed not at a rigorous attempt to determine and evaluate what occurred in the past, but rather to establish or develop the relationship between the conversation partners while accommodating most of their prejudices, a task to which the sharing of opinions and feelings is well suited. The trial implicitly says something like, "Before we start arguing about what our situation means, how we should understand it, and certainly before we argue about what is to be done about it, let's take the time to figure out *exactly* what occurred,[9] as best we can. And if we can't do even that, that means we don't have any real basis for opining or acting."[10] One path to that is to ask witnesses in some detail what they saw and did. Because accuracy is important, we ask witnesses to speak in the language of perception, in part because perceptions are less likely than opinions and interpretations to be products of the "anxious, usually self-preoccupied, often falsifying veil" that we usually spread over those aspects of what we see which offend our prejudices.[11]

## The Discipline of Direct Examination in Support of Formal Justice

There is much more to this. Testimony in the language of perception fosters accuracy, but it also furthers "the rule of law as a law of rules," as Justice Scalia is fond of putting it.[12] It supports the aspiration that state power be deployed only on the basis of preexistent rules of general application.[13] Testimony in the language of perception is more open to a jury's independent judgment on the basic legality of the human actions being evaluated than would be a flood of opinions and conclusions by a series of witnesses. Anyone who has done any interviewing knows how difficult, how artificial it is, to coax a witness or a client simply to recount what happened in a coherent and complete way. That's why there are books on the subject of legal interviewing. Without a set of conventions that allow the jury to hear the witnesses provide a coherent account of what the witnesses have perceived and now remember,[14] the trial would resemble at worst the Jerry Springer show and at best the *McLaughlin Report*. It would not allow the jury to make reliable determinations of what occurred and make the further judgment about whether what happened fell inside or outside the legal categories. Indeed the jury's judgment wouldn't be about a particular case at all, but merely an expression of generalized prejudices triggered by a few hot-button aspects of the case.

How and why should the trial support the rule of law as the law of rules? One important, though partial, view understands the trial exclusively as the institutional device for the maintenance of the rule of law in situations where there are disputes of fact. The law of rules that make up the rule of law is understood as a set of preexistent commands that assign determinate consequences to determinate classes of events.[15] The primary political good of law so conceived is the enhancement of citizen autonomy—the citizen always knows where the lines are and can always control how he may avoid the intrusion of the coercive power of the state into his pursuit of happiness. This is an important political value. Furthermore it explains and can be brought into reflective equilibrium with a range of actual trial practices.

Speaking broadly, this received view understands the jury to be engaged in two practices, distinct from one another and in sequence. First, it must create from inevitably circumstantial evidence,[16] through the mediation of purely empirical commonsense generalizations, an accurate and value-free narrative of what occurred. It must be accurate, because the rule of law will not prevail if citizens are punished or otherwise suffer the effects of the coercive power of the state when they have not in fact done what they are accused of. This would be true whether the officials deliberately misrepresent the underlying facts, were negligent in determining them, or were simply and innocently incapable of determining what actually occurred. The account must be not only accurate, but also value-free. If the account of what occurred was infected by norms that came from the jury's normative common sense or sensibility, then there would be no assurance that the case was actually being decided based exclusively on the legitimate norms found in the jury instructions.

According to the received view, after constructing a value-free account of what occurred, the jury must perform what we can call an act of fair categorization. It must decide whether or not the factual account that the jury has constructed, with the help of counsel, from the circumstantial evidence falls within or outside the categories defined by the rules to be found in the jury instructions, which in turn reflect the elements of the claims, crimes, or defenses as defined by the substantive law. The closer this operation comes to a deduction the better. This notion is "often thought to imply, further, that there are rules and procedures of inference according to which the features of the various concepts and the characteristics of various particular things . . . can be said to correspond to certain characteristics and not to others."[17] Thus, the verdict occurs as the result of what we might call an act of impartial conceptual "inspection," by which the jury determines whether or not its value-free account of what has occurred falls into one of the classes defined by the instructions. Thus, in the received view of the trial, the only rules or concepts linking the facts of the individual case and the verdict are the value-free empirical generalizations that allow the construction of the value-free account, on the one hand, and the legitimate legal categories, on the other.

The power of the received view stems not only from its connection with the basic values of the liberal state, but also from its coherence with a number of the most distinctive features of the American trial. It is consistent with the availability of a range of summary procedures in civil cases (though not with the absence of most of those procedures in criminal cases), the doctrine of materiality in evidence law, several other evidentiary doctrines that seek to ensure reliability, the availability of judgments as a matter of law after trial (though, again, not against the defendant in criminal cases), the use of jury instructions, and the strong preference for testimony in the language of perception. The law of rules has an important place in the structure of American trial practices. On the other hand, to understand the American trial solely in these terms is to commit the fallacy of misplaced concreteness, to assume that important rules or aspects of the trial exhaust its concrete reality. To understand the trial solely in the language of the received view is to impoverish our interpretation of the trial. To act as if the trial were equivalent to the rules and practices that stem from this understanding would be to return at the trial level to a species of mechanical jurisprudence. The trial is much more than that, as we will soon see.[18]

## Further Aspects of Trial Architecture

The requirement that the witness on direct speak in response to nonleading questions has significance. American, unlike British, trial lawyers are permitted to discuss the witness's trial testimony before the trial. This allows a rather high level of preparation with clients and friendly witnesses,[19] less with neutral witnesses, and virtually none with unfriendly witnesses, for example with relatives of the victims in a criminal case, who will often be actively hostile to the defendant and unwilling to talk with his lawyer.[20] On the positive side,[21] it allows the lawyer and the witness to focus the testimony on the relatively small number of the infinite aspects of any human situation that cut at the joints of the case, to resolve the ambiguities of expression that exist for all but the most articulate witnesses, and to refresh and clarify memories that often must reach back years. It produces a cleaner and clearer account of the witness's considered judgment on what he has to say. But the requirement that the witness testify in response to nonleading questions means that the words will still be the witness's. This should allow the jury to discern any artificiality in the witness's testimony and to deploy a broad range of tacit learning about who the witness is. The attorney cannot simply ask a sequence of leading questions evoking Yes or No answers from the witness. The jury gets to see something of who the witness is as a truth teller, something that is of very broad significance in the case.

Other rules are designed to raise the level of reliability of the evidence that each party presents. Exhibits have to pass tests of authenticity to be admitted. Scientific evidence must not be junk science; the judge must ensure that it, too, is reliable. If the proponent wants to prove what a document says, he must produce the original of the document or a reliable duplicate. (Notice that this "Best Evidence Rule" not only assists reliability, but also functions in the same way as does the requirement of testimony in the language of perception: it says, "Before we start talking about what a document means, let's be sure what it says!")[22] Some hearsay testimony is excluded because it is particularly unreliable.[23] In criminal cases some additional hearsay taken by agents of the state is excluded because our tradition understands it to be particularly dangerous.[24] Some of these rules are ineffective or misconceived, but we should admire their aspiration to enhance the accuracy of trial decision making.

It is easy to miss the contribution that the law of professional responsibility makes to this effort. Lawyers have an obligation to further the goals that their clients set, even if they are professionally or personally costly to the lawyer. True, this basic principle of loyalty may sometimes work against the reliability of evidence, but not always. ("How can you tell that a lawyer is lying?" You know the punch line.)[25] The potential indifference or sloth of a state actor charged with gathering evidence can pose at least as great a danger. To assure loyalty, lawyers are bound by rules prohibiting conflicts of interest that are much more stringent than those that bind other professionals and businessmen. On the other hand, to counterbalance these rules mandating attorney partisanship, there are others that require a respect for simple factual truth: prohibiting the presentation of false evidence and even requiring the disclosure of past client perjury.[26] Most lawyers take these rules very seriously.

The evidence must be not only reliable, but also relevant. The doctrine of relevance makes a qualified attempt to place the legal norms embedded in the jury instructions near the center of the trial. It focuses the discussion so that the argument will not be all over the place. All the evidence must have an arguable logical relationship with the legal rule that "controls" the case. This rule has a dark side that becomes apparent if the substantive law is in conflict with decency or justice. For example, where landlord-tenant law says that a tenant must pay his rent regardless of the condition of his apartment, then the fact that the apartment was in squalid disrepair is irrelevant at trial. Despite its dark side, relevance serves a central value in a liberal society: each citizen will generally be judged based on rules announced ahead of time, and no citizen will face loss of life, liberty, or property based on action that he could not possibly have known ahead of time was illegal.

If the legislature has been bought and sold—if it suffers from what economists cheerfully call "capture" or "agency costs"—then the law of relevancy may leave out too much of what justice requires to be in evidence. Mercifully, it is true that the legal rules cannot possibly anticipate every possible variation in the great, booming, buzzing confusion of the world. A great deal of background or contextual evidence must inevitably enter the case if the basic story is to make any human sense at all. All this additional evidence will carry meaning and significance that derives from the commonsense morality and the life world of the jury (or the judge).[27] Thus the legal norm from the law of rules can be only one center about which the evidence revolves.[28] It will be easy to present evidence close to that center, and, because what is talked about at trial tends to gain importance, the debate will tend not simply to be focused, but focused on what democratically enacted law determines is important. True, the doctrine of relevance cannot possibly serve with geometrical rigor to exclude all other moral significance from the case—something I will suggest is very much to the good[29]—but it imposes a significant discipline on the debate, a discipline far in excess of that which controls most debate surrounding public things.

So each party must present his or her case through witnesses who have something concrete to say about the details of these particular facts. Any documentary or physical evidence must not be misleading. Lawyers are ethically obliged to act vigorously on behalf of their clients, to gather and present the most persuasive evidence that supports the client's position, but to respect the truth (that which we cannot change at will, as Arendt liked to put it). The legal doctrine of relevance serves to focus the debate on what the law says is important and thus create a disciplined discussion, not one that is all over the lot, because accurate testimony may still be misleading. The conventions that surround the direct examination of witnesses, the key device for the presentation of evidence, provide for a detailed and disciplined description by witnesses with firsthand knowledge of what they did and what they saw.

## Cross-Examination

The important English legal philosopher H. L. A. Hart claimed that the Latin expression *audiatur et altera pars* (let the other side be heard) is at the heart of the common law's sense of justice. Cross-examination is one place where this right to present the other side of a case clearly manifests itself. The heart of cross-examination is the sequencing of short, clear, undeniable propositions that together suggest a conclusion that the witness has overlooked or deliberately obscured. The trial as a whole proceeds through the sequence of narrative and deconstruction of narrative. This sequence dramatizes for the jury not only that there are two stories to tell about most events, but also that there is always a discontinuity between any event and even the best telling of it. Cross-examination helps put the jury on the road to a truth *beyond* storytelling. It says, in effect, that the apparently disinterested tale the witness told was not quite the report of past perceptions that it seemed to be. It was rather a selective presentation of aspects of what the witness remembers, organized in a willful or at least a purposeful manner.[30]

When Augustine wrote "Omnis homo mendax est," he meant not only that "every man is a liar," that everyone tells outright lies, but also that we inevitably see things our own way and in our opinions and speech recount only the partial truths that serve our interests.[31] Our Puritan tradition could certainly appreciate that view of man, but our skepticism about government made us reluctant to trust judges to save us from one another's self-serving opinions.[32] When Madison wrote in *The Federalist No. 10* that our opinions are the objects to which our self-love attaches itself, he was showing himself to be a child of his skeptical tradition. The requirement of direct examination, that the witness testify in the language of perception, provides only a partial protection against this inevitable partisanship in important matters. And so the American trial provides individual citizens with some of the means to protect themselves against the inevitable half-truths that may be the basis of the loss of life, liberty, or property. It places in the hands of the cross-examiner some of the means to show the gaps between the truth and the telling of it.

What can the cross-examiner do? He may retell the entire story provided by the witness but use different descriptive language, a different
ordering of events, and a different selection of detail, all of which the witness must concede is fair,[33] to reveal an event with a profoundly different
significance than that which the witness sought to convey. (Any resistance
of this redescription, if it is truly undeniable, will only serve to show the
willfulness of the witness's initial description.) The examiner may not be
able to retell the entire story through admissions the witness may be unable plausibly to deny, but he or she may require the witness to concede
*some* few facts that the examiner's own witness will be able to place in
their proper context. Third, the cross-examiner may be able just to suggest
alternative ways of looking at the evidence offered on direct. A psychia-
trist who testifies that the defendant suffered from borderline personality
disorder as evidenced by her pervasive sadness can be reminded that she
had been incarcerated at the county jail for a year without a single visit
from home: "Make you sad to be there that long without a visit, huh, Doctor?" Fourth, the examiner may cast doubt on the assertions that the witness has made, using a formally valid method of basic logic:[34] if A, then B;
but not B; therefore not A. If the defendant had used a racial slur against
the plaintiff, the plaintiff would have complained to a close friend. But he
didn't complain, the witness must concede. Therefore, the examiner will
argue in closing, there was never any such slur. Fifth, the cross-examiner
can use the examination to manifest the character of those witnesses who
are often important players in the real-world drama that led up to the
trial. In particular, the witness's willfulness or casualness with the truth
will suggest a personal style that may not much care about others' rights
and interests. Finally, the cross-examiner may deploy a dozen or so methods of "impeachment" or discrediting of a witness that the conventions of
trial advocacy put in the hands of each party.[35] In the main, these are simply the commonplaces, or sources for arguments, rooted in common sense,
that suggest that there are reasons to disbelieve a person who claims to
be telling the truth. The examiner may thus attack the witness's opportunity to observe (it was a startling event which happened very fast on a
darkened street), his or her memory of the event (there was no particular
reason to pay attention to this event and you can remember no other similar events that occurred then) and the suspect artificiality of the way he is
speaking ("my report accurately recounts what it purports to memorial-
ize"). The examiner may elicit personal loyalties or aversions to a party
or a personal history that manifests racial or regional prejudices. Prior

inconsistent statements can be explored and careless straight-out errors in the testimony mentioned, even on relatively minor matters.

Entire books have been devoted to cross-examination.[36] It allows the jury to look through the spartan narratives of the witness's direct examination and to break the selectivity, the willfulness, and the manipulativeness that inheres in even the most disciplined storytelling. Where life, liberty, property, and political power are at stake, truth will often seem to those involved a truly ephemeral consideration. After all, Hobbes ends his *Leviathan* with the thought that only "such truth, as opposeth no man's profit, nor pleasure, is to all men welcome." And more wistfully, he warned, "I doubt not, but if it had been a thing contrary to any man's right of dominion, or to the interests of men who have dominion that the three angles of a triangle should be equal to two angles of a square; that doctrine should have been, if not disputed yet by the burning of all books of geometry suppressed, as far as he whom it concerned was able."[37] True, the self-interested narratives of direct examination, already disciplined by its conventions, may serve as pencil sketches that begin the trial's advance to a truth beyond storytelling. But it sorely needs the corrective of cross-examination. Sometimes the cross is wholly destructive. More often it offers additional perspectives from which to interpret, and thus to see, the evidence offered. Notice how discontinuous this kind of critical testing is with the flimsy means of questioning that reporters must use to challenge political figures or that political figures use to challenge each other in what often passes for political debate. Both of those forums permit politicians to talk continuously without affording the opponent the chance to define what facts the speaker is bound to concede. Continuous talk *is* important because coherence is a key criterion of truth: otherwise you do have the *McLaughlin Report.* But cross-examination says implicitly that the direct examinations themselves were interpretations, as indeed they were.[38] Cross-examiners remind the jury of those aspects of the situation that the witness or his or her counsel has chosen not to reveal. The assumption underlying cross-examination is that the witness has chosen to cut into the great booming, buzzing confusion of life in a way that is consciously or unconsciously willful, that he or she has left out something important that changes the meaning of everything. The autopoietic nature of a consistent and coherent direct examination—the suggestion, indeed the feeling, that it tells everything about a subject—can be undermined by cross-examination. After an effective direct examination the deconstructive shock of a well-wrought cross-examination can be stunning. To

anticipate, the death of the trial would mean the end of a forum where
each citizen can, subject to important constraints, tell the best story he or
she can, present the strongest evidence he or she thinks will support it, but
also have to submit to the strongest countervailing considerations.

## The Struggle for Meaning at Trial

So far, I have tried to provide an account of the trial as a simple device
for paying attention to the evidence. The death of the trial would mean
the end of the forum where we force ourselves to pay attention to brutally
elementary fact. This is a simple but a very big thing. Jeremy Bentham
famously called falsehood the handmaiden of injustice.[39] The devices of
the trial drive the mind of the juror downward, toward the specific details
of the case and away from unqualified and unrefined prejudice.[40] And the
empirical literature on the trial suggests strongly that these devices succeed. Jeffrey Abramson concludes after a review of that literature on the
subject that the "discipline of the evidence" is what determines the result
in jury trials, not any general characteristics of particular jurors.[41] Kalven
and Zeisel's monumental study of the American jury found that in most
cases where judge and jury disagree, it was due to differences in the consideration of the evidence. They found as well that the number of poten-
tially determinative evidentiary considerations in cases going to trial was
so large—the possible inferences among the evidence in even "simple"
cases so complex—that it was not possible, using the usual social-scientific
methods, to isolate and identify the factors that "caused" the verdicts.[42]
Jurors recognize the elevation of their capacity for commonsense reasoning and evaluation that their encounter with the trial's structure realizes.
In what Kalven and Zeisel referred to as a "stunning refutation of the
hypothesis that the jury does not understand," there was no correlation
between the complexity of the cases they studied and the likelihood of
disagreement between judge and jury as to the outcome. Social psychologists have found that juries have admirable powers of collective memory
for the evidence presented.[43] Perhaps the most prominent empirical investigators conclude, "Because jury performance of the fact-finding task
is so remarkably competent, few innovations are needed to improve performance."[44] Similarly, it appears that the devices of the trial, although
traditional, are designed to counter the sorts of systematic failures in reasoning identified by social scientists under the name "heuristics." Richard

Lempert sums up the social-science findings: "If there is any single finding that stands out in the 32 years of modern social science research on juries, beginning with *The American Jury*, it is that case facts are the most important determinant of jury verdicts. Ordinarily, their influence dwarfs everything else."[45] Or as Dwyer puts it in his clear-eyed but strong defense of the American jury trial, "[I]n well-tried cases, nearly all jurors find themselves caught up in the quest for justice."[46] The devices of the trial achieve that "*respect for the thing judged* and the notion of right" that Tocqueville found to be distinctive of the experience of the American jury.

The central activities of direct examination and cross-examination occur within a moral and factual context created by opening statement and closing argument. Respect for the things judged is achieved by constructing and then deconstructing lawyers' and then witnesses' narratives to allow the jury to understand how much pressure those constructions can stand. In many different ways, the truth is in between. For us, truth lies between the generalizations of law and morality that the lawyers urge and the detailed factual field that emerges from the trial's constructive and destructive devices. At the trial level this constructive task is assigned to the lawyers. They do not mechanically pile one fact upon another, but organize their initial presentation by the integrating insight—the inspired simplification—that is the theory of the case. The philosopher Bernard Lonergan argues that we know in both scientific and commonsense contexts through a sequence of two levels of insight. The first insight is the bright idea that organizes the material. Think of Archimedes in the bath: "Oh, I see now! I see how it hangs together!" Thus very good trial lawyers must have intelligence and imagination. But then there is a second level of insight that is necessary before the bright idea can be affirmed as true: insight into the adequacy of the evidence for the truth of the insight.[47] Bright ideas can be just that. Well-constructed narratives can be nothing more than pretty stories. It is only once the insight that is the theory of the case is concretely elaborated and all the implications and interconnections revealed that we are in a position to seek that second level of insight in reflective understanding. Of course each lawyer will have engaged in both steps before giving his opening, because each lawyer wants not just to present a bright idea, to gain the jury's admiration for his insights; rather, he or she wants the jury to accept his theory as true. Thus the theory itself and the evidence offered to support it will have gone through rounds of revision before the jury ever hears a word. It will be the most coherent presentation of the case, supported by the most persuasive evidence, most tightly organized and described. That enterprise serves the function of elaborating the factual and moral implications of the position the lawyer is presenting. To put it simply, a well-presented case gives the jury something worth thinking about. Or, more philosophically, it gives the jury exactly what it needs to exercise its power of reflective judgment successfully, to determine whether or not the theory presented is supported by adequate evidence. Fortunately for us, the powers of judgment are more broadly distributed than the powers of creation and construction: we the people can exercise those powers reliably once the more specifically gifted specialists have offered us their well-thought-out cases.[48] And, of course, they will be specialists not only in constructing the case, but in pointing out, through the deconstructive devices of cross-examination and closing argument, that however pretty a story the opponent is telling, it just isn't true.

## Opening Statement and Closing Argument: The Context of Meaning

As I said, the trial does not begin with the direct examination of witnesses. It begins with opening statements. Opening statements offer the lawyers the chance to explain to the jury what they hope the evidence will show. The best openings are, like good literary works, "vivid continuous dreams" in which all the factual details are chosen and characterized so as to demonstrate,[49] and actually to perform, the coherence and plausibility of the story the lawyer tells. It is in this oral performance that a story may fail to ring true. And it is a story: the thousands of inferences that the jury will be asked to draw in most cases are actually drawn by the lawyer and integrated into the story he or she tells. That is because, as Alasdair MacIntyre, has written, we necessarily understand human actions, the subject of every trial, in the language of narrative, and we necessarily see partial descriptions, such as the ones offered in the direct examinations of witnesses, as truncated parts of some more complete narrative.[50] The opening offers the jury an opportunity to see concretely, all at once, the account the lawyer asks them to accept. The juror can then ask concretely: "Does this hang together?" "Is this the way people act?" "Was this physically possible?"[51] The juror will thus be better able to evaluate each witness's testimony because he or she will be able to circle between the most local of details and the full story offered by the advocate.[52] If the lawyer's case is too weak to allow the juror to do that and the lawyer's opponent does offer a complete "theory of the case," the lawyer will, and rightly, begin to lose the battle for the jury's imagination. This theory is the precise cut, the inspired simplification, that allows the story to hang together, to be consistent with common sense, and to provide the jury a reason to *act*. The lawyer will try to bridge the inevitable factual, moral, and legal gaps among the episodes of the story and the facts by appeals to practical judgment. For the story told by the plaintiff or the prosecution is always an unfinished story, a story whose conclusion can only be the jury's righting of the wrong which the complaining party has suffered, so that the dimly perceived harmonies of the moral world will be restored.[53] An effective opening statement will, then, be sufficient as a matter of law;[54] it should have moral appeal; it should be internally coherent and consistent with common sense; it should anticipate the opponent's case and invoke more powerful norms; it should suggest, often implicitly, what is most important about the case and how it should resolved. Finally, it should be supported by admissible, credible, and ethically presentable evidence. It's not just a good story—it's a deeply constrained narrative. And that each party is entitled to give an opening statement ensures that there will not be One Big Story told by the state.

And the opening statement is not just a story. It is also a promise. The lawyer cannot simply tell the best story. He or she knows that the relatively short opening statements will be followed by the lengthy presentation of evidence in painstaking detail, evidence that will be subject to focused adversary testing. If the evidence does not support the lawyer's theory of the case, he or she will have broken his or her promise to the jury, he or she will have sinned against the jury's own obligation to find the truth and do justice. The trial itself will have served as a truthful lens and metaphor for the underlying events being tried. Indeed, one of the standard forms of argumentation in closing argument is to accuse the opponent of just this kind of moral failure, of "breaking his promise."

It will often be true that the criteria for choice among the standards that apply to a good opening statement will be in conflict. A morally compelling story may be legally insufficient and reliant on weak and self-serving evidence. A story that is well supported by credible evidence may invite the jury to follow a legal rule that seems mechanical and at odds with common sense. Typically the lawyer will have to resolve these conflicts and choose one story. In this choice, he or she will have to rely on an imaginative anticipation of how various stories will play out at trial in the crucible of oral adversary testing. The lawyer will know that by the end of the trial even the best of opening statements will seem tattered by the "brutally elementary data" that emerge from witnesses over whom the lawyer will not, thankfully, have the same kind of control that a writer of fiction, and even history, has over the characters. And that too, is to the good. The lawyer in opening provides an important service in trying to propose to the jury the best account, given the story expected to be told by the opponent and the anticipated evidence, of what the evidence means, what it adds up to.

But it will prove true that "the squirming facts exceed the squamous mind."[55] By trial's end, the openings will have proven helpful, but things will not quite have fit so nicely within even the most disciplined and careful opening statement. Each opening's simplification, however inspired, will usually emerge as just a bit *too* simple. Nonetheless, the storytelling of opening places the enormous detail of the evidence within the only context where it can be humanly comprehended. As MacIntyre put it, absent narrative we don't have access to "the real facts," only to "the disjointed parts of some possible narrative."[56] Opening provides each lawyer's candidate for that possible narrative. It will serve to reveal which element of each story a juror—under the "discipline of the evidence"—is bound to accept and where moral and political judgment must be in play.

The most obviously rhetorical aspect of the trial is closing argument. It is rhetorical not because of the exaggerated verbal pyrotechnics and emotional appeals found in television courtroom dramas, which are revealingly short, but because it must deal with uncertainty. Uncertainty—factual, moral, and legal—cannot be eliminated from our condition. It is precisely what defines us as human and not divine.[57] (Paradoxically, we reach as close as we can to the divine by sustained attention to the particular.) The devices of the trial, and finally closing argument itself, are designed to deal, as intelligently as possible, with the inevitable uncertainty we face in some of the most serious situations. We will never know even the "brutally elementary data" with geometrical certainty. Because the trial must always address a particular past event or series of events, not a universal law of nature, it cannot repeat the event experimentally. It can never achieve even the more limited certainty of which many natural sciences are capable. It is closer to historiography and the human sciences in being inevitably "abductive" and interpretive:[58] a true interpretation can be achieved only "by the mutual support of many considerations, of everything fitting together into one coherent view."[59] But further, the trial is a practical enterprise in a way that the human sciences are not. It leads directly to action.

In their study of the American jury trial, Kalven and Zeisel pointed out that moral values were necessarily implicated in trial decision making. Given this inevitability, the only concrete choice was whose values would influence the decision, those of the judge or those of the jury. They called their view of this feature of trial determinations of past events the "liberation thesis"—because jurors in triable cases were not compelled by logic alone to reach one conclusion rather than another, they were required to make, at the very least, a judgment about whether or not the evidence gave them a level of certainty that justified their action. They were responsible for at least that choice. Moreover, quite often the substantive law—the legal rules themselves—would assign to them other moral judgments as well: whether a defendant's behavior was "reasonable," for example,[60] and subtle evaluations about individuals' states of mind.[61]

Our trial courts achieve truth after the fashion of Peirce's metaphor: large cables support great bridges even though they are composed of vast numbers of thin wires, tightly wound. The rhetoric of closing proceeds by the gathering of the most salient particulars that have emerged in the course of the trial and binding them into a powerful whole. The lawyer here moves between facts and norms, between considerations of probable truth and of significance or meaning of the events tried. He or she will argue; will marshal undisputed facts and episodes in the courtroom drama itself ("Remember how Officer Peters grew angry when I showed him his earlier statement"); will invoke the allusions and analogies that are part of trial lawyers' lore or his own imagination creates ("You can call it circumstantial evidence, but if there are footprints in the snow, you *know* that someone has been there"); will intensify the moral value of the bits of narrative he or she offers, trying to make the jury feel just those emotions that reveal the human significance of the situation. After all, having the right feelings—indignation or sympathy or caution or even confusion—is part of seeing the practical situation truly.[62] Closing argument gives the lawyer the opportunity to reconstruct just enough of the opening to provide the jury with reason to act. There will now be doubt and uncertainty.[63] That's what makes it a triable case—a case in which there are truly debatable dispositive issues. But it isn't the trial that creates uncertainty, either factual or moral. It is our condition.

Closing argument also has a deconstructive aspect. This is the time when the advocate can point out the incoherence and implausibility of the

competing account and the opponent's failure to keep his or her promise
to present adequate evidence to support the story told in opening statement. The kinds of commonsense argumentation that go on in closing are
rarely designed to *compel* the jury to accept a logical conclusion.[64] They
are, rather, attempts to actualize largely tacit powers of integration that
are usually dormant, indeed usually anesthetized by popular culture. They
attempt to coax judgment by actually performing the case, by addressing
difficulties, and so restoring just enough of the narrative told in opening
statement to allow the jury to see its way clear to the decision sought.
The closing makes the implicit argumentation of the rest of the trial more
explicit. Never completely, of course, because "[a]ny situation which confronts me, and which is not a situation in a game, has an inexhaustible set
of discriminable features . . . over and above those that are mentionable
within the vocabulary that I possess and use."[65]

We will see that although closing arguments are not deductive, they
are hardly irrational. They appeal to our ability to integrate and interpret.
This ability we have, if structured and disciplined as it is at trial, and aided
by the commonsense argument of closing, actually can grasp "the cumulations of probabilities . . . too fine to avail separately, too subtle and circuitous to be convertible into syllogisms."[66] It allows the jury to "trust rather
in the *multitude and variety* of its arguments than to the conclusiveness of
any one. Its reasoning should not form a chain which is no stronger than
its weakest link, but a cable whose fibers may be ever so slender, provided
they are sufficiently numerous and intimately connected."[67] The ability to
argue well is not evenly distributed—that's why we rely on professionals,
lawyers, to do it. On the other hand, our powers of interpretation and
judgment, if offered the case in a disciplined and engaging manner and exercised with the anticipation of public justification, is in fact rather widely
distributed. Craft and judgment are thus joined in the jury trial.

At the end of the trial the judge will read the instructions to the jury.[68]
If well prepared, they will contain the clearest short statement of the legal
rules that apply to the case. Of course, the law of rules will already have
been well represented in deciding which cases get to trial and in determinations of materiality, which limits the evidence that the lawyers are
permitted to present.[69] So the legal rules are represented at trial, but they
are qualified and interpreted in a number of ways in light of the jury's
commonsense morality. In a democratic society, of course, discontinuities
between the legal rules and general commonsense norms should be rare
and short-lived. Very rarely will the jury engage in something that can

fairly be called nullification. It is inevitable that in making a concrete decision about how to respond to an event whose proper description and evaluation are fairly disputable we will rely on our common sense. But in deciding how fairly to address the inevitable uncertainty surrounding these events, we necessarily rely on our sense of importance. Again we must ask: How important would be error in one direction rather than in another? How important are the values underlying the appeals that both sides make, not in general, but in the very specific context of this case? It will sometimes be true, for example, that adherence to the letter of the law is of greater importance than more equitable aspects of the situation (e.g., where there are high levels of reliance on formalities in a morally indifferent context). And we must navigate these determinations of importance in light of the levels of factual uncertainty that surround all triable cases. These are determinations that must be made whenever we face the question of what we should do now in response to an uncertain event that has occurred in the past.

The journalists who distort the American trial pretend to know the correct resolution of the issues facing the jury based on a few stereotyped aspects of the situation. They pretend, in effect, that the details don't matter, and, ultimately, that the facts don't matter—because, of course, we already "know" what to do. That is the kind of sophistry that the Western philosophical tradition began by attacking. The critical devices of the trial are designed to make it difficult for the worse argument to defeat the better. They do so by actualizing the full range of the jury's abilities.

What could be a better way to address these important questions? Direct examination provides the jury the brutally elementary data that it must not ignore if it is to do justice in this particular case, data that must be provided to the jury before the process of reinterpretation occurs. Otherwise the symbolic significance of the case will overwhelm that right of each party to be treated fairly for what he or she did or did not do here. The rules of evidence are designed to raise the level of reliability of any of the evidence presented, especially the evidence that the methods of adversary presentation may fail adequately to evaluate. Each party is allowed to present any such evidence his or her own way through an agent knowledgeable about the rules and committed primarily to the client's perspective on the case. Each party may point out the willfulness and partiality in the opponent's presentation. The authoritativeness of democratically enacted law is represented in the judge's rulings on materiality and through the instructions. The decision is placed in the hands not of one person, but of a group of persons whom the parties have found acceptable and who represent a cross-section of the community with experiences similar to those of the parties and whose interests are not implicated in the resolution of the controversy. How could anyone object to this kind of a procedure?

What is the significance of these practices? We will come round to this question again, when we look, in closing, at the significance of their possible disappearance. But let's start with a positive and preliminary account: by the time closing argument comes around, each lawyer should know, once again, that the simplifications of opening statement, however inspired, are a bit *too* simple. No triable case is perfect, either on the factual or the normative level. A judgment has to be made, and that judgment will require the jury to say what is most important about the case. The genius of the trial is to prevent the jury from making the case a purely symbolic expression of some abstract commitment. The jury's immersion in the details of the evidence, the "discipline of the evidence," and the face to face nature of the encounter between the parties are designed to make that impossible.[70] And so the lawyer in closing argument must circle between the significance of what occurred and the truth of his factual theory. Both are important. Closing is an appeal to the freedom of the jury because "you cannot persuade jurors to do what they do not want to do. The goal of argument is to help the jury want to do the right thing, to feel comfortable in making the proper judgment."[71] But this freedom is not arbitrariness. It is an act of moral and political self-definition that can be more or less adequate, a better or worse integration of the relevant considerations, including the level of factual certainty, and their relative importance. This is inevitably a political matter. As Tocqueville put it, the criminal "jury is, above all a political institution, and it must be regarded in this light in order to be duly appreciated.... He who punishes the criminal ... is the real master of society."[72]

So much for a very compressed summary of trial's languages and practices. Because my contention here is that the trial has evolved into a precisely balanced forum, my argument must be carried largely by description. So far I have provided a brief account only of the constitutive rules of the trial and the linguistic performances that it comprises. But these have to be considered in the context of aspects of the trial that are so basic, so simple, that their extraordinary significance can easily be overlooked: "Those aspects of things that are most important for us are hidden because of their simplicity and familiarity. One is unable to notice something—because it is always before one's eyes. . . . [W]e fail to be struck by what, once seen, is most striking and most powerful."[73] First, trial presentation focuses on the concrete, the factual, and the multiple. The obsessive focus on *exactly* what took place drives the mind downward, away from lazy abstractions: "no ideas but in things."[74] It tells the jury implicitly that the details are important and that the ordinary modes of moral judgment that are extremely interested in those details are appropriate for understanding and evaluating the events being tried. Lawyers are obliged to seek and entitled to receive answers to all relevant questions, however embarrassing or uncomfortable for our dominant or "politically correct" (in the broadest sense) understandings. As the trial proceeds through time, each well-chosen detail can become the key normative perspective though which all the evidence is understood. The time compression that is characteristic of the American jury trial protects the unities of theory and theme from the predations of fading memory. It allows the lawyer to show what cannot be said and provides the conditions for "the cumulations of probabilities . . . too fine to avail separately, too subtle and circuitous to be convertible into syllogisms."[75] The succession of strategic choices that the lawyer has to make as to what gambits to accept, what evidence to engage, tends, as the case progresses, to focus the attention of the jury on just the most difficult and important questions. There is a taut balance at trial between continuous explication of a theory of the case, on the one hand, and criticism of that explication, on the other. Openings are counterposed; cross follows a continuous direct; parties may not usually offer their own evidence on cross; defendant's case follows plaintiff's, followed by plaintiff's rebuttal, and sometimes defendant's surrebuttal. We have to understand how a perspective holds together, but we need to keep our minds open enough to understand that there is another way of making sense of the situation. The trial is spoken and heard. It provides a momentary identification with all witnesses, but from a physical distance greater than that of ordinary conversation. It thus provides concretely the conditions for good judgment—sympathy and detachment. It is a dramatic event. It is a lens and metaphor that will allow a lawyer with a good case to be fairer to all the aspects of the evidence in all his or her performances. The trial's practices can actualize the full range of human feeling in a way that creates the conditions for good judgment.[76] Those practices will ring true, or not, in a way that is discernible by strong tacit powers.

Are these merely assertions? Social-science investigators, using a range of different methods, have identified the effects of the trial's rules, linguistic performances, and basic features. Mercifully, they have found that broad demographic characteristics of juries do not predict verdicts. Juries are bound by the "discipline of the evidence," which is understood with such subtlety that it overwhelms the usual means of multivariable analysis.[77] The norms implicit in the trial's linguistic performance are central to understanding its results. Juries are aware of the public significance of their role. Deliberation, though significant, is less important than the encounter of the individual juror with the evidence.[78] The trial's the thing.

The trial works because of the almost unbearable tensions created by the trial's practices. There are tensions between the roles of the lawyers, witnesses, judge, and jurors. There are, as we have seen, enormous tensions within the case taken as a whole and among different trial performances. Narrative is very important at trial, as a carrier of meaning, moral evaluation, and political identity, but the forms of narrative are distinctive. We have already seen the contrast between the narratives of opening and direct examination. But the conditions under which these stories are told pull them toward each other—the openings are not just "the best stories." They have to anticipate the other side's case. They have to anticipate the evidence that will soon be heard. (Otherwise, openings are "broken promises.") They have to be concerned with the law of rules—concretely with the possibility of a directed verdict and with the limitations the doctrine of materiality will impose on the evidence to come. The rules of the trial force the trial's narratives toward each other, toward the facts of the case, and toward the rules.

Those tensions create the conditions under which the jury may discern the meaning of the case, the practical truth of a human situation. They impose a real discipline. They eliminate the arbitrariness that often inheres in our ordinary lazy attitudes toward large undifferentiated classes of persons and events. They often achieve through public practices what only a few people are capable of through the refinement of their own moral judgment.[79]

The trial succeeds as well because it does not assume that all the meaning and thus the evaluation of events must be derived from the legal categories. Juries are typically instructed that they are to rely on their "common sense and experiences in life." That phrase may be given an interpretation that is consistent with a purely rule-centered view of the trial. Within that view, common sense provides a set of value-free empirical generalizations that allow the jury to construct a value-free narrative of what occurred. It seems to me, however, that an account of events that contained no evaluation other than those that could be rigorously derived from the jury instructions would probably be unintelligible. It certainly is not what the consciously structured hybrid of languages that we find at trial actually provides. The moral sources that are actualized at trial exist in the life world of the jurors. They are the negotiated truths that made a certain way of life possible. They are not arbitrary; neither is a decision derived from them, duly actualized and refined. Least of all is it "purely emotional."

## What It Adds Up To: Thinking What We Do

My next step is to offer a brief interpretation of the significance of what occurs at trial. The decision that the jury makes is a response "to the meaningfulness of the situation in which one is engrossed."[80] It is because the trial is so engrossing that the jury's decision is unlikely to be arbitrary, that it responds to the discipline of the evidence. It is true that I am interpreting an ideal trial, but not one so ideal that it is beyond the range of human accomplishment. I am interested in situated ideals, ideals that are consistently within the range of actual accomplishment. Those are also the ideals that point the way to possible reforms and allow us to see how the distortions of the trial, which I will consider shortly, have sadly prevented those ideals from being realized.

The trial proceeds, as I said, by the construction and deconstruction of narrative. What is the *significance* of the centrality of narrative at trial, both the relatively free interpretive narrative of opening statement and the greatly constrained narrative in the language of perception offered on direct examination? Narratives allow the jury to "organize and analyze the vast amount of information involved in making a legal judgment":[81] "[W]hat does not get structured narratively suffers loss in memory."[82] The trial wisely assumes that narratives are at least a reliable starting point for understanding a human event, that stories are "told in being lived and lived in being told,"[83] that narrative is congruent in some way with the actual structure of human experience. (It also wisely employs the whole range of devices that we have already examined to correct the possible distortions of free narrative.) Opening statements are necessarily simplifying, and that simplification necessarily involves a judgment as to relative importance that actualizes the meaning of the story: "[T]he judgment of importance, by getting rid of the accessory, creates continuity: that which

actually took place is disconnected and torn by insignificance, the narrative is meaningful because of its continuity."[84] Good storytelling can "reveal meaning without committing the error of defining it."[85] By allowing
lawyers to tell a relatively unconstrained story in opening, the law allows
more of the full human significance of the past events, as determined by
the moral sensibilities implicit in all practices that structure the life world,
to enter the courtroom.[86] It protects against the danger of bureaucratic
ossification that always haunts the law.[87] This morality is not the abstract
morality of principle, but can include everything necessary to the "complexity of the original moral problem."[88] Narrative is internally related to
issues of justice:

> Stories tell us how each one finds or loses his just place in relation to others in
> the world. And the communication of the story is confirmed when justice has
> been recognized. Is there *any* story we tell in which justice is not at issue[?] It
> is almost as if we constitute a jury out of our listeners, so that it falls to them to
> judge the particular view of the case that we present in our story.[89]

Stories are told when there has been a deviation from a traditional pattern
and the community needs to understand the event in light of an inventory
of commonsense beliefs about the sources of deviance. Otherwise the underlying offense would remain one of an "unbearable sequence of sheer
happenings" undermining the convictions that make our common life significant. Finally, the form of narrative used in opening statement places
the jury within the story being told. The story says that there has been a
disruption of the just patterns of life in which we all share and that action is necessary to restore those patterns. This is, of course, precisely the
structure of the commutative justice that is central to legal justice—the
restoring of the just balance that characterized the community before its
violent disruption.[90]

The battle for the imagination of the jury, we saw, begins with opening
statements. After the openings, the jury will be in a position to answer
three questions. The first is, "In what way is it more likely to have happened?" Here they are relying on their common sense, conceived as a set
of commonsense empirical generalizations. The second question the jury
will be able to answer is, "Which understanding of these events invokes
a more powerful norm?" This will be a moral judgment. The third question is, "Which understanding of these events invites us to act in a manner

more consistent with our public identity?" In answering this question, the jury is acting "politically" in a manner Tocqueville thought distinctive to the American jury.

Even in this preliminary stance, the jury is not reacting solely to "the best story the lawyer can tell" in abstraction from the evidence to come and the legal standards embodied in the law of rules. Each lawyer must anticipate the other side's case. The other attorney can be relied upon to inform the jury of any facts inconsistent with the story he or she wants to tell. Second, as I mentioned, openings have a performative quality as promises to produce admissible and credible evidence, a characteristic enforced by the rules of professional conduct. Third, the law of rules is represented in two ways. In civil cases, the parties' factual theory of the case will have to survive a motion for a directed verdict and so must be adequate "as a matter of law." And the evidence that each lawyer will present must pass the test of materiality, the standard for which is set by the rules embedded in the jury instructions. Although lawyers have relative freedom to invoke all the dominant moral values of the jury's life world in opening statements, the law and the evidence have strong impact even here.

So the jury can make preliminary determinations of the relative strength of the cases after opening statements. Structural elements of the theory of the case are weighed: "The inadequate development of setting, character, means or motive, as any literature student knows, render[s] a story's actions ambiguous.... In a trial it is grounds for reasonable doubt."[91] Further, the story is initially tested against the preexistent commonsense generalizations of the society. These are stored in the community's "web of belief," a set of generalizations that have the form, "Generally and for the most part, ..." (e.g., mothers will promote the interests of their children).[92] But, thankfully, these commonsense generalizations do not decide the case. Common sense very rarely confronts the level of detailed factual development that the trial provides. Every time one lawyer says, "Generally and for the most part ... ," the other lawyer is likely to say, "Yes, but not where...." Each new case requires a genuine insight, what Peirce called an "abduction," that must seek out the intelligibility inherent in these particular facts.[93] The jury will also begin to evaluate the case based on the openings' struggle for the higher moral ground in the particular circumstances that the details of the narrative reveal. Placing the facts in a narrative form "is a demand ... for moral meaning, a demand that sequences of events be assessed as to their significance as elements of a moral drama."[94] "The world of recountable events" is an ethical world,[95] and "narrative already belongs to the ethical field of its claim—inseparable from narration—to ethical justice."[96] Thus the tentative moral judgment that the jury makes after the openings is based not on a moral *theory* but on "an *ethics already realized*" (emphasis added) in the practices and institutions of the society.[97] Finally, the narratives of opening statement require the jury to consider the relationship of the case to their own public identities. In their opening statements, the lawyers are signaling to the jury that their decision in the case will determine the shape of the society for which they are now inevitably responsible: "By his manner of judging the person discloses to an extent also himself, what kind of person he is, and this disclosure is involuntary."[98] This identity is a public identity:

> Storytelling offers us the means of reconciliation with reality. But, in effect it also makes a common understanding of reality, and so, a world, possible for us in our plurality. . . . Stories tell us how each one finds or loses his just place in relation to others in the world. And the communication of the story is confirmed when justice has been recognized.[99]

This is precisely the place of the jury in American life of which Tocqueville has given the classic expression:

> The jury, as more especially the civil jury, serves to communicate the spirit of the judges to the minds of all the citizens; and this spirit with the habits which attend it, is the soundest preparation for free institutions. It imbues all classes with a respect for the thing judged and with the notion of right. . . . The jury teaches every man not to recoil before the responsibility of his own actions and impresses him with that manly confidence without which no political virtue can exist. It invests each citizen with a kind of magistracy; it makes them all feel the duties which they are bound to discharge towards society and the part which they take in its government. By obliging men to turn their attention to other affairs than their own, it rubs off that private selfishness which is the rust of society.[100]

The lawyers in a well-tried case, beginning with opening statements, are providing the jury with the means to perform an act of interpretation: "What we are interpreting is ourselves, and the past and present social worlds that make us what we are. . . . [W]e already possess a preunderstanding of our historical identity and social relationships. This we get from our past, from the cultural and linguistic traditions that compose our historical identity."[101]

The vast bulk of the trial is consumed with the presentation of evidence. I have described how the presentation of testimony in response to nonleading questions and in the language of perception serves to build the powerful tensions that are at the heart of the trial's genius, as does cross-examination. The evidentiary phase quickly moves the center of gravity at trial away from morally and politically significant stories to the inconvenient details of the facts and the multiplicity of the perspectives of the witnesses. Paradoxically, by giving particularity and empirical truth their due, the trial provides a strong critique of commonsense generalizations: "It is only when we are confronted by the demands of action *in the context of a particular set of circumstances* that we get a true understanding of what our ends really are, and reassess those ends in relationship to a new understanding of our life as a whole. Action in the particular circumstances of life is a continuing dialogue between what we think our life is about, and the particularities of moral and practical exigency" (emphasis added).[102] Jurors come from a world where mass-circulation journalism and sentimental mass-media fiction anesthetize common sense by eliminating most of the tensions between the general norms and the detailed realities of particular cases. One of the reasons so many jurors value their service is that through it they experience what their common sense, elevated by the discipline of the evidence, is capable of. The trial provides a self-criticism of the overgeneralized "scripts" within which much of our common sense is stored.

The consciously structured hybrid of languages at trial creates a fair contest among real values where the appropriate balance can be attained only by fighting it out. A legal system in which decision flows easily from the sort of case presented is a system in which there is relatively little internal tension and, I would suggest, relatively little justice. As in physics, where an infinitely more abstract point of view is appropriate, "only by entertaining multiple and mutually limiting points of view, building up a composite picture, can we approach the real richness of the world."[103]

The tension of opposites created by the trial actualizes the largely tacit powers of the jury. As Holmes put it, "[M]any honest and sensible judgments ... express an intuition of experience which outruns analysis and sums up many unnamed and tangled impressions—impressions which may be beneath consciousness without losing their worth."[104] Or in Judge Weinstein's words:

> The jury's evaluation of the evidence relevant to a material proposition requires
> a gestalt or synthesis of evidence which seldom needs to be analyzed precisely.
> Any item of evidence must be interpreted in the context of all the evidence,
> introduced. . . . In giving appropriate, if sometimes unreflective, weight to a spe-
> cific piece of evidence the trier will fit it into a shifting mosaic. . . . [C]onfirming
> evidence of that other line of proof may require a reevaluation of the witnesses'
> credibility and a complex readjustment of the assessment of all the interlocking
> evidence.[105]

The jury's cognitive operations at trial are holistic and interpretive. The
jury performs an integration of all the evidence within the horizon of its
own practical responsibilities. It grasps a literally indescribable constellation of facts, norms, and possibilities for action.

Jury determinations often have a quality of depth or substance about
them because the trial puts the jury in a position to judge with care and
skill. Why this is so requires an account of the ways in which the consciously structured hybrid of languages and practices at trial really illu-
minates what is at stake there. The different languages of the trial express
modes of understanding that are congruent with quite different norms that
find their natural homes in different spheres of social life.[106] They have a
foundation in the way we actually live, in our social practices and forms of
life. What is at stake at trial is the relative importance of the norms at play
and the relative appropriateness of moral judgment, legal categorization,
or public self-constitution to the resolution of the cause. Because we have
built a society that, like any decent society, has relatively different spheres
constituted by different norms, somewhere in our social practices we must
discern what is the most important aspect of this *particular* case. And we
often do it at trial. The unbearable tensions among the "language regions"
at trial conform to the great tensions among social practices in the world.
The trial does justice and creates the institutional conditions of the possibility of justice's accomplishment.[107] Although its power comes from its
conservative quality and the centrality of commonsense moral categories,
it performs a distinctively modern function for us, "less to create constantly
new forms of life than to creatively renew actual forms by taking advantage of their internal multiplicity and tensions with one another."[108]

Powerful philosophical positions support the view of the jury trial that I
have just sketched out. They serve, at the theoretical level, as those "fibers
ever so slender" to help justify that view. I can only sketch them out here.
On the cognitive side, philosophers have identified the human intellec-

tual capacities that juries must exercise to respond to the trial's languages and practices. The Kantian tradition speaks of "reflective judgment," the capacity we have to operate without given generalizations. This power is activated by multiplying the standpoints from which a situation can be understood to achieve a kind of generality—but not "the generality of the concept. It is, on the contrary, closely connected with particulars, with the particular conditions of the standpoints one has to go through in order to arrive at one's own general standpoint."[109] This multiplication of perspectives succeeds when "a particular issue is forced into the open that it may show itself from all sides, in every possible perspective, until it is flooded and made transparent by the full light of human comprehension."[110] The multiplicity of trial languages and performances is designed to create the conditions for that kind of illumination.

The Aristotelian tradition speaks of "practical wisdom" as relying on a kind of tacit judgment of perceptual identification—our ability to see something as it is. Human intelligence can dwell in the tensions of the particular to understand it for what it is beyond the capacity of principles likely to be established ahead of time. This ability so closely parallels the intelligence trial languages and practices activate that I must quote at some length:

> We reflect on an incident not by subsuming it under a general rule, not by as-similating its features to the terms of an elegant scientific procedure, but by bur-rowing down into the depths of the particular, finding images and connections that will permit us to see it more truly, describe it more richly; by combining this burrowing with a horizontal drawing of connections, so that every horizon-tal link contributes to the depth of our view of the particular, and every new depth creates new horizontal links. . . . This image of learning expressed in this style . . . stresses responsiveness and attention to the complexity; it discourages the search for the simple, and, above all, for the reductive. . . . [C]orrect choice (or: good interpretation) is, first and foremost, a matter of keenness and flexibil-ity of perception, rather than conformity to a set of simplifying principles.[111]

Finally, the interpretive or hermeneutical tradition stresses our ability to understand through circular codetermination of particulars and universals, on the one hand, and the details of a particular situation and our projects on the other. Again, Geertz speaks of "a continuous dialecti-cal tacking between the most local of local detail and the most global of global structures in a way as to bring both into view simultaneously."[112]

The particular situation is understood against a preexistent common sense, which is both a web of belief and also a "learned way of *acting*—or coping with things and situations—that renders the world meaningful" (emphasis added) and this because "the way human beings exist or 'dwell' in the world is fundamentally in a state of practical absorption in tasks and skills."[113] There are thus two circles of the understanding around which the jury moves. The first moves between the individual pieces of evidence and the whole theory and theme of the case. The second moves between the details of the evidence and the jury's practical options. For example, the defendant's actions may be found to be "knowing" depending in part on the risks of releasing him back out into the community.[114]

All three traditions provide accounts of "communal validity" for judgments. Arendt found in Kant's notion of reflective judgment a "mode of thinking that is neither to be identified with the expression of private feelings nor to be confused with the type of thinking that is characteristic of 'cognitive reason.' It is a mode of thinking that is capable of dealing with the particular in its particularity, but that nevertheless makes the claim to communal validity. When one judges, one judges as a member of a human community."[115] Likewise, Aristotelian practical wisdom involves a disciplined and careful perception of an individual situation in light of a complex web of public norms. And interpretive understanding involves an integrative understanding of a particular situation in light of shared modes of acting. All three achieve an objectivity rooted in a refined grasp of the relevance of basic norms to a particular situation.

Can the consciously structured hybrid of languages used at trial find the truth? I believe the answer is an emphatic Yes, though once again, such an affirmative answer depends on philosophical commitments, all of which are defensible. First, trial verdicts can be true if narrative is embedded in the nature of human action, which holds that stories are lived before they are told. The narratives of the trial, taken together and criticized ("deconstructed") by the acid of cross-examination and argument, can get close to the real human event. Second, though common sense must rely on commonsense generalizations and determinations of the probable, vigorous advocacy and well-wrought institutions can allow judgments of the probable to converge on the actually true. Recall the ways in which trial practices support this goal. The opening statement defines the meaning of the event being tried but is constrained by rules prohibiting "alluding to any matter of which there will not be admissible evidence."[116] More important, it is constrained by the trial itself: the opening statement is not only a story; it is also a promise. If the trial does not bear out the lawyer's statement, it is a broken promise. Lawyers may not fabricate evidence or suborn perjury. They may not assert matters on cross where there is no good-faith basis to believe the assertion. Testimony comes from live witnesses, under oath, who are subject to cross-examination. Each lawyer may offer evidence that supports his own case and also that undermines his opponent's. Further:

> The law of evidence, at least in the hands "of a strong and wise trial judge," serves to exclude both utterly unreliable evidence and the sorts of evidence that serve to dissipate the fruitful tensions of the trial with irrelevancy. So a lawyer cannot just tell the most plausible story, regardless of its truth. To the extent that a theory of the case is rendered initially plausible by a description which relies on the omission of details that ought fairly to be included, the correction will not be long in coming. To the extent that the jury was initially "taken in," then immediately disillusioned, to that extent will the general plausibility of the position be undermined, not only because of the performative offense, but also because of the implicit admission that such a distortion was the only way the position could be defended.[117]

In sum, "the ethics of the bar aim at dissuading 'puny' disputation, and the devices of the trial are designed to create the likelihood that the better argument and stronger evidence will prevail."[118] Third, the trial will work to the extent that it has the capacity to show more than it can tell, and correspondingly, that humans are capable of grasping a practical truth manifest in the tensions created by the trial's consciously structured hybrid of languages. Trial languages do not simply play off one another; they reveal something, "actually put us in contact with the sources it taps. It can *realize* the contact."[119] Fourth, the trial will be able to reach the truth of a human situation to the extent that fundamentally interpretive methods can converge on that truth. The trial shows us the meaning of the situation in a way that would be invisible without its methods, yet once we have experienced the trial, we cannot see the situation other than in the light the trial has shed. Finally, the trial will converge on the human truth of a situation to the extent that there exist no institutions better designed to achieve the practical purposes of the trial, and those purposes are rooted in the most important human interests. All those propositions are, I believe, more than defensible.

## CHAPTER TWO

# Historical Notes on the Trial's Importance

There is a unity in this centuries-old dialectic. —Thomas Green

In the first chapter, I showed the importance of the trial through thick description and interpretation of the kind of trial we have. I was beginning to show the significance of the death of the trial by explaining the power of its methods. But, true to the trial's own devices, understanding comes often from multiplying one's perspectives. In this chapter, I stand back from the contemporary trial, view it from the "outside," and provide something of an inventory of the ways in which it has been and remains significant. These perspectives are in the main historical, ways in which aspects of the trial have occupied the often passionate attention of the architects of our constitutional and legal order.

First, I recall the centrality of the trial, and in particular the jury trial, in the precious "rights of Englishmen" as they developed in the early modern world. More pertinent, I describe the ways in which the most "radical"—that is, democratic—strain of English thinking about the trial became particularly dominant in the United States. Indeed, Americans often pointed to the liberty and equality implicit in the shape of their own trials to distinguish themselves from the class-based oppression they saw in England. The shape of the trial for both civil and criminal cases was of the greatest concern in the debates that created the original Constitution and insisted on a Bill of Rights. The same was true in the states. At both the federal and the state levels, it was a matter of national identity that American trials were fairer and more democratic than were their English forebears.

So there are historical reasons to appreciate the trial's importance. There are also reasons that emerge from the structure of the legal doctrine that surrounds the trial. Its importance is reflected in the extent to which its shape has become a matter of constitutional law, that is, fundamental law. This reflects more than simply a guildlike proprietary interest on the part of judges in the procedures over which they preside: it suggests that the persons in closest contact with the ways of the trial perceive the intimate connections between those ways and the fundamental fairness of these important procedures, which should be beyond the reach of legislatures. This is true in criminal, civil, and even administrative contexts.

## English High Theory and Often Grim Practice

[I]t is not to be expected from human nature that the few should always be attentive to the interests and good of the many. —Alexis de Tocqueville, *Democracy in America*, trans. Philips Bradley, 1848, 1:297

The nature of the trial has been an issue around which Englishmen and Americans have established their political identity. The trial, as I described in the first chapter, is largely a creature of the late nineteenth century. By the beginning of the twentieth century, the trial's consciously structured hybrid of languages in sharp tension with one another had been set. But that trial had important continuities with earlier versions. It has always involved a face-to-face oral encounter among parties, judge, witnesses, and jury. Older forms embodied, sometimes in nascent terms, some of the most important qualities of our contemporary practices. Many of our attitudes toward the trial have deep roots in convictions surrounding these earlier forms. I cannot offer here anything approaching an historical narrative of the place of the trial in Anglo-American political culture. The best historical works have limited themselves to smaller pieces of this big story.[1] But aspects of the history are important for my purposes. They reveal perspectives on the place of the trial in our political culture that can easily be forgotten and must continually be recovered. This forgetfulness is fostered by the dominant instrumentalism of our intellectual and institutional world—the "onslaught of modernity" of which Hannah Arendt warned—against which the trial is one of the remaining ramparts.[2] We are historical beings, and some of the trial's contemporary importance can be gleaned from a recovery of key aspects of its place in our tradition.

The history does not contain any simple unidirectional trajectory. There appear to be complex ebbs and flows in the centrality of the trial in our political culture, in this "centuries-old dialectic." At several junctures,[3] as the trial becomes more powerful and more democratic and comes to realize, as I will suggest, its own internal ideals, it seems to lose political importance, as it becomes the target of powerful interests and sources of countervailing power. Given the tensions described below, this is something that should not surprise us. Quite recently, for example, the democratization of the jury trial has provoked a strong reaction from other sources of social power.[4] This reaction provides some of the force that currently threatens the death of the trial.

The languages and practices of our contemporary trial reflect competing values. Each set of values has its philosophical expression and defense. Which trial practices are legitimate and which decadent? Which political philosophy is fullest and which partial? The questions are inevitably interrelated.[5] And the answers to those questions both determine and are dependent on our historical narrative. We can converge on the truth on both matters only if such interpretive circles allow us real insight, as I believe they do.[6] And so my account on all questions can only convince "by the overall plausibility of the interpretation they give,"[7] by the "mutual support of many considerations, of everything fitting together into one coherent view."[8]

Historically, the trial has been an enormously important institution by any number of measures. There is a place for American particularism here: though rooted in the experience of our English forebears, the trial has had and continues to have unparalleled significance for American culture and society. As Dr. Johnson put it, it is more important to remind than to instruct. In the face of the decline in the numbers of trials that is my central subject, and in a related social-scientific perspective that relies on quantitative measures to minimize the trial's importance, a page of history may indeed, in Holmes's words, be worth a volume of logic. And so I will provide just a page or two simply to show how important the issues surrounding the extent and shape of the jury trial has been. The largely implicit conclusion is, of course, that we ought to attend carefully to its imminent death.

The Anglo-American trial has proven an enduring and adaptable institution, and the American forms have both continuities and discontinuities from their English forebears.[9] In England and the United States both, the trial was regarded as one of the nation's most important institutions, central to the enterprise of governing. Certain qualities of the English experience with the trial were intensified in the United States, making the trial, especially the jury trial, an even more significant institution in our political culture.

The centrality of the trial, though, begins with the English experience: "The English jury is as old as the English state itself."[10] Earlier forms of trial by battle and ordeal, which rested on religious commitments in an age of faith, disappeared after the Fourth Lateran Council withdrew church sanction for practices that were condemned as attempts to force the hand of God.[11] The power of the religious condemnation for perjury and the easy analogy to trial by battle fostered the next development in the trial form, a kind of competitive oath taking among parties and their supporting witnesses.[12] Centuries followed in which the local jury was largely "self-informing," that is, jurors were chosen because they came from the locality in which the events being tried had occurred and were thought to have personal knowledge of those events and the characters of the participants. During this period, roughly until the middle of the fourteenth century, the formal practices that characterize our "instructional" trial were far less important. The trial itself looked more like an informal discussion among neighbors, unconstrained by formalities designed to guarantee the reliability of evidence or in some way elevate deliberation. The medieval jury exercised enormous "law-finding" powers that largely derived from the "social and institutional circumstances" under which it arose.[13] The criminal jury trial served to mediate royal power exercised through the criminal justice system in two ways:

> In individual cases, juries prevented the imposition of sanctions they deemed too harsh in light of the defendant's behavior, reputation, or the hardship he had already suffered. More generally, and as the result of its role in individual cases, the jury reflected the interests of the local community as opposed to those of central authorities. The Crown required the jury to play a role the royal bureaucracy was as yet unprepared to undertake—the gathering of evidence; this, in turn, enhanced the jury's power to render verdicts that both blunted royal power and made what power there was relatively palatable.[14]

It is true to the dialectic within which we still stand that increase in the power of the central government during the Tudor and Stuart periods and the trial's capacity to offer a counterweight to that power led officials sometimes "to regard the jury as part of the problem rather than as a solution."[15] However, "the failure to contest the verdicts of merely merciful juries, seen alongside the determined attempt to overturn verdicts authorities viewed as corrupt and truly damaging, must have reinforced society's sense that jury insistence upon the former kind of verdict was appropriate."[16] This general authority of the English jury over the norms at work at trial took quite different forms,[17] but by the early modern period the "ideology of jury mitigation (the more modest law-finding tradition) was relatively stable even though the specific motives that underlay mitigation were ever-changing."[18]

According to John Beattie, "[T]he late seventeenth century was the heroic age of the English jury, for in the political and constitutional struggles of the reigns of Charles II and James II, trial by jury emerged as the principle defense of English liberties."[19] It was then that the jury, composed largely of men of modest property holdings, emerged as a self-consciously democratizing force in English life and claimed authority over central political norms well beyond the simple mitigation of harsh sentences.[20] A series of important political cases—Lilburne's Case, Pitt's Case, Bushell's Case, the Case of the Seven Bishops—and the pamphleteering around them placed the jury trial at the center of those forces throughout the seventeenth century. After the Glorious Revolution in 1688, Parliament responded with a number of statutes that expanded litigants' rights and limited the power of the judge to remove important powers from the jury. Bushell's Case established the principle that jurors could not be punished for rendering a general verdict of acquittal in the face of what the judge thought was overwhelming evidence of guilt. More significantly, the court recognized the inevitable intertwining of issues of fact and law and the inevitability of "complicative" determinations of both: "[Chief Justice] Vaughn seems ultimately to have responded almost viscerally to a deep-seated notion concerning the sanctity of the juror's conscience."[21] A strand of judicial thinking appeared that gave the jury the right, *in foro conscientiae*, to discern "true law," giving varying degrees of deference to the judge's instruction but always maintaining the ultimate determination. In the criminal context, the jury's ability to bring back a general verdict of acquittal had, after Bushell's Case, made its concrete determination of innocence unreviewable regardless of the norms on which the jury actually relied. Some conceded the jury's power to go beyond the instructions but viewed this power as illegitimate. Others rejected this distinction between power and authority.[22] At least some strands of seventeenth-century thought went further and saw the jury's role, in both civil and criminal cases, as the source of the norms by which the case would be decided, making jurors true "judges of the law."[23] These were the strands that proved to have the greatest appeal in the colonies. And the Americans resolutely set about creating procedural mechanisms discontinuous with those used in the mother country to ensure that jurors would, in fact, exercise a larger range of authority over the moral sources at play at trial.

In England, this strong theory of the jury's role stood in stark contrast to the truly awful nature of criminal trial procedure in the eighteenth century. This contrast between the ideals surrounding the trial and its all-too-human reality is something that pervades this history. John Langbein has written a wonderfully detailed description of the English criminal trial through the beginning of the nineteenth century.[24] Those details provide a corrective to the more philosophical or ideological accounts of what the British criminal trial was, accounts that can easily be derived from the arguments in and the pamphleteering around the great political cases of the eighteenth century that so inspired the Founders. To us, as to many of the founding fathers, English procedures appear to operate under deeply unfair constraints that could only distort "verdict according to conscience."

For example, criminal defendants were prohibited from testifying under oath in England until 1898.[25] Until the early eighteenth century, defendants could not retain counsel, and it was not until the end of the eighteenth century that counsel could engage in the full range of practices, including addressing the jury in an opening statement and cross-examining witnesses, that we see today.[26] Until 1836 prosecution counsel could make an opening statement, but defense counsel could not.[27] Defendants were often kept incarcerated under deplorable conditions and then pushed, starving and confused, before judges to respond to indictments that they were not permitted to see, even at trial. Realistically it was impossible for them to gather evidence to support the innocence they effectively had the burden of proving. It is no surprise, then, that defendants' responses to the prosecution indictment and evidence "very often took the form not of careful cross-examination but rather of denying the evidence as it was being presented," creating a trial with a "formless or wandering quality that resembles ordinary discourse, a conversation of sorts, lacking the crisp division into prosecution and defense case that we now expect."[28]

The judge, who served at the pleasure of the king and usually saw himself
as an agent of the executive, exercised extensive powers of commenting
on evidence through an ongoing "chatter" with the jury and seemed often
effectively to bully the jury into his view of the case.[29] He could "reject a
proffered verdict, probe its basis, argue with the jury, give further instruction, and require redeliberation."[30] Despite the democratic ideals implicit
in the great political cases, British judges generally accepted Lord Coke's
dictum that the statement of the law was completely within their province.
Capital punishment was the norm for felonies, and codefendants often
tried to bid their way to freedom by offering testimony that would hang
larger and larger numbers of their alleged conspirators.

Langbein attributes the domination of the trial by lawyers—with a relatively passive judge, that is—to the main lines of the trial as I described
it in the last chapter, a set of historical conditions in British criminal trial
procedure that prevailed in the eighteenth century. Prosecutions were
initiated by private parties who brought their complaints to the local justice of the peace. The justice of the peace came to be a "partisan" of the
prosecution case, rather than a "truth seeker."[31] His role was to create
and preserve evidence to support the prosecution. He was precluded from
searching out evidence that supported innocence or even from examining
"[w]itnesses that expressly come to prove the Offender's innocence."[32] He
conducted an uncounseled examination of the defendant (a "deposition")
that was often used effectively against the defendant at trial. Langbein recounts the complaint of defense counsel at a 1787 trial at Old Bailey that
"[t]he Magistrates at Bow Street never receive evidence for prisoners, only
for prosecutors."[33] He notes that "[m]agisterial questioning functioned as
police interrogation does today; it offered the government an opportunity
to get whatever information it could from an uncounseled and frequently
frightened and confused defendant."[34] The justice routinely committed
the defendant to jail pending trial. The conditions were appalling: malnu-
trition and disease killed large numbers of detainees. Often detained for
months and lacking the assistance of counsel, prisoners were disgorged
directly into the trial court:

> Beattie's account . . . of the ineptness that many felony defendants displayed
> when attempting to defend themselves at trial links their predicament in part to
> the horrific jail conditions. "[M]en not used to speaking in public who suddenly
> found themselves thrust into the limelight before an audience in an unfamiliar
> setting—and who were for the most part dirty, underfed, and surely often ill—

did not usually cross-examine vigorously or challenge the evidence presented against them." The degradation and distraction of confinement continued into the courtroom; defendants were kept in leg irons until called for trial.[35]

Defendants were prohibited from having a copy of the indictment either at or before trial, and their imprisonment made it all but impossible for them to discover and organize evidence of their innocence. The prosecution possessed compulsory process and the defense did not; defense witnesses were not permitted to testify under oath.[36] Trials were designed to pressure the defendant into speaking (though he was prohibited from testifying under oath in England until the very late nineteenth century) in response to the prosecution's case. Judges were very well—and often wrongly—satisfied that they and the jury could distinguish truth telling from falsehood. Judges were also far more active—overbearing, it seems to our sensibilities—commenting on the evidence, interrogating the defendant and the jury in what Langbein describes as the "altercation style" of trial, and sending the jury back to reconsider a verdict the judge thought wrong.

After some cross-examination came to be permitted in the eighteenth century, questions the defendant sought to put to the defense witnesses had to be screened by the judge.[37] The "altercation trial" of the seventeenth century "was an abrupt affair" lasting fifteen to twenty minutes, *including deliberation.*[38] A single Old Bailey courtroom in the early eighteenth century processed twelve to twenty jury trials per day. Procedures, to say the least, "bespoke a certain callousness toward the conduct of criminal business,"[39] because criminal trials were considered "the travail of the lower orders, a necessary evil that could be hurried along, unlike the civil business that deserved care."[40] Langbein describes the doings at the Old Bailey as a "conveyer belt"—one that led from unspeakable conditions of confinement to the gallows, unless some form of discretionary commutation intervened.

The English adversary trial as we know it emerged over the eighteenth century as a series of specific reforms to this deeply unfair system.[41] At first lawyers were permitted to assist the defendant solely on points of law; they were not permitted even to address the court or jury on the central issue of factual guilt or innocence. The lethality of the thieftakers and turncoat coconspirators led judges eventually to permit the cross-examination of prosecution witnesses. Judges then allowed lawyers to call defense witnesses and eventually to address the jury directly on the ultimate issues.

What Langbein descriptively calls the "defendant speaks" trial evolved into a proceeding in which the defendant rarely spoke. Judges' relative ignorance of the facts of the cases before them and the obvious clumsiness of their questioning led them to cede more and more authority to the lawyers, who had investigated and prepared the case and who could thus present a coherent theory of it in a way that judges could not. (In the United States, ceding an increasing level of responsibility for case presentation to the parties and increasing restrictions on the trial judge was also perceived to be consistent with many of the democratic themes that emerged during the colonial and revolutionary period, especially as they bore on suspicion of trial judges.)[42] Both in England and especially in the United States, the trial was assuming the shape that would make good on its historical promise of realizing the common sense of the jury, relatively unconstrained by disabling formalisms, structured by the ascendant law of evidence, and relatively free from authoritarian distortions. These developments could be justified on either moral ("natural law") or democratic grounds.

On the civil side as well, the potential that the trial held was constricted in England. The substantive law was in many ways undeveloped: the law of tort was virtually nonexistent, and vicarious liability (allowing recovery from the employer of damages resulting from the authorized actions of his employees) was "primitive."[43] Parties in civil cases—often those with the most reliable and relevant evidence—were disqualified from testifying.[44] The number of barristers, the attorneys actually permitted to try cases, was small and drawn largely from the landed gentry.[45] Civil cases were initiated by waves of extremely technical written pleadings unrelated to what we would call the substance of the claim. An error in the choice of writ at the pleading stage and so in the form of action would doom a case. Many cases did not survive pleading actually to reach trial. Indeed, Langbein describes the essential nature of early civil procedure as "trial avoiding": "The practical result was that the English civil courts were largely reserved for gentry and wealthy businessmen."[46]

As lawyers gained a wider range of functions in the British trial courtroom during the second half of the eighteenth century, conflicts with the older overbearing style of judging emerged. Prominent lawyers came to resent judges' clumsy intrusions into their cross-examination, intrusions that were based on judges' own misperceptions of the lawyer's purposes and theories.[47] But there was also a movement toward oral adversary presentation in both civil and criminal courts and some movement, already gaining momentum in the United States, toward resolution of cases on the merits. Most witness incompetencies—status-based prohibitions on testifying—including those of parties, were eliminated. Compulsory process increased. Cross-examination became the central device for the jury's newfound duty to determine relative credibility, and the growth of hearsay law was designed to support cross,[48] now understood as "the greatest legal engine for the determination of truth ever developed."[49] Inspired by a democratic self-understanding alien to the mother country, these practical developments were even more marked in the United States, as Americans proved determined to realize practically much of the power of the trial that had only been the aspiration of idealists and philosophers in England.

## American High Theory and a More Democratic Practice

The United States, too, had its "heroic" trials. They were rooted in the English tradition but were less disfigured by the English class system and the aristocratic nature of bench and bar. For example, the trial of the publisher John Peter Zenger for accusing the royal governor of malfeasance (including attacking the right to jury) and Zenger's subsequent acquittal were important events in American self-definition.[50] In the course of the trial the defendant's counsel was permitted to argue explicitly to the jury that it was up to them to decide whether or not truth was a defense to a charge of libel, regardless of what the English precedents known to the trial judge might say. In response to the trial judge's assertion that it was "very common" for the jury to provide only a "special verdict" on the bare issue of publication and "leave the matter of law to the Court," Zenger's lawyer replied confidently, "I know . . . the jury may do so; but I do likewise know that they may do otherwise. I know they have the right beyond all dispute to determine both the law and fact, and where they do not doubt of the law, they ought to do so. . . . [L]eaving it to the judgement of the Court whether the words are libelous or not in effect renders juries useless."[51] On the civil side as well, "juries became one of the agents of change helping to introduce new values into the law and society."[52]

American trial procedure emerged, of course, in a society without a feudal background or a relatively fixed class system formally represented in government. It was rooted in English practices but less distorted by England's class system and its aristocratic bench and bar. It is no surprise, then, that "the jury was the central instrument of governance."[53] Important distinctions between the vastly more democratic and egalitarian American society and the English class society had important effects on the importance the jury trial could assume. By the end of the eighteenth century, "two-thirds of white American families owned land, compared to only twenty percent of the English population."[54] Americans suffered little of the fear of an underclass rabble's bursting the dam of law that troubled the aristocracy in England.[55] Americans were by our standards poor, but they did not generally share that misery that overwhelmed the masses of urban poor in the great cities of Europe and toward whom officials often cast a nervous eye. As Jefferson put it (referring here to France), "of twenty millions of people ... there are nineteen millions more wretched [and] more accursed in every circumstance of human existence than the most conspicuously wretched individual in the United States." During his time in Paris, Franklin thought "often of the happiness of New England, where every man is a Freeholder, has a vote in publick affairs, lives in a tidy warm House, has plenty of good Food and Fewel." Visitors from England were shocked to find that "[i]n a course of 1,200 miles [they] did not see a single object that solicited charity."[56] In short, "the predicament of poverty" that overwhelmed the politics of Europe "was absent from the American scene but present everywhere else in the world."[57] There existed less of the desperate need for "social control" of the dangerous classes that was intertwined with criminal trials in England.

Further, the British bar itself was decidedly aristocratic,[58] while in the United States the new law schools opened the profession to a newly prosperous middle class. They came "to belong to the people by birth and interest" and "to the aristocracy [only] by habit and taste," as Tocqueville put it. The English judiciary, who all served at the pleasure of the king, viewed themselves as "advancing the royal policy," and the "Lord Chief Justice of the King's Bench remained a member of the ministry until the end of the eighteenth century."[59] The United States, especially after the Revolution, had a far sharper notion than did England of the importance of the separation of powers.

There was no doubt the colonists often clung to the historical "rights of Englishmen," but there was a powerful strand of thinking that interpreted those rights as the expression of the shared morality of ordinary citizens gathered in juries to decide both criminal and civil cases. Juries had begun in the colonies by exercising a broad range of political and administrative functions and retained their authority from their origins. The American suspicion of government found a natural expression in the jury trial and, as we will see below, made issues of "jury control" less pressing than in Great Britain.

Even in colonial times, there were marked differences from contemporary British practices. In "parts of British North America," the criminal defendant was, for example, permitted to have counsel at trial.[60] American writers after independence identified the presence of counsel, since constitutionalized in the Sixth Amendment, as a mark of the superiority of American ways: "We have never admitted that cruel and illiberal principle of the common law of England that when a man is on trial for his life, he shall be refused counsel, and denied those means of defense which are allowed, when the most trifling pittance of property is in question."[61] English judges enjoyed extensive privileges of commenting on the evidence that were denied judges in the colonies. "From the 1780s and across the nineteenth century" many states enacted statutes or constitutional provisions forbidding judges to comment on the evidence.[62] Indeed, the English judge's right to comment on the evidence can distract us from the way in which the judge could easily dominate the extremely informal discussion that was the English trial before the late eighteenth century. The English "altercation trial," in which the defendant was forced to answer often hostile questions from the bench in front of an often compliant (and illiterate) jury, provided the defendant none of the protection that increased formality brought in the United States.[63] Indeed, in the United States the motivation for that formality, including the growth of the law of evidence, seems largely to have been an attempt to control judicial interference in the proceedings. Unlike their English cousins, American judges didn't force juries to redeliberate about verdicts they disapproved of. Many American state courts gave up the prohibition on the defendant's testimony under oath decades before England did (in 1898).[64] And colonial experience tended to foster skepticism about that English fiction that the criminal court judge "represented" the criminal defendant, making individual counsel unnecessary.[65]

On the civil side, there was a drive for procedures that would allow substantive justice to emerge at trial. The right of the trial judge to grant a "demurrer to the evidence" and so take the case away from the jury was limited.[66] Even the judge's right to grant a new trial (and so a new jury) in cases where the trial judge believed the jury had gotten it seriously wrong, used more liberally in England, came slowly to the United States. Americans viewed the English common law pleading system in civil cases as a "petrified forest of arbitrary rules that did little to sharpen the thinking of either parties or courts,"[67] creating "a miserable state of intricacy, expense and confusion."[68] American courts were adopting a "'more liberal' approach to pleading, one that would assist them 'to Investigate the Merits of the Cause, and not to entangle in the Nets of technical Terms,'" as Alexander Hamilton put it.[69] Bogus notes that "[i]n 1799, Georgia enacted legislation declaring that a plaintiff could begin a lawsuit by filing a petition 'describing his claim 'plainly, fully, and substantially,' and a defendant could reply by filing an answer that set forth 'the cause of his defense.'"[70] William Nelson concludes that even in relatively conservative Massachusetts, "the emerging concern in pleading was with substance, not with form."[71] In sum,

> [i]n the span of a few decades, American courts created a functional procedural system, one that helped make the courts relatively accessible and focus the litigants and the court on the merits of the case. In retrospect, this seems so obviously sensible as to have been inevitable. And in fact, by 1830, England itself began moving toward a modern pleading system. At the time, however, it was a genuine revolution. The common law system had developed over centuries and was, for the most part, deeply revered by American lawyers and statesmen. Yet over only a few decades, an integral part of the system was radically reformed. Moreover, the change was related to a new conception of the role of the courts and the common law.[72]

The relaxation of pointless procedural formalism and the more egalitarian sensibilities of bench and bar in the United States both reflected and allowed the development of the place of the jury as providing a true "verdict according to conscience," in a way that matched the more radical English ideas. It was easy for American lawyers to embrace and develop the continuity between ordinary moral intuitions and the principles of "true law." After all, a conservative like John Adams could declare, "[t]he great Principles of the [English] Constitution, are intimately known, they are sensibly felt by every Briton—it is scarcely extravagant to say they are drawn in and imbibed with the Nurses' milk and first Air." And as Jefferson put it, "The great principles of right and wrong are legible to every reader: to pursue them requires not the aid of many counselors," and anyone could easily perceive "what violated decency and good order."[73] Procedural and substantive rigidity was sought to contain the discretion of judges, not of juries. The latter were thought to pose no systematic threat to the rights of the citizens who would likely appear before them.

## The Centrality of the Trial in the Formative Era

The political stature of the jury trial was also evident in its centrality in the disputes dividing the colonies and the mother country. Tensions often surrounded British efforts to remove proceedings into equity or admiralty courts, which were staffed by imperial appointees and sat without juries. The Stamp Act Congress explicitly protested the absence of a right to a jury trial under the provisions of the act.[74] The First Continental Congress strongly complained of a series of British "Intolerable Acts" in part because they provided for trials of colonial offenders in England, not before local juries. The Second Continental Congress's Declaration of the Causes and Necessity of Taking Up Arms protested English statutes "extending the jurisdiction of courts of admiralty and vice-admiralty beyond their ancient limits [and] depriving . . . [the colonies] of the accustomed and inestimable privilege of trial by jury, in cases affecting both life and property."[75] And the Declaration of Independence included the denial of jury trial in its bill of indictment against George III. In sum:

> By the time of the Revolution . . . the jury had become a symbol of the colonists' struggle for self-government. Its law-finding function made it ground zero in the battle between the king's ministers and colonial leaders. For the colonists, the jury had become an important weapon in combating royal oppression. Unable to fight unpopular laws in Parliament, America used the jury to nullify legislation. "Victimless" crimes, like sedition and smuggling, were essentially unenforceable because they lacked popular support.[76]

The colonial reverence for the jury trial and aversion to legal formalities unrelated to substantive ends continued after independence: "The right to trial by jury was probably the only one universally secured by the first American state constitutions."[77] That was true in both criminal and civil cases. As Hamilton conceded in *Federalist No. 83*,[78] many of the colonies had adopted a far greater use of the jury than had been the case in England, including in equity and admiralty courts, where the mother country tried cases to the bench. Procedures became far more deferential to the

jury's ability to provide "substantive justice" than the more rigid procedures in England. The English artifice of special pleading, which sought
to constrict trials artificially to a single issue, was little used in the colonies.[79] The special verdict, to which the trial judge alluded in the Zenger
case, seems to have been used only when both parties agreed, and juries
may have had the discretion to decline even an agreement of the parties.[80]
In most states, the English device of demurrer to the evidence,[81] which
avoided a jury determination by conceding the opponent's factual case
and resting its argument solely on legal argument presented to the judge,
was not employed.[82] Many American courts empaneled three judges, each
of whom gave his opinion as to the law, leaving it to the jury to choose from
among them. Furthermore, "[m]ost New England judges explicitly refused
to overturn a verdict on the grounds that the jury had ignored the court's
instructions."[83] Though such a conclusion must be qualified,[84] it appears
that colonial trials were far more oriented to allowing the jury to decide a
case based on its consideration of the facts and, after being informed of the
judge's best understanding of the state of the precedents, its own judgment
as to what "true law" requires. This contrast with the mother country was
self-conscious. As one Virginia judge put it, the practice of powerful English judges in controlling their juries "does not accord with the free institutions of this country."[85] The distinctive character of American democratic
self-understanding was affecting the details of trial procedure.

The original Constitution that emerged from the Philadelphia convention contained an explicit provision in the judicial article for trial by jury in
criminal cases in the state within which the crime had been alleged to have
been committed.[86] By contrast, the absence of a provision for trial by jury
in civil cases was a miscalculation by the Federalists that almost doomed
the Constitution.[87] As Hamilton conceded in *Federalist No. 83*, that absence was the most powerful argument deployed by the Anti-Federalists
in their arguments against the adoption of the Constitution. Indeed, the
rhetoric of *Federalist No. 83* provides a truly wonderful example of the
extreme delicacy and deference with which the Federalists had to address
the intense convictions of their audience about the importance of trial by
jury. Hamilton had to concede that "[t]here is no dispute about the excel-
lence of the institution" and sought to demur only on "whether it is the
very palladium of liberty."[88] "[A]t least seven state ratifying conventions
called for the amendments to the Constitution guaranteeing the right to
trial by jury in civil cases."[89] And in passing the Seventh Amendment, the
new nation explicitly understood that it was constitutionalizing a mode of

decision making that would sometimes be inconsistent with that likely to be favored by professional judges and that would lead to different results from those judges would provide.[90]

The arguments about trial procedure were fought out against broader developments in the political philosophy and rhetoric that had emerged from the Revolution to the ratification of the Constitution. The egalitarianism of the Revolution moved the new nation away from formalism and priestly forms of pleading and procedure. The distinctive political theory offered by the Federalists placed sovereignty in the people, not in the legislature. This was a departure from the inherited modes of thought that emerged from the constitutional battles of the English seventeenth century, where the goal was to put sovereignty in the legislature rather than in the king. In the United States, each of the branches of government was understood to be composed of "magistrates" who could pose a danger to the people's rights and freedom.[91] The jury served a fundamental role in providing a forum for that sovereignty that was the ultimate source of the constitution itself and was in a sense "above" the enactments of the magistrates serving in the legislature.[92] This sovereignty was not understood mainly as an expression of sheer popular will, but of the political and moral judgment of ordinary citizens on matters of justice, the most reliable consistent source for discerning natural rights.[93] Yes, government was inevitable, though itself "a reflection on the nature of man."[94] However, the devices needed to constrain men in their hostility to one another could be commandeered to do the very greatest harms. Checks and balances provided some security, of course, but the jury trial provided both a check on the magistracy *and* a reservoir of that preconstitutional medium of public judgment on natural rights.

Akhil Reed Amar has recently argued for a central role of the jury throughout the first ten amendments, "the paradigmatic image underlying the Bill of Rights": "Not only was it featured in three separate amendments (the Fifth, Sixth, and Seventh), but its absence strongly influenced the judge-restricting doctrines underlying three other amendments (the First, Fourth and Eighth)."[95] Amar cites the words of prominent Anti-Federalists, who urged that through juries "frequently drawn from the body of the people ... we secure to the people at large, their just and rightful controul in the judicial department," and that juries provide to the people "a share of Judicature which they have reserved for themselves."[96] And he recalls Jefferson's famous words: "Were I called upon to decide whether the people had best be omitted in the Legislative or

Judicial department, I would say it is better to leave them out of the Legislative."[97] Other contemporary constitutional theorists tried to understand
the jury as the lower house of the trial court, the "*democratic branch of
the judiciary power*—more necessary than representatives in the legislature" (emphasis added), analogous to the House of Representatives. And
contemporary advocates urged, cogently in Amar's view,[98] and consistent
with Wood's view of Federalist political theory, that because juries were
judges of the law as well as of fact, they possessed not only a more incho-
ate authority to nullify an unjust law in application, but also the right to
judge the constitutionality of acts of Congress in application.[99] That this
notion seems so alien to us is a function of the reconfiguration of the relationship between trial judge and jury and between trial courts and appellate courts during the nineteenth century, which I will describe briefly
below. Still, Amar finds echoes of this significant place for the jury in determining normative issues in the trial courts:

> But even today remnants of the Framers' vision remain, in doctrinal rules pre-
> venting judges from directing verdicts of guilty or requiring special verdicts in
> criminal cases; barring trial judges from reversing, and appellate courts from
> reviewing, criminal acquittals; allowing criminal defendants to escape govern-
> ment efforts to use collateral estoppel offensively; and prevent challenges to
> inconsistent criminal jury verdicts. In logic, each of these doctrines seems to
> bow to the criminal jury's right to go beyond merely deciding facts.[100]

The jury's "law-finding" role, noted below, thus migrated to an implicit
role determining the constitutionality of legislation.[101]

The tensions implicit in the nature of the trial continued through the
nineteenth century. In the early nineteenth century, several prominent
judges were impeached because they refused to honor the jury's role
as judges of the law.[102] In his reply to the impeachment charges, Justice
Samuel Chase conceded the jury's right to decide the law, limiting the
judge to a role in preventing counsel from misleading the jury on matters
of precedent.[103] And in arguing for a strong principle of *stare decisis*,[104]
Chase was careful to present the doctrine as a limitation on the judge, not
the jury. There remained a tension between the jury's highly individualized decision making to discern "true law" in the particular case and an
elevated notion of uniformity and predictability. The jury's authority over
law found its way into several state constitutions.[105] In 1790 Pennsylvania
Supreme Court Justice James Wilson lectured his Philadelphia audience

that the jury should "pay much regard" to the court's view of the law, but that if "a difference of sentiment takes place between the judges and jury, with regard to a point of law, . . . the jury must do their duty, and their whole duty; they must decide the law as well as the fact."[106] Supreme Court Justice Jay instructed a 1794 civil jury that "you have . . . a right to take upon yourselves to . . . determine the law as well as the fact in controversy."[107] As late as 1849 the Vermont Supreme Court reversed a trial court because it had instructed a jury that it was bound to follow the instructions as given, writing that the "opinion of the legal profession in this state, from the first organization of the government . . . has been almost if not quite uniform in favor of the . . . right of the jury to determine issues of law."[108] At the Massachusetts Constitutional Convention of 1853, delegates invoked the heritage of jury supremacy in language that the Anti-Federalists would have understood:

> Which is the best tribunal to try [a] case? This man who sits upon the bench, and who . . . has nothing in common with the people; who has hardly seen a common man in twenty years. . . . Is he the better man to try the case than they who have the same stake in community, with their wives, and children, and their fortunes, depending on the integrity of the verdicts they shall render?[109]

Another delegate invoked the tradition of "jury review" of the Fugitive Slave Law in exactly the way that Amar found for some situations: where "the rights which we reserve to the people are invaded by any law, . . . a jury coming from the people may be allowed to come in and give their judgment, and rescue the people, in the name of their declared rights, from an unconstitutional law, or from an unconstitutional interpretation of that law."[110] In the context of criminal law, the jury's explicit law-finding powers lasted longer and, in practical ways, still exist. As late as 1886 the Pennsylvania high court still held fast to the view that "the jury [were] not only judges of the facts . . . but also of the law."[111] In 1860 the Vermont Supreme Court explicitly praised the jury's role in criminal cases to protect "the security of the citizen against any impracticable refinements in the law, or any supposable or possible tyranny or oppression of the courts." Speaking directly to the cast of mind that sought to rely solely on comprehensive preexistent rules to protect a citizen's liberty, the court declared that the law-finding function is "one of those great landmarks . . . which . . . will always be likely to be characterized as an absurdity by the mere advocates of logical symmetry in the law, [yet] which will nevertheless be sure in the long run to constantly gain ground, and become more and more firmly fixed in the hearts and sympathies of those with whom liberty and law are almost synonymous."[112]

Before mid-century, however, one can also see Tennessee courts straining to set a middle position (despite a provision in the state constitution granting the jury the right to decide law and fact), one holding that the jury was required to accept the position of the trial judge "unless in their conscience they believed him to be wrong" and the other that "the jury as the judges of the law as it applies to the fact . . . but the court is the proper source from which they are to get the law, in other words, they are the judge of the law as well as the facts, under the direction of the court."[113]

The philosophical importance of the jury in the American trial had a social and economic correlate. The common law of England "was a body of rules and practices that were primarily concerned with the affairs of the rich and the powerful, the landed gentry of England."

> In the United States, of course, the situation was quire different. By the 19th century, law had an important meaning for the middle-class mass. Particularly in the northeast and the middle west, the average or typical family was a small landowner. At least the head of the family had some contact with the legal system—with the laws of inheritance, debt, and so on. Ordinary people in other words, were consumers of law and legal services. . . . Courts and judicial process were probably more accessible in the 19th century than they are today. Probably, a higher percentage of the population actually went to court, or appeared before a judge as a litigant, witness, or other participant.[114]

Countercurrents to the understanding of the jury trial as a source of law began weakly during the Confederation period, when populist political movements favoring debtors caused men of substance to be concerned about the conduct of state legislatures and courts: "[T]he esteem in which the jury was held appeared to wane somewhat . . . at least where men of property or substance were concerned."[115] Federalists urged that the end of the era of royal appointment of judges, the democratic legitimacy of American legislatures as sources of written law, and the need to develop a consistent body of law, often to support creditors' rights, had changed the landscape. By the end of the nineteenth century these countercurrents would prevail at least at the level of doctrine, first in the civil context and then in the criminal. The tension between the jury's right to discern "true law" and the interests of legal stability is acute in another portion of Justice Chase's reply, and for that reason is worth recounting in detail:

> [It] is the duty of every court of this country . . . to guard the jury against erroneous impressions respecting the law of the land. . . . [I]t is the right of juries in criminal cases, to give a general verdict of acquittal, which cannot be set aside on account of its being contrary to law, and that hence results the power of juries to decide on the laws as well as the facts, in all criminal cases. . . . [B]ut in the exercise of this power, it is the duty of the jury to govern themselves by the laws of the land, over which they have no dispensing power; and their right to expect and receive from our court all the assistance which it can give, for rightly understanding the law. To withhold this assistance, in any manner whatever; to forebear to give it in that way which may be most effectual for preserving the jury from error and mistake, would be an abandonment or forgetfulness of the judge, which no judge could justify to his conscience or to the laws.[116]

But as the century wore on, "[i]ncreasingly, many lawyers and judges came to view the jury as a drag upon stability in the law."[117] Juries tended to assess contracts on the basis of their "inherent fairness" rather than the bargained-for expectations of the parties, a more market-friendly standard. Harrington notes the interesting transitional case in 1796 of *Searight v. Calbraith*, which not only announced the new rule on expectations damages, but also instructed the jury that it might substitute its own sense of fairness for the intentions of the parties.[118] Judges began to think of law in instrumental terms and in particular sought to foster "the commercial character of our country."[119] Courts increasingly credited Coke's maxim that judges alone should address questions of law.[120] Other courts emphasized that the newly democratic nation no longer needed the protection that law-finding juries had provided during the struggles with England, an argument that Hamilton had anticipated in *Federalist No. 83*. Most significantly for the emerging commercial culture, it was contended that juries could not provide certainty and stability: "From the nature of juries composed of the people, taken indiscriminately from all ranks, professions, and trades, by turns and or a short service, it is impossible that they should be qualified to decide nice questions." Jury decision making would only "render laws, which ought to be an uniform rule of conduct, uncertain, fluctuating with every changing passion and opinion of jurors, and impossible to know until pronounced."[121] Courts began to grant new trials, even several new trials, in civil cases when they suspected that the jury had not followed the instructions. As one Connecticut judge put it, "What can be more preposterous than to say, that the verdict of a jury, often composed of men unaccustomed to weigh testimony, and peculiarly liable to local and personal prejudice and partialities, should never be re-examined and corrected, though opposed to the clearest evidence."[122]

Commercial litigation became an important part of the big-city lawyer's repertoire. Procedural devices were developed in insurance litigation that allowed lawyers to agree to by-pass the jury:[123] "For businesses . . . summary procedures were much more to their liking, and more suited their overall needs. Businesses that used the courts as collection agencies had no particular interest in trials."[124] Eventually, forms of summary dispositions, unknown at common law, allowed the court to take the case away from the jury when there had not been a judicially determined adequate level of proof, given law as determined by the court.[125] For the first time, New England supreme courts required their trial judges to instruct the juries on all relevant points of law.[126] The development of relatively elaborate doctrinal structures in what we now call "contract law,"[127] for example, served largely to achieve "the progressive dethronement of the jury" by producing detailed legal rules "where before there was little or none."[128] In fact, "there was very little law of contract at all before the [nineteenth] century, because there was no machinery for producing it and most of the questions were left to juries as questions of fact."[129] And Justice Story was eventually successful in his willful campaign to limit the Seventh Amendment jury right to those cases that would have been tried by jury in England in 1791, a narrower range than that prevailing in the United States. In the second half of the nineteenth century several state courts aggressively read English jury practice back into their own constitutions so as to limit the jury's law-finding powers to those implicit in the returning of a general verdict.[130] Between 1850 and 1930 most state appellate courts rejected their earlier adherence to the doctrine that juries were judges of the law. Finally, in 1895, the U.S. Supreme Court ruled in *Sparf and Hansen v. United States*,[131] over vigorous dissents, that a trial court was justified in instructing a criminal jury that it was obliged to follow the law as declared in the instructions, whether or not they agreed with it. Some courts give that instruction and some do not.[132]

Once they had the procedural devices to impose a set of judge-made rules discontinuous with general moral intuitions on the jury, nineteenth-century courts were not slow to use them. For example, they created the doctrine of contributory negligence. In its harshest form, it denied all recovery to an injured worker or citizen if his own negligence contributed, even slightly, to his injury. Not surprisingly, at the same time "judicial ingenuity" transformed a series of issues surrounding the doctrine from "issues of fact" to "issues of law,"[133] effectively removing them from jury consideration. One New York judge writing at mid-century put it this way:

> We can not shut our eyes to the fact that in certain controversies between the weak and the strong—between a humble individual and a gigantic corporation, the sympathies of the human mind naturally, honestly and generously, run to the assistance and support of the feeble, and apparently oppressed; and the compassion will sometimes exercise over the deliberations of a jury, an influence which, however honorable to them as philanthropists, is wholly inconsistent with the principles of law and the ends of justice. There, [sic] is therefore a manifest propriety in withdrawing from the consideration of the jury, those cases in which the plaintiff fails to show a right of recovery.[134]

Landsman concluded that contributory negligence "dehumanized the law" by excluding the jury's perspective from the trial and substituting "an abstract and often insidious set of principles."[135] As early as the turn of the twentieth century commentators were calling the doctrine "cruel and wicked" and shocking to "the ordinary sense of justice of mankind."[136] By the time of the New Deal, commentators were calling for "simpler and vaguer formulas in instructions to the jury,"[137] formulas that would have explicitly invited the jury to reach into its own commonsense morality in making its decisions.[138] In 1908 Progressives in Congress passed the Federal Employers Liability Act, which provided for trial by jury and a regime of comparative negligence, which allowed workers to recover from their employers the amount of their actual damages, reduced by the percentage of the total fault borne by the employee. But the refusal of juries under the older regime to enforce fully a contributory negligence rule was an important factor in effecting long-term changes in the law. Judge Wyzanski of the federal district court "confessed" that "juries are the device by which the rigor of the law is modified pending the enactment of new statutes."[139] Nancy Marder has argued persuasively that juries were throughout fulfilling an appropriate political role within our separation of powers by offering sustained criticism of the rules that the legislature had embraced, and that juries, "by declining to find contributory negligence, essentially created a regime of comparative negligence long before the legislature and judges had eliminated contributory negligence as a defense."[140]

What the trial was becoming in the nineteenth century could be read not only from the theorizing and the partisan debates surrounding the trial, but also from the procedural details of what occurred at trial. During the nineteenth century, while "true law" was becoming the law of rules, new procedural devices—motions for directed verdicts and for judgment notwithstanding the verdict and summary judgment[141]—were, in the civil context, allowing judges to decide cases that had previously been decided by juries.[142] American courts took a number of steps to recalibrate the tensions between jury determinations and "professional" determinations by judges. Conservative federal judges first took a limiting view of the availability of the civil jury trial in federal cases, linking it unjustifiably to the practice in England at the time of the adoption of the Seventh Amendment. Despite the literal language of the Seventh Amendment,[143] a range of jury control devices was recognized that the common law had not known. These went beyond the English practice of granting new (jury) trials and the risky "demurrer to the evidence." The latter allowed a litigant to ask the judge to take the case away from the jury and to decide the case "as a matter of law," but only at the price of admitting the truth of all the opponent's evidence. It was a very high-stakes game that only an extremely confident attorney could play: if the motion was denied, the moving party was declared the loser in the case as a whole. American courts came to allow a party (usually a defendant) to make motions for directed verdicts before jury deliberation or motions for judgments notwithstanding the verdict afterward. The moving party ran no risk by making such a motion: if he lost it, he could still win in front of the jury in the case of the directed verdict or in the appellate court in the case of the motion made after the jury presented its verdict.

The dissenting justices in the 1943 case of *Galloway v. United States* told the story of the continually increasing power of judges over "issues of fact" during the nineteenth century.[144] As late as 1835 the Court had ruled, "Where there is no evidence tending to prove a particular fact, the courts are bound so to instruct the jury, when requested; *but they cannot legally give any instruction which shall take from the jury the right of weighing the evidence and determining what effect it shall have*" (emphasis added).[145] Fifteen years later, however, in 1850, the Court for the first time permitted a directed verdict in situations where there was "no evidence whatever" on one of the key elements of the case.[146] The next major step occurred in 1871, when the Court ruled that it was not enough that there be "some evidence" of each key element in order to allow the case to go to the jury. Rather, "there must be evidence sufficiently persuasive to the judge so that he thinks 'a jury can properly proceed.'"[147] Tellingly, this came to be known as the "substantial evidence" test.

The century thus saw the standard for granting a motion for directed verdict decline, so that judges could direct a verdict even if there was some evidence on which a reasonable jury could reach its verdict. The law of evidence developed to place more authority in the hands of the judge to decide what the jury would see. The practice of summary judgment, which allowed judges to decide cases after a review of documents alone, arose and spread from its origins in limited commercial contexts to become universally available; it took deep root despite its questionable constitutional status.[148] And courts, including, finally, the United States Supreme Court, approved of instructions (even in federal criminal cases) mandating the jury to follow the law of rules whether or not they approved of that statement of the law.[149] However, these movements were not unidirectional, and American juries retained significant power into the twentieth century.

The law of rules in its increasing complexity could provide an explanation, and certainly an excuse, for why more and more determinations should be made by the judge, as opposed to the jury. After all, the legally salient aspects of a case could be exhaustively caught in the net of legal rules so long as they were applied by someone who knew them well, or so the argument went. There remained, however, a doubt that judges actually decided cases according to the methods that supported these devices, all of which allowed the judge to weigh the evidence.[150] Was the judge "following the rules laid down" in a mechanical way and without real discretion, or was the invocation of complex forms of legal reasoning often a smokescreen for the exercise of a discretion that tracked the judge's class interests and often conservative political philosophy?

Throughout the nineteenth century the shape of the trial reflected and shaped the enormous political and social changes affecting the nation. The trials forged in the crucible of the egalitarianism of the revolutionary generation came slowly to be cabined. These restrictions occurred, as always, both in more philosophical (or polemical) self-understanding of "true law" and in the procedural devices that reflected (and caused) those understandings. The appeal of clear preannounced rules may have been greatest among the commercial classes, but it also proved powerful elsewhere.[151] The increasing diversity of perspectives in the quickly growing

nation and the perceived increased complexity of social organization convinced some elites that older forms of trial needed to be restructured. In
large part, the trial changed because of the two most important social and
political issues of the nineteenth century. In the first half of the century, it
was slavery. The "pact with the devil" that inserted a legal recognition of
slavery in the original Constitution came in the northern states to be seen
as incompatible with certain of the most democratic features of the trial.[152]
In the second half of the century, it was the increasing size and sophistication of the system of finance capitalism, whose legal skeleton was often
at odds with the ordinary moral judgments of most jurors. In both cases
judges, committed to a law of rules discontinuous with commonsense morality, sought to control the responses that juries would likely give and
developed the procedural machinery to achieve that control. In neither
case, however, was the triumph of the law of rules over the trial complete.
In both cases, the values implicit in the trial were more or less effective in
pushing back to limit what the law of rules could achieve.

By the beginning of the twentieth century the main lines of the trial I
described in the first chapter had been established. In both civil and criminal cases, the trial was becoming a dramatic oral adversary encounter,
quite unlike the British trials of the eighteenth century. The nineteenth
century had seen a countermovement against the populist trial celebrated
in the period of the founders. But this was not so much as a swing back to
earlier procedures—the writ pleading system or the altercation trial—as
it was an attempt to recalibrate the point of equilibrium among the unavoidable tensions I will soon describe in more general terms. If lawyers
were to be allowed to represent their clients vigorously and to tell their
stories in opening statements and argue them in closing, if lawyers were to
be permitted to present witnesses under oath and cross-examine opposing
witnesses, all of which could appeal to "true law," and if more cases survived the thicket of pleading, then devices would emerge that expressed
the interests underlying the law of rules. That is what occurred during the
nineteenth century.

Throughout this history two visions of the trial were struggling with
each other in arguments couched in procedural terms. One understanding, of which Tocqueville gave the classic expression, saw the trial as a
forum where citizens could gather, stand face to face with fellow citizens,
hear evidence limited only by rules identified by common sense and free
of artificial distortions, and take on the burden of "magistracy." They saw

in their own moral tradition and sense of responsibility for public matters powerful resources for self-governance. Citizens expected that "the law" would generally be consistent with that tradition and sense of responsibility. Where there appeared to be some discontinuity, they expected that the judge (or judges) would explain it to them, so that they could take the reasons for that discontinuity into account in their deliberations. But there would be few circumstances where "technicalities" would ultimately interfere with "judgment according to conscience."

The other view had a number of different rationales, but its effect was to remove decision making from the commonsense moral judgment of ordinary citizens. It sought to rely on an "artificial reason," on procedural mechanisms that did not rest on the commonsense judgment of jurors. These mechanisms operated "autopoietically"—on their own—and would remove decision making from jurors' own intuitions. (Lord Coke famously spoke of the law's "artificial reason.")[153] Those mechanisms allowed the judge to make dispositive rulings on purely legal grounds, which always posed the risk of masking the intuitions and prejudices of an elite judge, then rationalized by legal technology. And some of those procedural devices, made on a paper record behind closed doors, spared the judge from trial's more contextual confrontation with the human situation underlying the case.

The twentieth century again saw readjustments of the essential tensions that defined the trial, but without any fundamental change. The trial remained structured by the tensions between its being an oral dramatic event designed to actualize the practical intelligence of the jury and a kind of machine designed to decide the case by stamping the rule of law on an accurate version of the facts. But some changes did occur. The Federal Rules of Civil Procedure, adopted in 1938, further reduced the importance of pleading. This would seem to continue the elevation of the importance of the trial as a decisive oral event save for the drafters' inclusion of the summary judgment device as a newly significant step in the course of civil litigation. Until the mid-1930s the summary judgment device had been deployed primarily as a means by which plaintiffs who were collecting debts could eliminate sham defenses to the collection of definite amounts to obtain judgment without trial. Edson R. Sunderland, who had written an earlier piece decrying the inefficiency of the American jury,[154] and its "economic extravagance,"[155] drafted the new summary judgment rule. He embraced the combination of notice pleading, relatively full discovery,

and summary judgment that has come to characterize civil practice in
most American courts. There was support in the Advisory Committee
to limit the kinds of cases where summary judgment would be available,
consistent with its origins as a device for resolving commercial disputes,
in particular liquidated debt claims.[156] One member of the committee responded to a comment by Morgan (which reflects the current Supreme
Court's view of the subject) that summary judgment was appropriate
where a directed verdict would be appropriate, a position that discounted
the importance of the distinctive characteristics of the trial: "There is a
great deal of difference between getting the facts on affidavits and getting
them on cross-examinations. . . . As I understand it, the real thing is that
the motion should be used only if there is no real difference between the
parties as to the material facts."[157] Another member insisted on the significance of "hav[ing] it clear that we are not trying to introduce a rule which
will substitute trial by affidavit for trial by jury."[158] Another member, who
was a former judge, seemed to speak from the heart when he said:

> I am in favor of retaining trial by jury inviolate and not in an instant substitut-
> ing trial by affidavit, whether the party is in good faith or not. I think this is one
> of the most serious rules in our whole group, and it will be the one subject to
> the most criticism unless you throw every safeguard around the man who wants
> his case tried by a jury. Trial by jury is the safeguard of the man who otherwise
> would not get a square deal. I am very much opposed to giving any color to the
> charge that these rules in any way encroach on that right.[159]

Stephen Burbank concludes that these concerns were unduly mollified in
the imagination of the committee by the factual association of summary
judgment with the routine debt cases where it was most often used. We
will see that the current decline of the trial is intertwined with the increasing attraction of this summary judgment device.

The law of evidence is itself an important jury control device. Judges
may choose to deny the jury knowledge of some aspects of the truth that
may be of significance not to the substantive law of rules, but to moral or
political sensibilities that have not found lodging in that law. Of course,
this is a clumsy device: to omit some important aspect of a situation may
completely distort the jury's basic understanding of what has occurred
even from the perspective of the law of rules. With the adoption of the
Federal Rules of Evidence in 1975 and derivative state codes, the trial
courts moved to a more liberal regime. This regime was more respectful of

the jury's ability to weigh the probative value of problematic evidence and to resist the grosser forms of prejudice that could distort judgment.

The twentieth century also saw an increased recognition that important aspects of the civil and criminal trials are matters of constitutional law. The law is in many ways structured by constitutional interpretation in ways that take its form out of the hands of legislatures. The right to compulsory process, the right to counsel in criminal cases, the right to present a defense, the right of a criminal defendant to testify, the right to cross-examine opposing witnesses and to argue to the jury in both civil and criminal cases, and limitations on reducing the size of the criminal jury and on qualifications of the unanimity rule are all of constitutional dimension. The newly reinvigorated confrontation clause provides for the right to confront and cross-examine "testimonial" statements,[160] even if they would be permitted under state and federal hearsay definitions. The *Batson* line of cases recognizes the place of the jury as a means of self-governance by prohibiting racial and gender-based peremptory challenges. It has insisted on the removal of barriers to minorities and women serving on juries, so that, for the first time in our history, the jury is truly cross-sectional.[161] The Court has recognized a preeminent place for the jury in capital sentencing, an area of the law that is rapidly developing. The Seventh Amendment, itself interpreted more aggressively in the last half century, after one hundred years of judicial evisceration, provides for a jury right in federal civil cases even where such a right would not have existed under analogous English chancery and law practice in the eighteenth century and where no close analogy exists. Constitutional rights to due process control, albeit in a more indulgent manner, the conduct of adjudication within administrative agencies.[162] In all these ways, our fundamental law has recognized the central status of trial procedure in affording protection of individual rights. Not only is the trial one of the great achievements of our public culture, but many of its most important features have explicitly constitutional status. We will see, too, that our constitutional commitments give aspects of this history continuing normative force, a force that resists the functionalism and instrumentalism of our age.[163] Once again, several commentators have noticed that it is a recurrent historical pattern that as the trial seems to realize its internal ideals, countervailing pressures seem to emerge. The "centuries-old dialectic" reasserts itself.

To the extent that aspects of the trial are of constitutional dimensions, they are beyond the reach of the legislatures and the interest groups that often control them. It may be that constitutionalizing fundamental aspects of a fair trial has itself released the antibodies from the surrounding organs—market and bureaucratic—that have placed the trial in mortal danger. That is a topic to which I will return in the final chapter.

So the availability of trial, and in particular trial by jury, was a central aspect of Americans' political self-understanding during the first sixty years of the republic. Contemporaries recognized that changes in the shape of the trial designed to accommodate the legal recognition of slavery in the original constitution and then the interests of industrial expansion were important changes in a basic institution. The legal and political battles that surrounded these developments were hard-fought. The Civil War and the Thirteenth, Fourteenth, and Fifteenth Amendments rescued us from slavery, and the Progressive Movement and the New Deal rescued us from the worst excesses of the Gilded Age and laid the groundwork for recovery of the essential American values embedded in the jury trial.

My point here has been a simple one: that the shape of the trial has played an important role in the most important political issues the nation has faced. It is likely that this central importance will continue. This account will prepare us for the conclusion of the book, where I will argue that that debates surrounding the frequency and nature of the trial continue to reflect some of the most important issues facing the nation. The twentieth-century trial was a major achievement, one that balanced sharply competing values in a comprehensive way. I next turn to a somewhat more general statement of what those competing values are.

CHAPTER THREE

# The Fundamental Tensions
# the Trial Defines

[F]rom the outset of the common law period, trial juries were prepared to voice a sense of justice fundamentally at odds with the letter of the law. —Thomas Green

A wide range of social and political considerations points to the trial's importance and the likely significance of its demise. These tend to have the character of tensions, conflicts between powerful human values that exist in broader society and are mirrored in the trial's availability and shape. In this chapter I will review those tensions and suggest their absolute centrality to our forms of life and modes of self-governance. They include the tensions between face-to-face argument and governance by autonomous systems, between public and confidential decision making, between personal responsibility and organizationally diffused responsibility, between citizen participation and deference to authority, between reliance on contextual judgment and protection by rules, between rule by citizens and deference to experts of one sort or another, between moral-political decision making and deference to a more or less self-regulating market, between law as value and law as fact, between what we might call a morality of identity and instrumental rationality, between adherence to ideals and acceptance of a reality that systematically falls short, and between rigorous factual analysis and broad generalization. There is some value on each side of each of these tensions, but there are vast differences in the way of life created by shifts in the balance that we inevitably strike. The availability and shape of the trial creates that fateful balance.

I have provided a short history of the continuities and sharp discontinuities surrounding the English and especially the American trial. *Why* has the trial been the focus of such violent disputes and sometimes jagged discontinuities? That is the issue I address below. I don't believe that they are the function solely of unique historical circumstances unrelated to our current quandaries. I try to demonstrate that it has stood astride major conflicts in our modes of social ordering and, even more deeply, in the forms of life that they reflect. I am convinced that the deeper issues are at stake in our current situation and will not yield to technical fixes and reforms alone, as important as some of those may be.

My focus in the first chapter was on "the inside game," on what we actually do at trial and its significance for us. We are in a far stronger position to describe the contemporary trial than we are to inform our understanding of what trials were in the tradition within which we stand. Although we have enormous masses of statutes and decided cases, there are few verbatim transcripts of trials from before the end of the nineteenth century. We have had very little detailed sense of the specifics of what occurred, the tone of the dialogue in court, until recently. Once again, an understanding of institutions and practices becomes possible only through a "continuous dialectical tacking between the most local of local detail and the most global of global structures in such a way as to bring both into view simultaneously."[1] From a normative point of view, the critical evaluation of social institutions will almost invariably involve something like the attempt to achieve "reflective equilibrium" by moving back and forth between general moral principles and the balances among competing principles struck in the concrete social institutions and practices in which we have the most confidence.[2] These notions apply to the recovery of the significance of the trial that I have been seeking to achieve here.

The jury trial has not been a single thing. Thomas Green has provided us a nuanced understanding of the way in which the jury evolved from the Middle Ages through the beginning of the nineteenth century. His emphasis throughout is on the ways in which the tensions between royal power and local moral sensibilities coexisted in the trial. These included ways in which the actual practice within the trial court, in which judge and jury generally cooperated in a common enterprise, seems in some ways at odds with the very strong claims made for both royal power and jury sovereignty that seemed to make such cooperation unthinkable. At different times, indeed in different courtrooms, the balance was struck in different ways. Green's focus is on what we may call the intellectual history of the trial court and its relationship to the evolution of English society. Major cases and pamphleteering around them offer a window on this central institution. Jeffrey Abramson has done something similar for the United States. Here, too, major cases allow us to understand the larger political and philosophical issues of the age.

The trial is a forum within which, on the one hand, *face-to-face argument goes forward in ordinary language appealing to common morality* under rules designed to assure that the decision maker actually *listens* to both sides.[3] On the other hand, the issues that find their way into court are often posed by practices *belonging to large systems steered by mechanisms that are embedded in markets and bureaucracies and are discontinuous with the ways of the trial court.* The trial's availability and shape determine the norms and means by which we will govern ourselves or, less optimistically, be governed. Relatedly, the trial's availability and structure answer the question of the form of intelligence or "reason" that will be allowed to have public force.

The trial's character also concerns the range of *public, as opposed to private or secret, decision-making.* There are decisions and deliberations best made in relative privacy and there are those that should remain public. "Sunlight is the best disinfectant" is a popular bromide. More ominous is federal Judge Damon Keith's warning that "democracy dies behind closed doors."[4] The American trial, supported by a comparatively large range of pretrial discovery devices,[5] provides for a high level of public decision making, or at least public review of decisions made in private, decisions often driven by strong private interests. The trial's availability and shape implicate this issue of publicity and therefore of public justice.[6]

Hannah Arendt famously declared that bureaucracy was "rule by nobody." (Of course, our bureaucracies are both publicly and privately owned.) Bureaucracies allow for the dissipation of human responsibility for decisions and deference to systems that seem to function independently from human judgment.[7] *The trial requires a public judgment from one or a (usually) known group of persons.* Its commonsense language and rhetoric assume that human beings are responsible for the actions and the policies they establish. The trial's availability and shape determine the range of public behavior for which individuals can be called to account.

Then there is the *tension between trial actors as pure instruments of the sovereign or his rules*—bound only by "role morality,"[8] we might say—*and*

*actors as moral agents.* The oral character of the trial was closely related
to its perceived moral dimension from the start:

> The fact that the trial remained oral and personal reinforced the popular con-
> ception that the trial was as much an assessment of just deserts as it was a search
> for the truth in the case at hand. This was not, of course, the way in which the
> authorities viewed the matter. The oral and personal trial was also consistent
> with the view that the jury was bound to find the facts and nothing else.[9]

The Levellers, members of a powerful seventeenth-century Christian egalitarian movement, complained that certain devices of jury control turned
them into "ciphers." They complained as well that slavishly following the
dictates of the law of rules with lethal effect where the law was skewed or
the punishment was excessive would turn them into "murderers." So, particularly in the United States, it was often urged that not only did jurors
have the right to follow their consciences as to the meaning of "true law,"
but it was their moral obligation to do so. Because they were assigned
the burden of judgment, they were obligated to exercise it "according to
conscience." As John Adams put it, "[I]t is an absurdity to suppose that
the law would oblige jurors to find a verdict according to the direction of
the court, against their own opinion, judgment, and conscience."[10] In discerning the rightness of the cause, jurors were understood to have several
advantages over judges. They were not "magistrates" who might seek to
curry favor with the powerful. They probably were not "public men" at all,
whose loyalties were likely to reflect the "spirit of faction," as they might
put it.[11] Even Hamilton had to concede that they were harder to corrupt
through the cruder methods.[12] And, as Chesterton taught, trials were sufficiently unusual events in their lives such that jurors could see what was
before them with fresh eyes. As it has played out, this tension most often
expresses itself concretely as a kind of presumption in favor of the judge's
statement of the law,[13] which only compelling circumstances could over-
ride.[14]

Another set of tensions that has always constituted the trial is that between *ruler and citizen.* The jury trial was initially an instrument for the
exercise of royal power, for which it provided necessary information and
local support. In different ways at different times, "[f]or the government,
jury discretion was tolerable only within the context of a centrally administered, closely overseen, and highly managed system of criminal law."[15]
Whatever else effectively enforced law is, it is always an expression of the

power of dominant individuals or groups, "the will of the stronger." Rulers have an interest in the effective expression of lordship, if for no other reason than to gain the deference of those ruled, to establish and solidify their power. The trial and the effective enforcement of its results have always served that purpose. Indeed, it has been suggested that the participation of the people in the administration of justice actually increases the effective authority of the ruler. Of course, rulers have always justified the exercise of power in the interests of social order, and order is a social good.[16] But maintaining either power or order may be in tension with a contextual evaluation, doing justice in the sense of making delicate determinations of individual desert in particular cases. Rulers concerned with maintaining power are natural utilitarians, at least in their rhetoric. This may explain in part the English satisfaction with enormously draconian rules of homicide and theft that were systematically nullified by juries over centuries. Notice how this tension may justify the denomination of increasingly high numbers of issues as "legal" issues in order to place them in the hands of the judge who, like the English judge until the end of the seventeenth century, saw himself as an agent of executive power.

Tocqueville celebrated the American jury trial in part because it conferred on jurors a share in the "spirit of magistracy," that is, the burden of making public decisions affecting real people for which one is responsible. (In his wonderful metaphor, that responsibility could "scrape off the rust of selfishness" that is the real danger to democracy.) It has recently been suggested that this experience is no longer necessary because of the higher level of formal education about the legal system. The availability and shape of the trial, however, determine the range of opportunities for a certain *kind* of knowledge that responsible participation brings, a kind of understanding that has been thought to be an essential element of citizenship. It is not identical with the notional knowledge one derives from books and lectures. One may characterize the issue as the appropriate balance between participation and passivity (or perhaps we could call it "deference to authority").

The trial as we have it plays an essential part in the debate over the extent to which we can rely on *rules, as opposed to what we may call disciplined judgment*, to protect our way of life. For almost a century skeptical voices have argued that "general rules do not decide particular cases" and that the efflorescence of legal rules according to which we live merely disguises the discretion of judges and bureaucrats. Traditionalists have complained about the "nihilism" of that view, even to the point of urging that those who hold it should be banished from professional education for inevitably corrupting the youth.[17] As we saw in the first chapter, the American trial offers a range of languages and practices that are not reducible to rule following but are not merely a disguise for the exercise of raw will either. The availability and shape of the trial must be of concern to anyone who understands the limits of rules but who cares deeply about a concrete, realistic, and meaningful sense of the rule of law.

Judges could easily forget the admission of Chancellor Kent, invoked by the Realists, about his mode of deciding civil cases, that "[h]e made himself 'master of the facts.' Then (he wrote) 'I saw where justice lay, and the moral sense decided the court half the time; I then sat down to search the authorities . . . but I almost always found principles suited to my view of the case."[18] The danger, then, lay in the growth of procedural devices that would flatten out the human story to which the law would apply and anesthetize our largely tacit powers for discerning its human significance. Legal technology could easily be seen to be all that was necessary, so that trials became less and less important. The functional significance of these developments would be the same as that of the writ system, though to a different end—to disconnect the legal outcome from the way a disinterested person of realized common sense might view the case. To the extent to which the formalists were right, the law of rules alone would dictate the conclusion. To the extent that the realists were right (and they mainly were on the descriptive side), the judge could choreograph the increasingly large ballet of bloodless categories to reach the conclusion that his politics dictated. And in either case, the summary procedures could spare the judge the almost inevitable tug of the discipline of the evidence in particular cases.

So the tensions implicit in the trial can be understood as emerging from the conflict between *natural justice on the one hand and authoritative political purpose and policy on the other*. It can also be understood as a *tension between the contextual understanding of human events and clear rules with predictable consequences*. The latter was the emphasis of the American commercial classes in the early nineteenth century, who decried jury determinations in matters of tort and contract that sought to create fair outcomes as measured by canons of ordinary morality. Those kinds of contextual determinations could not provide investors with the sorts of predictability that would enable them to engage in rational calculation. That sort of contextual determination is in sharp tension with the multiplication of preexistent rules. (Green argues that the institutionalization of jury discretion in the seventeenth century slowed the development of criminal law doctrine, and Simpson argues that the invention of much of contract doctrine in the nineteenth century "where there was little or none" before occurred as part of "the progressive dethronement" of the jury in that century.) The notion was that the ability to plan in light of such rules—whether in criminal law or contract law—allowed the individual a broader range of power over his own destiny. For good or ill, each person's choices and their consequences could be free of the effective condemnation of his neighbors, so long as he played by the rules. In the criminal context, a citizen could avoid the intrusion of the state into his affairs by steering clear of the prohibitions clearly announced in the rules.[19] Individuals did not have to be concerned about the predations of popular justice. This is the interest that Justice Story invoked in *United States v. Battiste*, a criminal trial of a sailor accused of violating a federal law prohibiting aspects of the slave trade. Story instructed the jurors that they did not enjoy any "moral right to decide the law according to their own notions, or pleasure," and therefore "[i]t is the duty of the court to instruct the jury as to the law; and it is the duty of the jury to follow the law as it is laid down by the court."

There remains an unending controversy about the extent to which such rules can or ever could serve this purpose. The radical realist critique has suggested that this efflorescence of rules served only as a justification to shift decision-making power from the jury to the judge through jury control devices. The difference, so the radical argument goes, is not between rules and context, but between juries and judges, whose just-as-intuitive sensibilities were aligned with those of the prosperous classes.[20] The sane middle ground on the power of rules to ensure predictability, which is not all that intellectually satisfying, seems to be: "only to a limited extent and often not at all in the actual circumstances that are likely to find their way into the trial courtroom." Most scholars accept a version of Holmes's dictum that "general propositions do not decide individual cases." It goes too far to say, "We are all realists now," but few serious students of the law accept all of the elements of legal formalism Leiter identified: that law is rationally determinate in that the class of legal reasons justifies one and only one outcome to a legal dispute; that the judge is mechanical in that judges exercise no discretion and that they do not render decisions by reasoning in ways that are not sanctioned by legal reasons or reach judgments that legal reasons do not justify;[21] and that legal reasoning is autonomous in that legal reasons determine a unique result without recourse to nonlegal reasons.[22] On the other hand, it would, in my view, be foolish to say that the contents of the positive law, mediated through the procedures we now employ, do not, put most minimally, change the likelihood for a ruling one way or another at or before trial.

Kalven and Zeisel argued that there were limits on the social scientific explanation of trial determinations owing to the vastness of the normatively significant details in most cases.[23] Those details can well form a constellation that is persuasive to a judge or jury. After all, Aristotle emphasized that practical reasoning focuses on particulars, and rhetoricians have always known the importance of details. At the very origins of the natural-law tradition, Plato reminded us in the *Statesman* that the rule of law would always be second best, because any manageable rules would have to be overgeneralized.[24] That means that if the legal rules were actually to provide the basis for decision making, they would have to do so by enormously simplifying the full significance of what occurred. And this is where this second way of understanding what is at stake in trial decision making connects up to the first. If legality is to trump natural justice, then it can only be by *removing morally significant aspects of the situation as effective bases for decision making*.[25] That simplification can be in the service of either predictability or interest.

The public-relations attacks on the trial often present it as a wholly irrational appeal to emotion. In reality, trial presentations involve a level of linguistic and logical rigor quite alien to most public discussions. It is certainly distant from the sloganeering, untested by fair adversary marshaling of inconvenient fact, that occupies too much political appeal and mass-circulation journalism. The latter are easy on preconceptions and make no attempt to challenge, and so to realize, the powerful common sense that we all share in. T.S. Eliot famously told us that we cannot bear very much reality. It is more widely known that Jack Nicholson told us that we cannot handle the truth. But in the context of American public debate, those seem relatively untested hypotheses. The trial's availability and shape determine whether they will remain untested. Or as Judge Dwyer put it more straightforwardly:

> My admiration for the jury, strong while I was [a] trial lawyer, has only deepened during my service as a judge. Imperfect and battle-scarred though it is, the jury, as I see it, still is able to reach fair and honest verdicts, to say "no" to official power when that word must be uttered for the sake of freedom, and

to legitimize hard decisions for a questioning public. It still "contributes most powerfully," as Tocqueville wrote a hundred and sixty-five years ago, "to form the judgment and to increase the natural intelligence of the people." And it sheds light on two other democratic institutions, the ballot box and the initiative and referendum. If jury trials as a rule produce sounder results that we can count in elections—which I believe they do—one reason may be the quality of information given to the citizens who must decide. In contrast to the chaos and mendacity of much political campaigning, and to the scattergun delivery of thirty-second television commercials, a jury hears testimony that is kept to the point by an impartial referee, tested by cross-examination, and offered throughout the day. We should be able to learn something valuable from the differences in communication.[26]

The trial is interested in accurate determinations. Narrative structure inevitably provides our path toward historical truth. Narratives can be persuasive for many reasons, but they are inevitable means for reconstructing the past. Any attempt to understand human actions or events "in themselves" before or "beneath" narrative will produce only the "disjointed parts of some possible narratives."[27] Generally, the more details the jury hears,[28] the better position it will be in to make a relatively accurate judgment of historical fact. But the more details are included, the more likely it is for those details to invoke norms other than those embedded in the jury instructions and so in the law of rules. Thus the judge may be inclined to exclude details that really do bear on "pure accuracy" in order to protect the law of rules (or pure sovereignty). This is an enduring tension. Each and every piece of evidence "has two faces," as trial lawyers like to say; each may be interpreted in a way that furthers one or other of the two competing theories of the act. This means practically that there is some absolute limit on the degree to which the jury's normative judgments can be screened out of a trial and still present a basically coherent understanding of the human event that has occurred for purposes of deciding the case in any manner. At a certain point the attempt to formalize the presentation of the case will so distort the underlying event that one is not really true to the rule of law, even as it is understood within the received view of the trial. Furthermore, John Dewey explained,[29] mere consistency in the legal formulas invoked will not achieve the stability and predictability of the law of rules unless one deploys the methods and languages to grasp concretely the events being evaluated. This cannot be done in solely nonnormative terms, and the norms in the substantive law alone will *never* be enough to fully characterize a human situation. Some part of the drift away from the trial that we see today may have to do with these dynamic tensions playing themselves out.

As we saw, reverence for the jury trial was an important element in the "radicalism of the American Revolution." The trial, both criminal and civil, was thought to offer an important protection against all the vices of lordship, from simple and focused abuse of power to the carelessness with which those who have grown bored with its exercise can treat "little" people. The trial is structured by the *tension between citizen participation in governance and deference to experience and authority*. The trial's availability and shape determine the balance between direct citizen participation and rule by politicians and experts.

In the late 1960s the political scientist Theodore Lowi identified free-market capitalism as America's dominant political philosophy through the 1930s and interest-group liberalism as that which succeeded it.[30] (He claimed that Justice Holmes was a very bad historian when he wrote that the "Fourteenth Amendment did not enact Mr. Herbert Spencer's *Social Statics*," though quite a good prophet.) Since then, the champions of the free market and its associated deregulation have staged something of a counterrevolution. With deregulation, the devices of the legal system, and the trial in particular, have remained an even more lonely counterweight to the internal norms of the market. The availability and shape of the trial determine, in part, how much of our national life will be controlled by *market forces, qualified only by what interest-group liberalism can provide through legislation as a means of limitation*. Without trials, the market would become more truly "self-regulating," in Polanyi's phrase, and there would be *less attention to background institutions and the politically determined framework within which market institutions have functioned*.

Our academic and popular legal culture has struggled in different idioms with what legal scholars call the *endless struggle between natural law and positivism*. We can put aside the complexities surrounding both doctrines and the great variations in historical forms they both have taken. For our purposes, what is at issue is the continuity between an ideal of legality (the law of rules) and moral judgments that have a foundation deeper than the simple fact of enactment by an entity with legally conferred authority. These moral judgments are often quite inconvenient when judged by the norms of enacted law, which is always, as I mentioned, the will of the stronger. We saw in the first chapter how the trial is constituted by the tension between authoritative rules and the other moral sources that are incarnate in narrative and argument. The availability and shape of the trial determine the *balance between political will and moral judgment*.

These tensions are among the deepest that we experience in public life. Some were given their classical expression in Sophocles' *Antigone* as the *tension, sometimes conflict, between natural law and state purposefulness*.[31] The appeal to natural right often invokes a historical "myth of a founding" that creates a more fundamental law that neither king nor legislature may transgress. So the Levellers initially asserted the jury's right as "judges of the law as well as of fact" to be rooted in the fundamental Anglo-Saxon liberties long since covered over by Norman bureaucracy.[32] In later stages of the debate, the partisans of jury power claimed that the jury had the right to "evaluate" even a statute in the light of English fundamental law. These claims were hardly the result of historical scholarship, of which jury partisans did precious little. It is as if they understood Arendt's point that in the modern world "nature" has provided far weaker protection than have historical claims about the "entailed inheritances" provided by the "rights of Englishmen."[33] But it is clear that religious, philosophical and historical modes of thought were being conflated in Lilburne's statement:

> [B]ut you must know that the law of England is the law of God. . . . It is the law that hath been maintained by our ancestors, by the trial rules of reason, and the prime law of nature; for it does not depend upon statutes, or written and declared words of lines. . . . Therefore I say again, the law of England is pure primitive reason.[34]

This "pure primitive reason" could stand in opposition to political purpose, even if that purpose was legitimate:

> The radical reformers were not primarily concerned with a national crime wave, with judicial administration, or with interpretation and enforcement of parliamentary statute. For them the criminal law was primarily a process of community self-identification, and only second a system of rational self-defense.[35]

Direct appeals to common sense in trial decision making had great appeal in democratic America. "A clear head and an honest heart," instructed a New Hampshire judge, "are worth more than all the law of the lawyers."[36] But we also see the same conflating of jury determinations based on "primitive reason" or "common sense" or "natural reason" with questions of constitutionality (a level between absolute morality and positive law) in the American context.[37] Amar finds evidence of both in the founders' understanding of the place of the jury in the Bill of Rights, though with important differences. The Englishman could rely on the mists of history to hide evidence of any divide between his own moral judgment and Anglo-Saxon foundations. The American written Constitution, with its relative positivity, in some ways resisted that identification, particularly on the key issue of slavery, which many continued to denounce. Nonetheless, we see in Amar's conclusions the same sort of elision of ordinary moral judgment with fundamental law, in opposition to executive action and statute. Indeed, in a philosophical climate where the sovereignty of the people was accepted as key to the self-understanding of the new republic, the radical English notion that jurors were "more ancient" than mere officials had special poignancy.[38]

Moral judgments are not instrumental judgments. And so, the trial patrols *the borderland between a purely instrumental rationality concerned with choosing the effective means to predetermined ends, on the one hand, and a form of intelligence that seeks to determine an appropriate response to a situation, a response that is continuous with the moral identity of the actor.* The trial's absorbing "consciously structured hybrid of languages," as I described it in the first chapter, provokes a response from the decision maker that is discontinuous with a rational calculation of consequences. It stakes out a limit on instrumental rationality in public affairs. The jury is invited to make a decision based on who we are and want to be as revealed by a range of narrative, argumentative, and dramatic devices, not simply the specific social consequences we want to achieve. It provides a traditionalist counterweight to the dominant mode of rationality in our larger institutions.

It is true that law as a device of bureaucratic power can be less concerned about a refined determination of the human event than is a judge or jury engaged in "doing justice." Certainly, if the goal of the ruler is solely to "monarchize, be fear'd and kill with looks," a kind of carelessness about the application of his rules might actually keep citizens from coming anywhere close to the lines the sovereign has drawn and have the added benefit of projecting a terrifying lordship at many turns. On the other hand, to the extent that the rules express the will of the sovereign, carelessness may lose the benefits that come in actually shaping society in accordance with his purposes. In all cases there will inevitably be logical gaps between the legal rules and the evidence that supports a verdict. The formulas expressed in burdens of proof provide very rough guidelines for how these gaps ought to be handled. Determinations of relative importance inevitably come into play here. Where what is most important is the message that the case sends to others, whether it be an expression of pure lordship or a utilitarian message of general deterrence, it is less likely that trial practices will bear down with enormous care on the facts of particular situations. The *tension between the obsessive regard for accuracy* that Iris Murdoch says is almost equivalent to love *and the instrumental uses of the trial* is an enduring one.[39] Billy Budd, though innocent, is unable to tell his story effectively in a proceeding necessary for the good of the fleet. As John Langbein's account implicitly demonstrates, it is *only in the recent past that the trial's internal ideal of accuracy has expanded to rival the bureaucratic needs of social control.*

James Boyd White has pointed to the benign "hypocrisy" that pervades many of the best appellate opinions.[40] They invoke high ideals while implicitly rationalizing the failure to achieve those ideals. White argues that this is far better than merely invoking the realities of power politics as an explanation of the result: it keeps the ideal alive and maintains it as a legal source for subsequent cases in an imperfect world. There is something similar in our thinking about the trial. Several commentators have mentioned that the trial seems to come under political pressure just as its internal ideals and the quality of its methods improve.[41] Jeffrey Abramson's account of the quite recent democratization of the jury trial, when placed beside Marc Galanter's account of decline in the numbers of trials, provides the example that has occasioned my efforts here. The nature of the trial thus remains a focal point for the resolution of endless *tensions between judgment and power*, while allowing the former some oxygen to survive in a world of power.

The history of the trial sketched in the previous chapter is then necessarily intertwined with political and philosophical argument about the tensions identified in this chapter. Indeed, history and philosophy express the same tensions in different idioms. We will now turn to the present and examine what appears to be a dramatic shaking of the foundations of the contemporary trial and so of the particular balance among the important tensions that define our public life.

## CHAPTER FOUR

# Decline and Criticism

It's happening quietly in state after state, in court after court, and in several different areas of the law. But make no mistake, the right to trial by jury is slipping away. —Ronald J. Cohen

## The Collapse of the Trial System

Marc Galanter of the University of Wisconsin performed the key empirical research that traced the recent "implosion" in the numbers of American trials. He found that the percentage of federal civil cases that ended in a trial declined from 11.5 percent in 1962 to an amazing 1.8 percent in 2002.[1] He found even "more startling," given the increase in the absolute numbers of filings, "the 60 percent decline in the absolute number of trials since the mid-1980s." Although civil rights trials came to dominate tort trials during this period, the number of trials in "every category" declined. The decline in trials was evident as well in criminal cases and in bankruptcy. A similar decline has occurred in state cases. Galanter observed that "[a]lthough virtually every other indicator of legal activity is rising, trials are declining not only in relation to cases in the courts but to the size of the population and the size of the economy."[2]

In 1962 there were just over 50,000 dispositions or endings in federal civil cases.[3] By 2002 the number of dispositions had increased to almost

260,000, reflecting a significant increase in the amount of federal civil litigation. Astoundingly, however, the number of trials had *decreased*, even in absolute numbers, by about 20 percent, from about 5,800 to about 4,500, "[s]o the portion of dispositions that were by trial was less than one-sixth of what it was in 1962—1.8 percent now as opposed to 11.5 in 1962." Jury trials declined from 5.5 percent of all dispositions to 1.2 percent, while bench trials declined from 6.0 percent to 0.6 percent.[4] Although the decline in the percentage of cases going to trial has been consistent since 1962,[5] the rate of decline has accelerated rapidly since 1985. In the federal courts, there has been some shift in the case types constituting the trials that do take place, away from torts and commercial cases to civil rights cases. Although the recent decline has fairly been described as an "implosion," it is actually an intensification of a much longer historical decline.[6] When the Federal Rules of Civil Procedure went into effect in 1938, almost 19 percent of dispositions were through trial.[7] Some detailed historical studies suggest that the percentage of civil cases going to trial in the nineteenth century and through the end of the first quarter of the twentieth century was over 25 percent.[8] The percentage of trials in both contract and tort cases has fallen sharply.[9] Even in civil rights cases, where the "greater emotional intensity" may make settlement difficult and which remain the kind of case most likely to be tried,[10] the percentage of cases tried fell from nearly 20 percent in 1970 to merely 3.8 percent in 2002.[11] In part because of restrictions enacted by Congress, the number of prisoner petitions in the federal district court has fallen dramatically since the mid-1990s, but the number of trials on these petitions has fallen even more sharply.[12] The decline in federal civil trials applies to proceedings presided over by magistrate judges as well as to those presided over by federal district court judges.[13] The results for state courts are similar: from 1992 to 2001 the number of trials in the seventy-five most populous counties fell by 47 percent, even while the average jury award to a winning plaintiff also fell almost 50 percent.[14]

Galanter explored the possibility that the increasing complexity of the trials that did take place was somehow related to a decreasing number of trials. There is some evidence of an increase in complexity, though the lack of historical data makes broad conclusions difficult. However, "[c]ivil trials that last four days or more were 15 percent of trials in 1965 and 29 percent of trials in 2002." Yet it is still true that more than 40 percent of trials are over in one day and 70 percent in three days.[15] In a number of studies of state courts in urban areas, there seemed to be an inverse relationship between the number of trials and the median jury award, though more recent studies showed a mixed pattern.[16] It seems reasonable that "the causality may run in both directions: not only would the settlement or abandonment of smaller cases tend to produce larger awards, but higher awards could provide greater inducements for defendants to avoid trial."[17] Although the time it takes to end cases that are disposed of short of trial has remained constant or declined, the time it takes to get from filing to trial increased 25 percent from 1962 through 2000.[18] So one of the costs the plaintiff must pay for trial is a significantly delayed disposition.

The data also show that a declining percentage of federal cases are now resolved without any court action. These are cases that are voluntarily dismissed usually because the parties have settled: this category fell from over 50 percent of cases in 1963 to approximately 20 percent in 1982. The big change has occurred in the great increase in the percentage of cases resolved through judicial action short of trial. The major category here appears to be an increase in the percentage of cases resolved by the judge without a jury through summary judgment and other pretrial motions, that is, solely on a written record and without the participation of a jury. Although full data are not available, studies of representative districts for 1975–2000 showed that "the portion of cases terminated by summary judgment increased from 3.7 percent in 1975 to 7.7 percent in 2000."[19] Comparing the summary judgment data with the trial data showed an absolute reversal in the percentage of cases resolved through trial and summary judgment over that twenty-five-year period. In 1975 twice as many cases were resolved by trial as by summary judgment; in 2000, three times as many cases were resolved by summary judgment as by trial.[20] Another empirical investigator, Stephen Burbank, concluded that the percentage of cases resolved by summary judgment increased some 350 percent—from 1.8 percent to 7.7 percent. He also found that in another federal district, summary judgments increased from 4.1 percent to 4.7 percent of dispositions from 2000 to 2003, a 14 percent increase *in four years*. Meanwhile the percentage of trials dropped from 2.5 percent to 1.0, a 60 percent decrease in those same four years.[21] In sum, we seem to be moving "from a world in which dispositions by summary judgment [are] equal to a small fraction of dispositions by trial into a new era in which dispositions by summary judgment are a magnitude several times greater than the number of trials."[22] The data show that the decline in trials is not related to the number of filings (which has increased) or the kinds of cases most likely to go to trial (also increased).[23]

The picture on the criminal side is similar, if slightly less dramatic. The number of criminal filings over the same forty-year period has more than doubled, while the percentage of cases going to trial has declined from about 15 percent in 1962 to 5 percent in 2002.[24] The percentage decrease in trials overwhelms the increase in filings to produce a 30 percent decrease in the absolute number of criminal trials in the federal courts. Most of the decrease in the number of criminal trials seems to have occurred since 1991.[25] As with civil cases, the decrease in bench trials is more dramatic than that of jury trials.[26] There has been no dramatic increase in the length of federal criminal trials: 80 percent are completed within three days and 95 percent are completed within nine days. Shrinkage has recently occurred in the number of bankruptcy trials, comparable to that in federal district courts.

One consequence of the reduction of the number of trials is a similar reduction in the number of appeals that occur on the fully developed records that trials create. Although tried cases are more likely to be appealed than cases that are resolved short of trial, the dramatic decline in the number of trials has meant that only about one in eight appeals during the years from 1987 to 1996 was from a trial. Defendants tend to appeal more from trial outcomes than do plaintiffs, and they succeed on those appeals at a rate higher than do plaintiffs. Although much of the commentary on the vanishing trial focuses appropriately on the decline in the trial by jury, once again, the decline in bench trials has been even more dramatic. It is the trial itself that is dying.

The vast majority of trials, perhaps 98 percent,[27] occur not in federal court, but in the states. Here the data are somewhat harder to come by, but definite trends are still discernible: "[T]rends in the state courts . . . bear an unmistakable resemblance to the trends in federal courts." In the states studied, which contain 58 percent of the American population, from 1976 to 2002 "the portion of cases reaching jury trial declined from 1.8 percent to 0.6 percent of dispositions and bench trials fell from 34.3 percent to 15.2 percent" and the "absolute number of jury trials is down by one-third and the absolute number of bench trials is down 6.6 percent."[28] Other studies corroborate the basic trends:

> Although the state data is less comprehensive, it is sufficiently abundant to indicate that the trends in state court trials generally match those in the federal courts. In both there is a decline in the percentage of dispositions that are by jury trial and bench trial. In both there is a decline in the absolute number of

jury trials and bench trials. In the federal courts, nonjury trials have declined even more dramatically than jury trials; in the state courts, it is jury trials that are shrinking faster.[29]

The decline in state criminal trials has also been dramatic. It is true that "plea bargaining's triumph" is an old story and that the criminal trial has been vanishing for over a century. Since the turn of the twentieth century, with some variation over time and from court to court, about 90 percent of criminal cases have been plea-bargained. But here too the more recent decline has been dramatic: from 1976 through 2002 trials as a percentage of dispositions declined from 8.5 percent to 3.3 percent. Bench trials as a percentage of dispositions fell from 5.0 percent to 2.0 percent, while jury trials fell from 3.4 percent to 1.3 percent.[30] Similar declines occurred in jurisdictions where only the more serious felony trials were studied.[31]

Judith Resnik, who has been a major critic of the decline of adjudication, has provided a graphic portrayal of what this means on the ground in her description of the new federal courthouse in Boston:

> In this courthouse, some twenty-five trial courts look more or less like ... [this]: A judge's bench is placed at the back, a bit lower than is common, in a self-conscious (if subtle) effort to portray law as accessible and not unduly hierarchical. Each wall has an arch of equal height, to suggest the equality of all before the law. The designers of this courthouse [Harry Cobb was the principal architect] chose the arches and the courtrooms as central icons of their building. ... Yet a disjuncture exists between this new building, its courtrooms, and the rules and practices that now surround processes, which have also been re-shaped many times during the twentieth century. Judges are now multitaskers, sometimes managers of lawyers and of cases, sometimes mediators and sometimes referral sources, sending people outside of courts to alternative dispute resolution by judges and lawyers. ... When that courthouse opened in 1998 in the District of Massachusetts, 142 civil and 48 criminal trials were completed. With approximately twenty-five trial courtrooms for district and magistrate judges available ... *about seven or eight trials were held per courtroom per year in the new courthouse.* (Emphasis added)[32]

And so it is not surprising that federal investigations have revealed what many unscientific walks around many American courthouses have shown: "that federal courtrooms have their 'lights on'—meaning lit for at least *two* hours a day—about *half* the time." There is no doubt that in the federal system, judges try fewer cases:

> In 1962, there were 39 trials for each sitting federal district judge (18.2 criminal and 20.8 civil). Twenty-five years later in 1987, near the height of the boom [in absolute numbers] in trials, there were 35.3 trials (13.0 criminal and 22.3 civil) for each sitting district judge. In 2002, there were just 13.2 trials (5.8 criminal and 7.4 civil) for each sitting district judge—roughly one-third as many as in 1962.[33]

The implosion in the number of trials does not at all mean that there is any withering away of the law:

> Every other part of the legal world grows: there are more statutes, more regulations, more case law, more scholarship, more lawyers, more expenditure, more presence in public consciousness. In all these respects the growth of the legal world outstrips that of the society or the economy. But trials are shrinking, not only in relation to the rest of the legal world, but relative to the society and the economy. . . . From 1962 to 2002, federal trials per million persons fell by 49 percent; from 1976 to 2002, trials in 22 state courts of general jurisdiction fell by 33 percent.
> Since the economy was growing more rapidly than the population, the number of trials per billion dollars of gross domestic product (GDP) has fallen more steadily and precipitously. By 2002 federal civil trials per billion of GDP were less than one quarter as many as in 1962, even though spending on law as a portion of GDP had increased during that period.[34]

And so the decline of the trial does not apply to the legal world considered more globally. There are almost three times as many lawyers now than there were in 1960. Charges for legal work by law firms quadrupled during that time to the point where legal work probably represents about 2 percent of the gross domestic product.[35] There has been an increase of 133 percent from 1962 to 2002 in the number of pages devoted to case law.[36] It is true, of course, that the trial has never been the statistically most common method of resolving disputes, or even civil cases, but "common law procedure has been defined by the presence of this plenary event, to which all else was prelude or epilogue." It was, as White put it, the "central institution of law as we know it,"[37] the sun around which all the planets in our procedural system revolve. This plenary public dramatic event has been replaced by various pretrial and post-trial procedures, largely conducted behind closed doors and often in a technical language far from ordinary modes of speech.

## A First Attempt at Explanation

Scholars have made a few first attempts to locate explanations of or causes for the decline. Most broadly, "[p]lausible causes for this decline include a shift in ideology and practice among litigants, lawyers, and judges."[38] "The decline of trials is not an isolated meteor flashing across the legal skies" but is connected with "changes in elite ideology, institutional practice and legal culture that have transformed the legal environment."[39] Although my focus in this book is the meaning or significance of the death of the American trial, some light may be shed on that matter by a consideration of likely causes. Some of the meanings of the death of the trial are independent of the causes of the decline, while others are closely intertwined with those causes. The notion of explanation in this context is quite fluid, as we will see. Some of the explanations are simply descriptions of the decline in more inclusive or theoretical language, while others seek to identify what we might call efficient causes of the fall. In all, there seem to be about a dozen possible explanations, most of which are not mutually exclusive.

The first explanation (observation, really) points to a convergence between American and continental procedures.[40] Of course, this itself doesn't identify a cause of the development. Rather, it provides a descriptive comparison. The question is why legal actors are choosing or being pressured toward procedures that have generally been thought to reflect more authoritarian and organic, and certainly less democratic, political cultures. On the continent, the *Prozess,* to cite Kafka's often mistranslated masterpiece, continues from date to date until the judge, who has received a pretrial dossier created by a state official and is himself actively developing the record and asking most questions, is satisfied that he is ready to rule (or that the parties are ready to settle). In the United States the "process" is becoming "a series of encounters with more judicial control, more documentary submissions, and less direct oral confrontation."[41] The case often comes to be resolved, or "disposed of," through strategic judgments by the parties in reaction to (1) the judge's pretrial rulings on discovery and evidence, (2) the emergence of information in discovery itself, and (3) determinations of cost. The legal norms or rules have only a background existence in this process.[42] The parties may no longer even be "bargaining in the shadow of the law" and, as appears to be true in securities litigation, "all cases settle" based on settlements in other cases where strategic considerations have set a "going rate" distant from either official or commonsense norms.[43] And so we have a set of dense and complex judge-dominated written procedures with ever fewer trials. The question is whether the constitutional protections surrounding the jury and the "deep cultural attachment to it—at least as a symbol" will impose limits on the convergence with continental processes, as Galanter seems to hope.

The second explanation is the displacement hypothesis. Here the notion is that trials have migrated elsewhere, primarily to administrative agencies or alternative dispute resolution (ADR) forums, including both arbitration and mediation. Indeed, there are almost three times as many trial-type proceedings in federal administrative agencies than in federal courts, even if one includes proceedings before magistrate judges among trials in federal courts. These "trials" can vary enormously in quality and structure.[44] Many are quite discontinuous with the practices of the common law trial described in the first chapter. But the threshold problem with the notion that trials are being displaced to agencies is that there seems to be no evidence of an increase in trials in these alternative locations that would counterbalance the decline in the courts.[45] Although we don't know much about the effects of referrals to ADR within the federal courts,[46] we do know that "the caseload of [private] ADR institutions remains small in comparison to that of the courts."[47] Even in libertarian Los Angeles, ADR caseloads were only about 5 percent of that of the public courts.[48] On the other hand, the numbers are growing faster than in the public courts and the case size seems larger, while arbitration in particular is taking on some of the formal characteristics of traditional litigation.[49] Other commentators bemoan "adhesive arrangements imposed by the economically powerful on their weaker antagonists," prominently the growth of arbitration clauses in a growing number of form contracts for consumer goods.[50]

The nineteenth century saw general judicial hostility to arbitration as lawless and informal. This attitude began to dissipate in the early decades of the twentieth century with the encouragement of Congress, which passed the Federal Arbitration Act in 1925. For a time courts remained at least skeptical of and grudging toward arbitration, especially when it served to waive federal statutory rights.[51] In 1985 the Supreme Court, in an about-face, "enforced an arbitration contract even though federal statutory rights were at stake" while celebrating its flexibility.[52] Though its embrace is not absolute, the Court has made it progressively more difficult to avoid the effect of arbitration clauses by ruling "that arbitration waivers could be applied to preclude discrimination claims of employees, that opponents of arbitration bore the burden of showing that the costs of arbitration made it unusable as a technique to vindicate statutory rights, and that arbitrators (rather than judges) should at the first instance interpret agreements to consider whether contracts permitted aggregate processing."[53]

Resnik believes it important to divide the displacement explanations of the vanishing trial into two broad categories, which have quite different implications for the meaning of the trial's demise. The first, which she terms the "proliferation thesis,"[54] is that trials (or proceedings that may reasonably be called trials) have migrated to other, still public forums. The strength of this theory, in her view, is that it is consistent with the evidence implicit in "national and transnational agreements" that there exists "a worldwide political consensus that transparent adjudicatory processes are a prerequisite to successful market-based democracies."[55] But she also emphasizes how much we don't know about these "displaced trials" and whether they have even the main lines of the features I described in the first chapter. The second is the "privatization" thesis, the notion that disputes are increasingly resolved outside the context of public adjudication. This explanation also finds support in rules and practices and reflects views, broadly held if not consensual, that public justice is unresponsive, over-lawyered, and intertwined with a drive to create and impose public norms offensive to libertarian sensibilities. Resnik finds that both theses are supported by significant evidence. She emphasizes, however, the depth of our ignorance of the nature of trial-type proceedings in agencies other than the federal courts.[56]

The third possibility, an extension of the convergence explanation, is termed "assimilation," a process by which "law is less an autonomous, self contained system distinct from the surrounding institutions that it controls or monitors, while at the same time these institutions become legalized—they adopt due process and mimic legal procedures. Law mingles with other forms of knowledge."[57] The picture that emerges here is one of an increasingly complex but monolithic society with fewer differentiated spheres. This too is more a general description than an identification of causes. One result is that "the decision-making process of adjudication may be swallowed up by the surrounding bargaining process," as in securities litigation and child-support litigation (where, once again, the expected level of payment is derived not from prior adjudications, but from prior settlements).[58]

Commentators who emphasize the assimilation hypothesis point to the growth of long and complex pretrial procedures and often endless discovery combined with highly discretionary "managerial judging." This has given the judge enormous power to determine the outcome through incremental decisions on matters of procedure detached from the merits of the claim. It has also placed the center of gravity in litigation in bargaining with opposing counsel and often with the court. Of course, trials have been understood as providing a distinctively discontinuous ritual space, "isolated, hedged round, hallowed, within which special rules obtain . . . temporary worlds within the ordinary world, dedicated to the performance of an act apart."[59] This centrality of bargaining during the pretrial stage (and the often inconclusive and expensive briefing that goes along with it)[60] allows the economic and political pressures of the broader society to press in on the legal sphere and compromises its distinctiveness. We will return to this in the last chapter. This assimilation occurs in the other direction as well. Arbitration, at least, has come to look more like traditional adjudication, while, conversely, the processes of arbitration and mediation have come to be ordered by courts and reflective of the norms that prevail there,[61] "[s]o other locations, too, lose their distinctiveness and their independence and function as auxiliary courts while in the courts it is more difficult to get a definitive adjudication and there is more pressure to go along and make a deal."[62] But, once again, these other "trials" can lack many of the characteristics of twentieth-century trials that I described in the first chapter.

A more theoretically driven redescription of the decline of the trial continuous with the assimilation hypothesis sees "a fundamental change in the character of the legal system" reflecting the "momentous shift of the capitalist political economy towards economic and financial globalization."[63] This shift is from law as "an accountable expression of national policy to an informal and flexible economic and political instrument that links public and private power."[64] It is not a benign development: "Corporate and government actors manage to have it both ways—they enjoy the legitimation of law while being able to exert their economic and political power," yielding "governance in legal garb."[65] Galanter concludes that "[d]irect evidence of such a transformation is elusive," but "the vanishing trial is suggestive of a shrinking of the role for definitive adjudication in the whole complex of governance."[66] As he puts it:

> In the "bargaining in the shadow of the law" that underlies settlements, the influence of legal doctrine and tested facts is always thoroughly mixed with considerations of expense, delay, publicity and confidentiality, the state of the evidence, the availability and attractiveness of witnesses, and a host of other contingencies that lie beyond the substantive rules of law. The diminishing role of trials and the greater indeterminacy of doctrine provides [sic] more space for the play of enlarged judicial discretion and the stratagems of intensified lawyering.[67]

I will return to this possibility as well in the last chapter.

A fifth explanation of the vanishing trial tells a story that Galanter terms "evolutionary." It is mainly a happy tale in which our new pluralism of dispute resolution methods allows us to step up to a higher ethical level than does adversary trial procedure. In this view,[68] the decline of the trial results from citizens' "seeking more tailored, complex, and future-oriented, as well as more conditional and contingent-to-be-revisited-if-things-change outcomes," and so looking "to places other than courts to help them resolve their disputes."[69] Galanter wonders whether "all this 'seeking' and 'revisiting' and 'tailoring'" is "being undertaken primarily by one sub-set of 'parties'—corporate and governmental repeat players—who are with increasing success imposing those choices on individual claimants."[70] The plausibility of this story would require an extremely complete assessment of the adequacy and appropriateness of the other means through which disputes are resolved and social ordering is occurring. Any such assessment would have to take into account the enthusiasm of large corporations for some forms of alternative dispute resolution and the relative lack of freedom that many people have to avoid the contracts of adhesion that require resort to those alternative procedures.

A sixth explanation focuses on economic causes. It has always been true that the vast majority of cases have ended in settlement, for a number of reasons: "This reflects the exigencies of litigation, which lead parties to trade off the possibility of preferred outcomes for avoidance of the costs and risks of proceeding through trial."[71] And the legal system has its own exigencies, which it translates into incentives directed at the key actors:

It also reflects the architecture of the system, which has the capacity to give full treatment to only a minority of the matters entitled to invoke it. Instead, it relies on a combination of cost barriers (not only out-of-pocket expenditures, but queues and risk) to induce parties to abandon claims or negotiate a settlement on the basis of the signals and markers that it generates.[72]

But strictly economic considerations are only part of the picture. It is not apparent that devices other than trial always reduce the time and expenditures of all the parties.[73] And economics may only be the "language" within which other causes—ideological self-understandings, for example—express themselves. Thus legal actors acting for ideological reasons may be in a position to raise the various costs of trial in ways that make it less eligible.

Various sorts of costs associated with trial have indeed risen. These include experts of various kinds, including the $400 million jury-consultant industry, and higher priced counsel. The simple economics of settlement show that such costs raise the defendants' bottom lines and lower the plaintiffs' (the legal costs avoided can be thrown into the pot available for bargaining), making settlements more attractive. It is sometimes suggested that "the risks attendant to litigation" have been "jacked up to so high a level that no litigant in his or her right mind would choose to take them."[74] This seems to be true in securities litigation. The growth of plea bargaining has long been based on the ability of prosecutors to expose defendants to penalties very much higher than the sentence they are offering on a plea.

Seventh, the perception that trial awards (and jury awards in particular) are rising may lead to higher settlement rates, though this notion is strongly undermined by the most reliable studies.[75] The perception may be supported by views that "juries are arbitrary, sentimental, and 'out of control.'"[76] It is consistent with the enormously distorted bias of mainstream mass-circulation journalism, which has reported plaintiffs' awards many times more often than defendants' awards in both tort and civil rights cases:[77] "Notwithstanding occasional efforts to debunk some of the 'litigation explosion' legends, the regular consumer of media reports would be badly misinformed about the number of product liability and medical malpractice cases, the size of jury awards, the incidence of punitive damages, and the regularity with which corporate defendants succeed in defeating individual claimants."[78] The legal profession itself seems not to be appreciably better informed.[79] I believe one must be skeptical of this explanation, especially as it applies to well-counseled corporations and insurance companies with fairly sophisticated data retrieval and analysis capabilities and who ought to know the actual facts about jury awards. (I suppose, though, that one can eventually come to believe one's own public relations material.)

A good deal weaker are "diminished supply" explanations based on the notion that cases are not being brought or, once there, are finding their way elsewhere. There has been some decline in the absolute numbers of state civil filings, but the decline is significantly less than is the decline in the number of trials. It has no applicability in federal court, where, as we have seen, the number of filings has increased while the number of trials has collapsed. Furthermore, the kinds of cases filed are the kinds of cases that have historically had the highest trial rates. Given the expansion of resources devoted to the courts,[80] and the fact that, in the federal courts, half the judges were trying 30 percent more trials in 1962, the explanation of simple lack of resources there seems strained.

Ninth, a powerful, though more subtle, set of explanations focuses on the self-understandings of the courts themselves. These explanations focus on a "changing institutional practice and ideology that justifies that practice."[81] Such changes are continuous with the "assimilationist" explanation described above. Stephen Yeazell, for one, has emphasized the ways in which modern civil procedure has conferred on the "trial" judge enormous unreviewed discretion, leading to a style sometimes criticized as "managerial judging": "[T]he discretion of trial judges has expanded partly because of increased complexity, but even more so from the multiplication of discretionary procedural, evidentiary and management decisions."[82] Galanter whimsically quotes a Colorado Supreme Court Justice: "While an appellate court may have the opportunity to reverse any individual trial judge every few years, I know that trial judges, in their numerous workday rulings, reverse appellate courts every day."[83] Procedural rules that strongly discourage interlocutory review (review before the judgment entered at the very end of the case in the trial court, leaving only enforcement) and an extremely deferential "abuse of discretion" standard of review insulate these managerial decisions from effective review. The trial courts' willingness to exploit their discretionary managerial powers grew as a result of changes in prevailing ideology and bureaucratic incentives: "[I]nfluential judges and administrators in the federal courts embraced the notion that judges were problem solvers and case managers as well as adjudicators."[84] Judges were praised as "good case managers" and criticized for failing to "dispose" of a sufficiently high number of cases, often through settlement, sometimes through "muscle mediation" by a judge who would clearly be seeking settlement and who the parties knew would continue to make many unreviewable decisions as the case proceeded. Some judges may come to relish the feeling of power that comes from operating free of the confining conventions of the trial, where, as we saw in the second chapter, the American tradition and American political sensibilities have tended to impose constraints. And some relish the reputation for being "strong judges" that may accompany that style. Acting publicly as a "passive" adjudicator may come to look less attractive. After all, as Bentham put it, "Publicity is the very soul of justice ... It keeps the judge himself, while trying, on trial."[85] Some judges may prefer not to be on trial too often.

And so "[t]he '*normative valence*' of going to trial has changed, as leaders of the bench and bar bemoan the need to take cases to trial."[86] Judge Herbert Will, of my own Northern District of Illinois, wrote, "One of the fundamental principles of judicial administration is that, in most cases, the absolute result of a trial is not as high a quality of justice as is the freely negotiated, give a little, take a little settlement."[87] Resnik recounts that the saying "A bad settlement is almost always better than a good trial" has been repeated in a number of published opinions. She believes as well that costs and the pressure of increasing numbers of cases are factors in the anti-trial rhetoric of some judges, but not the key factor. Rather, she identifies a set of additional considerations consistent with the criticism brought by others of the bureaucratic scaffolding of the contemporary trial.[88] Judges "shifted from an understanding that their role was to move cases toward trial (with settlement a welcome by-product of these efforts) to a view that it was their job to resolve disputes; they also embraced process pluralism—i.e., the notion that there was more than one right way to deal with a dispute—and accordingly they welcome 'alternative' processes in the courts and in forums outside the courts."[89]

The causal suggestion that judges' self-understanding, bolstered by institutional pressures, has resulted in fewer trials is consistent with deeper, more structural explanations such as the notion of assimilation. On the other hand, at a certain point avoiding trial can become cumulative and self-sustaining, for judges, especially the state court judges who must stand for election and face increasingly partisan publicity campaigns by opponents, may become averse to the exposure to public scrutiny and the possibility for reversal that comes from trial. A similar suggestion has been made about trial lawyers. Here an "atrophy of advocacy skills ... may both lessen future trials, as inexperienced lawyers are unwilling to undertake the risk of trial[,] and also distort settlements as lawyers without trial experience are less able to evaluate cases accurately."[90] (Lawyers who still try cases like to smile at the self-description of lawyers who spend most of their time on discovery disputes as "litigators.") And consider the plaintive defense of the activities of "trial judges" that has been urged by the Administrative Office of the United States Courts in its attempt to sustain congressional funding for the courts:

> In addition to research and opinion drafting, many case-related events not classified as "trials"—such as hearings on motions of summary judgment and other dispositive motions, hearings on sentencing issues, *Daubert* hearings on expert witnesses, evidentiary hearings in pro se prisoner and other cases, supervised release and probation revocation hearings, and activities related to alternative dispute resolution (ADR) and settlements—involve substantial judicial activity.[91]

Tenth, there are explanations that focus on the dramatic democratization of the American jury. Beginning with the congressional mandate dismantling the "key man" system for assembling "elite" juries in the federal courts,[92] and continuing on to the Supreme Court's requirement of more representative jury pools across racial lines and to prohibitions on race-based and gender-based peremptory strikes, the American jury has rapidly become much more representative of American society as a whole—more democratic. This is a very important development. A truly democratic jury may be incongruent with the distribution of power in economic and political spheres, causing what we may call a lack of institutional equilibrium. As we saw in the first chapter, even without the recent broadening of representation, the contemporary trial privileges traditional life-world moral intuitions, which are always in tension with the norms dominant in other spheres. The latter are partially represented at trial through the law of rules, but they are truly dominant in other modern American institutions, notably our public and private bureaucracies and the market.[93] The trial is, as we have seen, designed to encourage a kind of penetrating fact finding and evaluation enormously more serious than the clichés of mass-market political discourse, and a kind of evaluation continuous with the moral world rather than with the implicit norms of our public and private bureaucracies. Such an institution, though an irritant, may be tolerable,

especially after the recalibrations of the nineteenth century, if the prem-
ises of evaluation employed by jurors are skewed by an overrepresenta-
tion of jurors identifying with those holding economic and political power
in this society.

The conflict between this institution and others may reach a point of
crisis, however, if the jury becomes truly representative *and* maintains at
least some of its traditional role of engaging in highly contextual moral
evaluation. The judgments likely to emerge from real deliberation of
such juries may be feared to be doubly discontinuous with the modes of
thought embedded in other powerful institutions. The jury would not only
be engaging in evaluation incongruent with the principles of modern bureaucracies, but also would embody sensibilities that would diverge from
those of the elites, who possess economic and political power. (This is
not to say that juries were anything but traditional; those elites may well
have absorbed instrumental modes of operating that were inconsistent
with ordinary moral intuitions.)[94] One would then expect to see various
attempts to constrict the trial as an important means of social ordering:
"tort reform," limitations on the jury's ability to assess damages, mandatory arbitration, and schemes of administrative adjudication where judges
are subject to bureaucratic controls may all provide forums that are more
harmonious with other forms of institutionalized power. One would also
expect economic and political pressures within the conduct of litigation,
pressures that elevated both bureaucracy and bargaining over trial presentation and deliberation.

Paul Butler has even more provocatively suggested a race-based explanation for the vanishing trial. Butler comments that it does not seem
coincidental that the trial began to vanish soon after the jury was effectively democratized: "[O]ver the last hundred years, the civil jury has
grown into perhaps the most diverse and representative governmental
body in America."[95] He argues that there may well be a racial element in
the declining attractiveness of the jury trial and that, from the perspective
of an African American scholar, the vanishing trial bears a resemblance
to white flight.[96] It is also continuous with the conscious strategy in some
quarters to starve all the organs of the public sphere of effectiveness. The
key issue, he suggests, is not that black and working-class jurors may be
more willing to nullify or stretch the law, but that potential litigants may
perceive that they do.

The eleventh explanation suggests that there are fewer trials because
there are fewer resources with which to conduct them. It does not seem,

however, that the legal establishment as a whole is starved for resources. After all, much of what the courts do is wholly continuous with the needs of other sources of social power. And so the picture here is very mixed. There have been recent reductions in expenditures on the courts, but the sheer number of dollars expended increased "from $246 million (1996 dollars) in 1962 to $4.354 billion (1996 dollars) in 2002."[97] The number of federal district court judges increased from 279 in 1962 to 615 in 2002, and the latter are "assisted by 95 senior judges and more than 500 magistrates." Still, this increase has not kept pace with the increase in case filings, so that number of filings per judge has actually doubled.[98] Although the number of judges has doubled during this period, the number of other employees has increased fivefold,[99] suggesting a much larger bureaucracy surrounding a number of judges that has not kept pace with the increase in filings.

A more limited speculation is that the increase in the number of class-action filings—in which most of the action occurs at the pretrial stage, and which are rarely tried—may represent a successful attempt by defendant corporations, with the implicit aid of "sections of the plaintiffs' bar," to "manage the risk of multiple claims."[100] The aggregation of claims in the class action, the results of which preclude individual class members from filing their own claims, may serve to reduce the number of truly triable cases. Similarly, the emergence of the Judicial Panel on Multi-District Litigation as a device for consolidating a large number of cases for both discovery and trial seems to have reduced the number of cases likely to go to trial.[101]

Finally, any general explanation of the death of the trial would have to account for the historic growth and triumph of plea bargaining in the criminal context. This, too, involves a long historical decline followed by a very sharp recent decline (though not quite so sharp as in the civil context). The most comprehensive attempt to explain the dominance of plea bargaining historically offers a two-step explanation.[102] The first step saw prosecutors and then judges come to understand in the nineteenth century that a regime dominated by plea bargaining was in their own narrow interests. Plea bargaining reduced the number of cases that prosecutors could be criticized for losing and increased the conviction rate, something that could be touted at the next election. Part-time prosecutors could spend more time on their remunerative civil caseload. Mandatory minimum sentences gave prosecutors the ability to "charge bargain," to offer to charge at a lower level and so, even without the judge's cooperation, to expose the defendant to a smaller range of possible sentences. When legislatures removed the prosecutor's ability to dismiss ("noli pros"), plea bargaining all but disappeared, but prosecutors were ingenious about improvising effective methods of reinstituting the practice. Foster believes that all nineteenth-century prosecutors would have improvised some form of plea bargaining because it so strongly served their interests. For good or ill, this allowed determinations of sentences to be made behind closed doors: for good, it allowed prosecutors to avoid the posturing that public performances by officials who had to stand for election sometimes brought; for ill, it offered prosecutors tremendous discretion in determining what the ultimate sentence would be. Another enormous boost to the practice was the institution of probation. Not that probation came into existence solely to serve the interests of plea bargaining, but its availability fit nicely into a system where bargaining was central:

> By the last quarter of the nineteenth century, plea bargaining had become a valued tool not only of prosecutors, but of judges as well. Serving the interest of all those with real power, plea bargaining became a dominant institution by winning their protection. Prosecutors and judges nurtured plea bargaining by promoting other procedural reforms, such as probation, that helped plea bargaining thrive.[103]

Countermeasures were necessary to promote plea bargaining because of the emergence of other developments, notably higher levels of representation, more effective advocacy, and rule changes that for the first time permitted the defendant to take the stand and testify under oath. Additionally, judges were coming under pressure to "dispose" of criminal cases because of vast numbers of injuries, which created a "crushing civil caseload from transportation and industry":[104]

> [The great expansion of the civil caseload] represents . . . one of the great transformations of American law. It did not respond simply to the booming population growth of the era, but rather to the suddenly expanding mechanization of production and transportation. It is a measure of the human carnage wrought by massive but still primitive technology deployed by industrialists and railroad barons bent on profit and untethered by government safety regulations.[105]

The advent of indeterminate sentences (which put the ultimate sentence in the hands of corrections bureaucrats) gave judges the excuse to denigrate the need for a searching, individualized hearing to determine a just sentence: "With their moral guard down and with alarming civil caseloads pressing them to cut deals were they could, judges perhaps gave in to temptation and dealt."[106] Other procedural devices, such as the right of defendants to withdraw pleas and the end of indeterminate sentencing, accelerated the dominance of plea bargaining.[107] In short,

> [p]lea bargaining entered the twentieth century with all the staying power that comes from serving the interests of power. Its course through the century proved to be one of the consolidation of power, as institutions that might have threatened the dominance of plea bargaining fell by the wayside and others that fed its preeminence took hold.[108]

Plea bargaining's power is "its derived power, for the power of plea bargaining is the power of the courtier—the influence it has gained by serving well the interests of those in high places."[109] He suggest that the "sheer efficiency of plea bargaining as a means of clearing cases has frozen it in place."[110] Legislators, themselves hard-pressed by popular opposition to raising taxes, were unlikely to consider increasing the resources going to the courts when those same courts had in their hands a cheap and effective means to keep their costs down. The importance of realizing the values implicit in constitutional guarantees to trial came to seem quite ethereal: "This multiplicity of mechanisms [of evasion] makes it highly unlikely that the historical correlation between plea bargaining's rise and the indeterminate sentence's fall was simple coincidence. By various devices, the forces that impelled plea bargaining's progress also compelled that the indeterminate sentence make way."[111] Indeed, "[n]ot a single important procedural innovation . . . threatened to choke off plea bargaining and yet flourished."[112]

What about the more dramatic recent decline in the rate of trial in federal criminal cases? Foster agrees with Galanter's suspicion that the federal sentencing guidelines have decreased the number of trials by providing an additional incentive for the defendant to avoid trial.[113] First, the guidelines make sentences almost fully determinate. Second, they give prosecutors greater power to make attractive, definite offers and have their promises stick:

> Not only are these mandatory sentencing laws rigid, they are harsher than what went before. Together with the Guidelines themselves, they have produced far

longer sentences that in pre-Guidelines days. In the process, they perhaps have made it easier for prosecutors to widen the gap between the sentences they offer on a plea and the one they demand should the defendant risk trial and lose.[114]

Finally, a 1990 amendment from the commission made a downward reduction in the sentence available to a defendant who "accepted responsibility" for his crime, a reduction that was only rarely available to a defendant who insisted on putting the government to its proof in a criminal trial. Thus, "the Guidelines have set off a plea-bargaining frenzy,"[115] which has contributed to the sharp recent decline in the number of criminal cases.

In short, the triumph of plea bargaining was accomplished by public officials who had control over legal mechanisms and who could bend them to serve their own interests.

## The Trial Deformed by the Litigation System

Finally, there is a possible explanation for the death of the trial that I have not yet considered. The trial may be dying because it deserves to die. Despite my idealizing description of the trial in the first chapter, it may be that it has proven incapable of achieving its human purposes. As I intimated earlier in this chapter, this incapacity may be the very complex matter of disequilibrium with other dominant institutions, which may cause the trial's decline without justifying it. Or the trial's defects may be something simpler. The trial as we have it may simply be costly, inefficient, incapable of achieving factual truth, and at odds with the values underlying the rule of law.[116] I believe that none of this is true.

We must make two important, though sometimes subtle, distinctions here. First, there are weaknesses in the trial that stem from the bureaucratic and market institutions within which the trial is embedded. These disfigurations of the trial's internal ideals continue to plague us and, quite frankly, may help hasten the death of the trial.[117] Second, we must understand the essence or core of the contemporary trial and how it may be better realized by relatively minor improvements in the way in which we actually try cases. I briefly survey some of the more plausible reforms, some of which would actually strengthen the trial and likewise the argument for the importance of the trial I make throughout this book. In the first chapter I identified the heart of the trial. The trial is a highly constrained dramatic event constituted by tensions between broad narratives and, more particularly, testimony in the language of perception. All narratives are subject to harsh deconstruction and are limited by the values embedded in the law of rules. Most of the criticism of the trial, we will see, does not go to this heart of the matter, but rather attacks the bureaucratic and market institutions surrounding the trial. The practices of the trial may be distorted by the institutions within which they are encased.

Judge Dwyer identified "six deadly sins" of the American litigation system,[118] none of which implicates the core of the trial: overcontentiousness, expense, delay, fecklessness, hypertechnicality, and overload. The O. J. Simpson criminal trial, with its two and half months of voir dire and endless and undisciplined proceedings, remains the poster child for overcontentiousness. Expense, Dwyer's second deadly sin, has a number of aspects, most of which have little directly to do with the conduct of trials. One concern may be the sheer size of the expenditures for legal services. The statistics presented earlier in this chapter clearly show that those expenditures (even if they do not "add value") are going for services other than trials. Within the world of litigation, costs of discovery and legal research and writing dwarf those of trials. Indeed, the death of the trial may well funnel more resources into high-billing enterprises such as endless discovery, disconnected from a reasonable relationship to a possible trial, and lengthy written summary judgment proceedings.

But the concern about expense may be a concern not about total expenditures, but rather with the maldistribution of legal services. The United States spends about $1.70 per capita on civil legal services, compared to $30 per capita in England and Wales.[119] On the criminal side, public defenders are overworked and underpaid. In some states, lawyers with little experience or interest are appointed from the private bar to represent felony defendants. This, along with the rare case where the prosecution is outspent by a wealthy defendant, is the basis of the complaint that "[m]oney is the defining element of our modern American criminal justice system."[120]

This "wealth effect" is, of course, extrinsic to the practices of the adversary trial itself.[121] It is rather a defect in the market for legal services. The wealth effect can distort the trial because of the effects of the market institutions within which the trial takes place. If parties had equal resources to pay legal fees, the insurance to pay them, or public funding of those services, the wealth effect would disappear. The consequences of the wealth effect, especially at the pretrial stage, can distort the accuracy of trial decision making and therefore endanger the rule of law in the trial court. Serious reform efforts, which will be quite different in the civil and criminal contexts and will require the greatest imagination and political will, are called for here.

It seems to me that the trial's practices and languages are less autonomous and more dependent on the market and bureaucratic institutions within which the performances take place when their task is to determine "brutally elementary data."[122] These are cases that concern not the meaning of events, but the basic perceptual "data," such as in criminal cases where identity is the key issue. Underfunded, sloppy, willful, or deliberately deceitful behavior at the pretrial stage can produce skewed verdicts at trial. The trial's devices provide some defenses here, but they are not impregnable. Results may also be skewed by formally inadequate discovery methods, such as the lack of any compulsory pretrial deposition practice in most serious criminal cases and realities such as the crushing caseloads in public defenders' offices.[123] Most of the failures of the rule of law that occur because trials are without truth stem from these sources. The uneven skills of trial lawyers at trial, once a threshold of competence is reached, are less likely to have an effect.

Trials should not be an expensive luxury that only the rich can afford. The institution is too important an element of our public culture. Yes, it is a scarce resource, in the way all costly resources are scarce. Trials should not be conducted in a wasteful way—that offends both fiscal responsibility and the internal ideals of the trial itself. But to say that we should not have trials because we have not devised a fair system for funding them will do little to alleviate the wealth effect as it affects litigation in general.

What we know about wrongful convictions also shows that most of the disfiguration of the trial stems from the surrounding bureaucracies, especially as they function in the pretrial process, though only some of it stems from inadequate funding. No human procedure will be infallible, but we have seen too many persons freed after serving long sentences, often on death row. Long ago Judge Learned Hand opined reassuringly that "[o]ur [criminal] procedure has always been haunted by the ghost of the innocent man convicted. It is an unreal dream." Justice Scalia recently opined that American criminal convictions have an "error rate of .027—or, to put another way, a success rate of 99.973."[124] The latter assumes that the relatively few false convictions that have been discovered are all the false convictions there are, which is surely wrong.

For various reasons, there is much here that we do not and cannot know. The convictions that have been proven incorrect to a high level of

certainty are almost all death penalty and rape cases,[125] very poor proxies
for the actual cases tried where false convictions have occurred. Plausible
estimates for the percent of death penalty cases where there have been
false convictions range from 1.5 percent to 2.3 percent to 5 percent.[126]
There are good reasons to believe that the pressure on police and prosecutors to solve these cases perversely increases the likelihood of false convictions in these most serious of matters. What are our best guesses—and
educated guesses are all we have here—as to the causes of false convictions in the unrepresentative cases about which we know the most? The
consensus seems to be that there are four causes. Eyewitness misidentification is probably the most important. We suspect strongly that much of
this eyewitness misidentification has been created by faulty and suggestive lineup and show-up procedures before trial: "[O]nce a witness has
identified the suspect in a lineup, she may convince herself that the person
was indeed the offender. Defense counsel, especially those appointed by
the court, cannot always be counted on to know of and reveal these various improper procedures in trial."[127] For example, few police departments
conduct "blind" lineups, where the officers in communication with the victim do not themselves know who the real suspect is and therefore cannot
either intentionally or inadvertently signal the identity of the right person.
Intentional perjury—by police and by jailhouse snitches offered deals for
testimony[128]—looms large as a source of false conviction. False confessions, especially by young and mentally limited suspects, are another major cause; they were cited in "nearly a quarter of the DNA exonerations
studies by the Innocence [P]roject."[129] Methods of police pressure toler-
ated by the courts can be extremely effective in producing confessions.
Some of the confessions are clearly false,[130] and police have been very
slow to take the steps to reduce their numbers. Finally, there is sloppy or
deliberately falsified forensic evidence, usually supplied by labs affiliated
with the police. Recent cases in Oklahoma and West Virginia resulted in
findings of irregularities and overturned convictions. And then, pervading
everything is the bureaucratic incentive structure that drives police (and
sometimes prosecutors) to engage in the behaviors correlated with false
convictions:

> What may be the most pervasive source of errors of due process in homicide
> cases is *beyond the reach of the court*: informal rewards and formal incentive
> systems that often put the police under undue pressure to solve high-profile

cases. The pressure has led, clearly, to the arrest of many a leading suspect who has turned out to be innocent. In their zeal to justify an identification arrested as the true offender, police often persuade themselves of the correctness of the decision. A variety of errors have followed: witness inquiries and lineup procedures that produce false identifications, use of untrustworthy snitches, overlooking and (occasionally suppressing) exonerating evidence, inducements to false confessions; and shopping for laboratory technicians who are more inclined to find incriminating evidence against the suspect. (Emphasis added)[131]

My only point here is that the problem of false conviction cannot be laid at the door of the jury and the trial's methods. Especially when what is at stake is "brutally elementary facts," the jury is dependent on the bureaucracy that brings the case to trial, and that bureaucracy can sometimes defeat even the best of trials. But bureaucratizing the trial itself by adopting more inquisitorial methods is likely, in my view, just to make things worse.

With only a few exceptions, delay, Dwyer's third deadly sin, occurs not at trial but because of endless and contentious discovery and motion practice before trial in civil cases and sometimes by endless continuances in criminal court. The appellate process can likewise add years to the length of a lawsuit. Trials themselves are usually a small part of the problem of delay, as the statistics noted above on the average length of trials show. Occasionally a trial—and parts of a trial such as voir dire—are allowed to drag on to truly unreasonable lengths. This is an issue that a "strong and wise trial judge" should be able to control by imposing reasonable time limits on the parties (which are far less intrusive than micromanaging the evidence presented by evidentiary rulings) and by using available procedural devices to prevent parties, including the government in criminal cases, from joining too many parties and too many issues into a single trial. Once again, these disfigure the trial by making it impossible really to join issue on the key questions in the case, and they dissipate the productive tensions that the trial offers. Dwyer's fourth sin, fecklessness, is closely related and occurs when there is no time discipline imposed at the pretrial stage or at trial.[132]

Hypertechnicality, his fifth sin, occurs, thankfully, less and less often in the application of evidence law, though it does persist there. More often it crops up in the course of motion and appellate practice in the hands of the lawyers and judges. It is true that evidentiary rules are sometimes complex, may be without secure justification, and often fail to cut at the joints of the facts of the case. They can disfigure the evidentiary base in a number of ways.[133] With relatively few streamlining devices such as limits on jury selection methods, simplification of evidence law, and imposition of time limits for the presentation of cases,[134] it would seem possible to conduct many more jury trials. In the hands of competent practitioners, the conventions of both direct and cross can reveal both the strongest and weakest aspects of the witness's evidence, as it bears on the inevitably either-or issue usually before the jury. As I tried to show in the first chapter, they improve the discipline of decision making.

The trial I described in the first chapter is not an elaborate affair. It is quite simple. The arts it demands of lawyers and judges are learnable and powerful. The simplifications necessary for effective trial work improve deliberation by forcing both parties to emphasize what is most important. Yes, there will be fact patterns that can be complex, but the trial's devices are up to that complexity. The encrustation of legalisms, especially at the pretrial stage, is the work of the lawyers and judges seeking to avoid trial.

Dwyer's final sin is overload. This is a function of the mismatch between what we have come to expect from the legal system and the resources it works with. But this sin, if it exists, does not bear on the trial at all. He concedes that we would not want to go back to a world where "poverty, injury, unfair treatment on the job, ill health, [and] loss of savings in a failed bank" saw no remedies. Likewise "cases about employment rights, child abuse, social security benefits, professional malpractice, product liability, consumer protection; cases about race discrimination, sex discrimination, endangered species, [and] toxic waste disposal" have come relatively recently to the trial courtroom.[135] Few of us would want to roll back a key development of the twentieth century that has increased the number of cases, one in which "governments recognized greater obligations to subject themselves to regulation, to be bound by their own rules, and to treat persons with dignity and respect,"[136] and the ability of citizens to enforce that recognition in court. On the other hand, the war on drugs has put sometimes unbearable pressure on the federal and state courts. As Galanter's work showed, the raw number of lawsuits, criminal and civil, has increased dramatically. But the resources to handle fairly those cases have not, and largely for political and ideological reasons.

Most of the criticisms of American litigation do not, then, reach the trial itself at all. By attacking the very idea of adversary presentation, John

Langbein provides an exception. Though he recognizes the unfairness of the pre-adversary English criminal trial, Langbein laments the shape that the Anglo-American trial has taken as a result of the reforms of the eighteenth and early nineteenth centuries:

> Two-sided partisanship may indeed have been better than one-sided partisanship, but it was still a poor proxy for truthseeking. Adversary procedure entrusts the responsibility for gathering and presenting the evidence upon which accurate adjudication depends to partisans whose interest is in winning, not in truth.... The adversary dynamic invited distortion and suppression of the evidence, by permitting abusive and misleading cross-examination, the coaching of witnesses, and the concealment of unfavorable evidence. This attribute of adversary procedure, the combat effect, was worsened by the wealth effect inherent in privatizing for hire the work of the adversaries to gather and present the evidence. We recall the chilling lament of the woman tried and sentenced to death for forgery at the Old Bailey in 1757, who told the court "I have not a six penny pence to pay a porter, much less [enough] to fee counsel." For her, the message of adversary justice was that "I must die because I am poor."[137]

Langbein's basic criticism of adversary justice is its lack of "a coherent theory of truthseeking. Adversary procedure presupposed that truth would somehow emerge when no one was in charge of seeking. Truth was a byproduct."[138] He laments the failure of Anglo-American procedure to embrace the methods of reformed continental procedure, where the judge has the wherewithal and authority to conduct his own pretrial investigation and guide the testimony of witnesses solely to achieve truth and a result consistent with the law.[139] As the above quote suggests, he argues that the "combat effect" and the wealth effect continue to plague our trial system.

I have already discussed the wealth effect. Evaluation of the combat effect, which, unlike the wealth effect, is intrinsic to the trial, is more difficult. It may, of course, be viewed solely as a function of the wealth effect (lawyers for the party best able to reward them will do more of the bad things that distort the truth). I doubt that Langbein would be satisfied by Milner Ball's provocative argument, which has some basis in actual practice, that lawsuits need not be battles.[140] But if taken independently of the wealth effect, his broadest claim is that under the conditions that prevail in litigated cases, the presentation and mutual critique of two interested parties is less able to allow the truth to appear to a passive and disinterested judge or jury than the sustained inquiry of a single investigator following the line of investigation where it takes him. But it is not so clear that truth is more likely to appear to a single mind directly seeking it than to a disinterested judge or jury engaged with the best case to be presented on each side. If the essence of justice is *audiatur et altera pars*, isn't it more likely that the other side will be heard when it is urged by an advocate all of whose energies are directed to making it heard? That, at least, has been the assumption of the common law system. Sloth, bureaucratic indifference, or political animus can distort the truth more easily than misdirected energy.[141] Our values are embedded not only in the ideas of any one person—the inquisitorial judge, for example—but in our practices themselves: "The meanings and norms implicit in these practices are not just in the minds of the actors but are out there in the practices themselves, practices which cannot be conceived as a set of individual actions, but are essentially modes of social relation, of mutual action."[142]

We return to our problem of mixed ideality here. Much, although not all, of the criticism of excessive adversarialism points to conduct that is *mis*conduct under current procedural and ethical norms. This is conduct that our legal rules and bureaucratic regulatory mechanisms have not always been able to control. Such inability counsels skepticism about our ability to control any public actor and points to the wisdom of institutionalized oppositions. Our tradition is duly skeptical of a state official, the judge, exercising power *sine ira et studio* (without anger and zeal), solely in the interests of justice. The Federalists taught us that officials in all three branches are "magistrates," officials who have aspired to and achieved political power and from whom we should not expect too much too consistently. The behavior of judges and prosecutors in establishing plea bargaining is not encouraging. Our tradition generally resists comparing that conduct with the idealized inquiry of an inquisitorial judge because of its general skepticism about state power. We are unlikely to find many idealized inquisitorial judges. The centrality of competitive and critical methods within a joint enterprise in modern science provides an important example of their general power.[143] Finally, it is important to distinguish adversary presentation at trial and the adversarial discovery of information. Adversary presentation works best when it is a competitive interpretive enterprise that proceeds on the basis of common access to the underlying information. Disfigurations of the trial may occur when the bureaucratic and market devices distort that evidentiary base.

## Reasonable Proposals for the Reform of the Conduct of Trial

A general critique of the methods of the trial does not, I believe, survive a descriptive, interpretive, and social-scientific account of the discipline and comprehensiveness of its practices. I have supplied a summary of that account. But there is a whole range of specific suggestions for improving the adversarial trial. These are incremental, and many of them make good sense. Recently the American Bar Association assembled a distinguished committee to make recommendations for the improvement of the actual conduct of jury trials. Their work deserves serious attention.[144] For example, the commission recommended extension of a right to trial by jury to "minor" crimes not currently covered by constitutional rules, one-day-one-trial rules for jurors, return to the twelve-person jury whenever possible, and purging jury instructions of legalese.[145] It also offered excellent general guidelines for assembling a fair, impartial jury.[146] The committee wisely recommended provisions for controlling the length of jury trials by reasonable time limits rather than the overuse of evidentiary rulings. Trials of outrageous length dissipate the institution's power. The committee made a number of additional housekeeping provisions as well.

I also generally endorse the recommendations for the conduct of the trial itself that Jeffrey Abramson made some years ago.[147] The unanimous verdict should be reinstated, the peremptory challenge should be eliminated,[148] juries should be instructed they have the authority to set aside the written law to acquit a defendant, the practice of routinely disqualifying potential jurors because of exposure to the standard kinds of pretrial publicity should end, and citizens should not be able so easily to escape their jury obligations. The spectacle of jury selection that lasts as long as the trial itself should end. Although I am not sure anything will come of it, I would like to see a sustained attempt by experimental psychologists and other social scientists to identify those systematic failures in human cognitive capacities (heuristics) about which there is the highest level of certainty in the scientific community and which pose special dangers of distorting jury reasoning.

As is by now obvious, I am a strong defender of the power of the jury's common sense when it is disciplined by the trial's devices. However, we already instruct jurors about what may fairly be considered in weighing evidence. Jurors are, for example, told that they should, in assessing credibility, consider a witness's interests, demeanor, and any prior inconsistent statement a witness has made. They are told about the significance they may or should attach to a witness's failure to produce evidence within his control. Yet as with the exclusionary rules of the law of evidence, there is precious little empirical evidence to support these instructions about how to consider evidence. I can imagine a day in which judges helpfully provide to jurors instructions identifying the circumstances under which we know that eyewitness identifications or confessions by juveniles are especially likely to be unreliable.

I would also repeat that the trend to admissibility in the law of evidence should continue.[149] Because most evidence that a reasonably competent lawyer would consider offering has *some* probative value, and because exclusion deprives the jury of that significant evidence, we should rely primarily on the critical devices of the trial itself to enable the jury to properly evaluate the evidence. Only when those devices are for one reason or another inadequate should we consider exclusion. As one of our most important evidence scholars, who is also a trial court judge of great distinction and experience, put it:

> Excluding information on the ground that jurors are too ignorant or emotional to evaluate it properly may have been appropriate in England at a time when a rigid class society created a wide gap between royal judges and commoner jurors, but it is inconsistent with the realities of our modern American informed society and the responsibilities of independent thought in a working society.[150]

The goal of evidence law should be to maintain the productive tensions that I described in the first chapter. I understand that this is not an easy recipe for deciding what evidence serves only to dissipate those tensions and so should be excluded, but I believe that some such regulatory ideal actually informs much of the best of the current "discretionary controls in the hands of a wise and strong trial court."[151] However, implementing these suggestions would not change the heart of the trial, nor would they address the most important sources of its current limitations, the market and bureaucratic systems that surround it.

## Conclusion

The trial system is imploding for reasons we are just beginning to glimpse. It is not because of defects in the core practices of the trial, though there are significant problems in the bureaucratic and market institutions within which they are encased, problems that may distort the trial's practices in particular cases. And a number of sensible reforms in our current trial practices that are completely continuous with its core values could easily be implemented. It does not seem likely that the trial system is collapsing because of those characteristics of the trial often addressed as candidates for incremental reform. The key question for us concerns the meaning or significance of the trial's death. That is the subject to which I now turn.

## CHAPTER FIVE

# The Meanings of the Trial's Death

James Boyd White has argued that the trial is the sun around which all of the planets in the law's solar system move. Lawrence Friedman writes with a whiff of Marxist idiom that the trial has always been the "ideological core" of the common law, though not the "working core of the system."[1] (He does add that "whether this is good or bad is another question," a normative query unavailable in that idiom.) When considering the meaning of the decline of a social practice, we may find it too easy to slip into deterministic modes of thought—which is the one way in which we must not think of the trial's death. It is easy to see the trial solely as a dependent variable conditioned and constituted by vast social, economic, or political forces. That is not my intent here. The trial itself is a "space of freedom," to use Arendt's term: its practices allow for autonomous action by lawyers and juries, among others, in the public sphere in their treatment of parties. To some extent, our appellate courts and legislatures remain spaces of freedom as well, in the way they, at the next level, treat the trial itself. That they may be objects of social-scientific inquiry doesn't mean that they may not also be sources of political initiative and autonomy. I offer my account of the important meanings that the death of the trial would have to legislatures and courts, which will themselves decide whether the trial lives or dies, hopefully after considering seriously what its death would mean. I address these remarks to public actors and scholars, not thinkers intent on explaining or understanding a fait accompli.

Several authors have mentioned that the death of the trial is of a piece with the "turn against law" and the "recoil against expanding accountability" that began about a quarter of a century ago.[2] Thankfully, however, the broader context may be changing again. We have recently endured waves of corporate misbehavior and seen the effects, in many theaters, of deliberately denying resources and talent to public institutions. This "starve the beast" strategy has worked all too well. There appear to be signs that American legislatures and courts are newly open to the importance of maintaining and strengthening public institutions, the infrastructure on which we all depend. The significance of the collapse of a bridge or the destruction of a city is easy to see, and we have begun to respond politically to those events. The significance of the collapse of a public institution is less clear, but I intend to shed some light on that danger in this chapter.

The death of the trial would have a number of meanings for us. We would lose *the forum that has traditionally been the place where the rigidity and sometimes harshness of written law was softened.* Green showed how the jury trial was fulfilling that function during the Middle Ages. Kalven and Zeisel showed that the American jury trial is still carrying out that task by discerning the significance of "legally irrelevant" aspects of an individual situation (that the defendant was seriously injured at the time of the crime, or that the victim was not enthusiastic about prosecuting, that the behavior is rarely prosecuted, that the conduct is not illegal across the river in the next state, that the defendant was not represented by counsel, that he was suffering personal tragedies at the time he "knowingly" failed to file an income tax return, or that he used a toy gun rather than a real gun at a robbery)—even though the law of rules does not recognize any distinction.[3] True to Chesterton's understanding of the jury trial,[4] these are the kinds of details that may be of great significance to fresh eyes but are likely to be overlooked in the bargaining process by busy lawyers or, in analogous civil contexts, by judges looking only at a paper record.[5]

The death of the trial, especially by an assimilation to inquisitorial methods, would mean the end of a place where *a citizen can effectively tell his own story publicly in a forum of power,* one of our "few official forums for story telling."[6] Some of this storytelling will be through the citizen's lawyer, but a trial lawyer is simply a person who knows how to tell an individual's story in a public forum where perspectives other than those of the client have authority. (Trial advocacy has been called "trial diplomacy.") In the first chapter I emphasized the discipline under which each party must present the evidence to support his or her story and the power of the trial's devices actually to obtain a hearing for each party. *Audiatur et altera pars* is the first principle of procedural justice.[7] The conventions of trial procedure assure that a party to a lawsuit, civil or criminal, may present any reliable and relevant evidence, as determined by fairly liberal preannounced rules applicable to both parties,[8] that the citizen himself or herself chooses to present. He or she does not have to rely on the interest, judgment, and intelligence of a state official, the judge—who, with his or her settled prejudices and decreasing involvement in the specifics of each case, has "got used to it"—to do the preparation and ask the questions that manifest the citizen's perspective on the issue. This is, of course, continuous with American individualism and skepticism about people who have sought and achieved positions of power.[9] It recalls Arendt's observation that preserving a space for the presentation of the most basic of factual evidence can be far more important than forums for philosophical debate: "In Hitler's Germany and Stalin's Russia, it was more dangerous to talk about concentration and extermination camps whose existence was no secret, than to hold and utter 'heretical' views on anti-Semitism, racism, and Communism."[10]

This right to tell one's own story and present the evidence to support it runs deep. Stories are to be found "in the midst of experience and action, not in some higher level of linguistic reconstruction of the experiences and actions involved . . . told in being lived and lived in being told."[11] Arendt maintained that "[n]o philosophy, no analysis, no aphorism, be it ever so profound, can compare in intensity and richness of meaning with a properly narrated story."[12] Because "[a]ction produces stories with or without intention as naturally as fabrication produces tangible things . . . it is part of the concept of action that actions form themselves into stories," which is, in turn, "why only narration of stories can give meaning to history,"[13] even when that history is a history of an individual life or, more commonly at trial, a history of a particular event. Ball observed that "[s]tories nurture apperception and the discernment of a guiding presence between the lines of legal texts and between the facts of situations."[14] From the perspective of the judge or jury deciding the case, giving each party authority over his or her own narrative may "nudge law toward art and transformation" and foster "understanding, the development of judgment, and the enlivening of imagination—the things that carry us through the unstructured places of the world and the heart."[15] In sum, "to say what *is* always requires telling a story; that narrative reflects or supplies the necessary order of things."[16]

Our European cousins do not generally place this role of telling the story and choosing the supporting evidence so completely in the hands of the parties themselves. On the continent, inquisitorial judges have much greater control over the documents to be discovered, the witnesses to be called, and the questions to be asked. They thus have much more control over what facts will be allowed to appear in public. We take a different path, one that seeks to balance party autonomy with discipline through a certain level of formality.[17] Which is more effective? Comparative judgments are treacherous because they usually cannot take into account the differences in culture and background institutions that may justify different procedures.[18] American adversary procedures implicitly agree with the conclusions reached by one continental legal philosopher after his study of transcripts in continental criminal cases:

> [I]n continental criminal procedure the likeliness of equal communication still leaves much to be desired. The asymmetrical distribution of speaking roles rather restrains forensic communication. The course of courtroom interaction can even be considered coercive communication. The judge is leading the interrogation and generally directs the verbal interaction to a confirmation of the charges through the use of suggestive and—sometimes even—insinuating questions and of "indisputable" assertions from the police records. The defendant is forced to comply with both factual and normative presuppositions underlying the speech-acts of the judge that afford him or her hardly any opportunity to give an own view [*sic*] of the situation.... Therefore, it can be said that the asymmetrical role-division does interfere with the (inner) logic of argumentation in that certainly not all aspects of the legal conflict are openly debatable. Moreover, the pragmatic condition imposes restraints on forensic communication, since the indictment is already formulated in strictly juridical terms in which framework "reality" has to be reconstructed. This reconstruction of reality in court does not allow for another—particularly the defendant's—version of the situation.[19]

We can consider that statement a very abstract version of the American trial lawyer's classic complaint to intrusive trial judges: "Your honor, I would prefer that you allow me to try my own case. But if you insist on trying it for me, I would ask that you not lose it for me!" The assimilation of American procedure to continental procedure described above as a possible "explanation" of the death of the trial would *reduce the spaces for effective individual speech.*

More globally, one has to evaluate our form of relatively formal, participatory, and adversarial trial procedure *in light of our broader institutions.* We are probably the most capitalist large country and our capitalism is the least qualified by welfare state institutions. Our corporate executives' incentives are the most short-term-profit maximizing, with the fewest obligations to other "stakeholders." In the furtherance of those interests, our public relations machinery is the most sophisticated and, of course, wholly instrumental, driven not by the truth but by getting the job done. Our politics are the most driven by interest groups. Powerful interests can gain a disproportionate hold on the now scientifically gerrymandered legislatures, as they did in the Gilded Age. That style of politics is likely to extend increasingly to elected judges, as more professional restrictions on advertising and campaigning are lifted.[20] The trial, and especially the "populism" of the jury trial, has, from the beginning, been envisioned as a partial counterbalance to other aspects of our national life, as it still is.[21]

All decent societies divide their common life into discontinuous social spheres—economy, neighborhood, school, church, family, and so on. In the United States, those discontinuities are probably sharpest. One doesn't have to be a relativist to say that in our kind of society there will be a broader range of perspectives, even "truths," than in (even somewhat) more organic societies. To a larger extent than in more organic societies, for us "justice is conflict,"[22] that is to say, it achieves the fairest tension among each of the incommensurable norms that finds its natural home in one aspect of our social life and whose extension to other realms is always possible and always likely to be contested. (What is the sense of "fraternity" in the economic realm? What is the place of "political" considerations in law?) That is another reason why, in our kind of society, in contrast to those of European nations,[23] it is more appropriate that parties invoking the values of these often conflicting spheres be able to tell their *own* stories in court and have a higher level of control over the evidence they present than they do on the continent. These are normative as well as descriptive issues. In a sufficiently individualist and adversarial society, a justice system that is not adversarial will likely ease the imposition of the will of socially dominant groups,[24] the "tyranny of the effective majority," if you will. There is a tension between law as the instrument for social control by dominant groups—put more darkly, Thrasymachus's "will of the stronger"—and law as a medium for the realization of the justice revealed by its internal practices. Again, whatever else effectively enforced law is, it is always "the will of the stronger." We have seen that this has been a recurring tension in our history, and the nature of the trial has often been a focus of that controversy.[25] In particular, the appropriate procedures for applying the law of rules have often seemed discontinuous with the procedures that will allow "true law" to emerge. The death of the trial would lead us closer to a society that reflected only the will of the stronger.

The death of the trial would also mean the end of a proceeding in which *facts, not overbroad abstractions, are taken seriously*. Lon Fuller's classic defense of adversary presentation emphasized the quality of the factual development that it allows.[26] Without that development, the common sense of adjudicators is not challenged, and so not realized. Instead, judgment becomes a mechanical application of legal rules that are themselves not refined in application to factual material. Inconvenient truths can be assumed away in a manner that weakens the process of the common law development of legal doctrine and allows judges to hide behind stereotyped factual narratives that remain unchallenged. This suppresses the real bases of decision making, gives another blow to law's public nature, and so places it beyond serious criticism. As one philosopher put it, "there can be no ethical mass production," no mechanical stamping out by rule-like press brake on purely plastic or unformed material in any legal order that aspires to justice.[27] Without the consciously structured hybrid of languages that the trial deploys and the discipline brought about by adversary presentation, we will become increasingly lazy about facts in important matters. Even simple accuracy does not come easily: "Accurate facts are hard to come by, and the harder they are, the more they entail some costly equipment, a larger set of mediations, and more deliberate proofs."[28]

The death of the trial would have a broad effect on *citizen participation in governing*. As Stephen Landsman put it, the jury trial is "an expression of America's faith in its citizens":[29] "[N]o other institution of government rivals the jury in placing power so directly in the hands of citizens. Hence, no other institution risks as much on democracy or wagers more on the truth of democracy's core claim that the people make their own best governors."[30] The jury "is drawn from the community at large and speaks with a voice unmediated by either a political appointment process or a requirement of professional training":[31]

> The jury is the most effective instrument for incorporating the diverse ethnic, economic, religious, and social elements of American society into the justice system. It is far more effective at this task than the judiciary, which despite progress is a far less all-encompassing body.[32]

The jury has a unifying quality and has always been understood as representing a cross-section of, and so the entire, community. The unanimous verdict tells Americans that we really can have a shared perspective on important public issues, even though, and perhaps because of, our diversity of perspective.[33] Even Hamilton, perhaps the least populist of the founders, had to concede that juries are less likely to be corrupted than office holders.[34] That remains true even when "corruption" takes the form of the systematic capture of administrative agencies by the companies they are charged with regulating or of arbitration by adjudicators who are too eager to please the repeat players who bring them business.

Landsman notes as well that the jury's check upon the judiciary actually tends to increase the authority of the judicial branch of government by allaying fears of excessive judicial power and activism. The jury may have the effect of "[i]nsulating judges from sole responsibility for unpopular decisions" and so "helps protect their independence and defuse socially corrosive hostility to the justice system."[35] He has also suggested that judges are likely to lose authority as they morph into a cadre of investigating magistrates and ADR administrators.[36] Exercising formal authority through the formal proceedings at trial enhances the courts' authority. For those of us who believe in the high quality of trial decision making (by either juries or attentive judges), the participation of the jury will have a broadly legitimizing effect for those decisions. We are better governed because we govern ourselves in part through trial.

The death of the trial would also deprive Americans of an *occasion to develop political maturity*. It would likewise signal a change in the extent to which we potential jurors—few of us will be judges—have the self-confidence to make decisions on public matters, even under uncertainty and even with serious consequences. This is what Tocqueville meant when he made the conservative argument that the jury trial "invests each citizen with a kind of magistracy."[37] Experiencing the burdens of judgment elevates a citizen and makes him or her more than a disengaged critic or complainer. The disappearance of the trial could involve a kind of bad faith, an abdication of responsibility to elites who have spent perhaps too much time and attention achieving power.

The death of the trial would mean the end of a forum where *newly enfranchised citizens have a major role in self-government*. It was only forty years ago that, owing to legislative changes and constitutional decisions, minorities and women began to serve on juries in significant numbers. It may be extreme to analogize the death of the trial to a form of "white flight," as Paul Butler does,[38] but there does seem to be a relationship between the advent of truly cross-sectional juries and heightened attacks on the jury system followed by the collapse of the trial system altogether. Developments that have occurred over the past fifty years have, to some small degree, reversed the decline of the jury during the nineteenth and early twentieth centuries. Seventh Amendment jurisprudence has broadened the availability of the civil jury in the federal courts. Most important, a series of Supreme Court decisions and congressional enactments has democratized the American jury so that jurors are now much more likely to be representative, if not of the country, at least of the electorate. It is no accident that opposition to the jury has grown since this last development.

The death of the trial would signal a *transfer of power to elites, either scientific or political*. Lawrence Friedman has argued that "it is a characteristic of many different kinds of proceedings that they end up vesting enormous discretion in somebody. This is particularly true for cases where there is and can be no right answer."[39]

> The vanishing trial is, in many regards, the vanishing jury. Power and discretion have shifted away from the jury and more and more now is in the hands of the judge. To put it another way, the long-term historical development is to shift decision making from amateurs to professionals. The jury decides few felony cases; prosecutors and public defenders do it now, in the process of plea bargaining. Lawyers and the parties dicker and settle. The judge, or the parties themselves, now answer most of the unanswerable questions.[40]

He argues—in fact asserts—that in the era of the administrative state, there is more and more determinateness in rules, along with fewer and fewer "interesting questions that the legal system handles, manages or determines though actual trials."[41] The loss of the trial would take from us "that most characteristic and constitutionally favored of American adjudicatory mechanisms, the jury."[42] We would lose the institution through which, as Tocqueville taught, "the real direction of society [is] in the hands of the governed."[43] Ironically, this is more true the more literate, educated, and diverse our juries become.[44] Kalven and Zeisel demonstrated the high level of convergence in decisions between judges and juries, one that does not decrease with the complexity of the case. Nonetheless, it is the availability of the jury trial that keeps judges from becoming utterly "used to it" and improves the quality even of bench trials. It is because judges know that the parties may choose a jury that they are likely to resist somewhat the slow corrosion of their ability to listen. I know from my Chicago experience that judges may become bureaucrats or party men, impervious to any of the trial's appeal. Then the first principle of procedural justice may disappear, for the other side is no longer heard. Blackstone, surely no radical, saw the jury as an important counterweight to the elitism of the judiciary, whose "decisions, in spite of their own natural integrity, will have frequently an involuntary bias toward those of their own rank and dignity; *it is not to be expected from human nature that the few should always be attentive to the interests and good of the many*" (emphasis added).[45] Judge Dwyer quotes Robeson Davies: "The power to argue strongly and what I may call the puzzle-solving and examination-passing cast of mind, is often the possession of people of arid and limited perception and uneducated heart."

The death of the trial will *skew the process of settlement* by which most cases have ended and will continue to end. Its loss is disorienting for lawyers seeking to value and settle cases: without trials we would have a context "suffused with . . . legal uncertainty [because] the disputing parties' assessment of both the merit and magnitude of their case would correspond only coincidentally."[46] There will be a larger percentage of areas where all cases settle without any relationship to determinations that have been made on the merits of disputes. Similarly, Butler has suggested that the pressure to settle—to bargain away every principle, as he would more polemically put it—has a corrosive, even relativizing effect on public morality. It sends the message that we think that there are no principles worth standing on or, perhaps worse, that we do not trust that we have the means by which reliably to ascertain and defend them.[47] The full assimilation of the trial to the endless process of negotiation in the broader society can *impoverish our modes of social ordering*.[48]

Overwhelming pressure to settle everything can have additional corrosive effects. The increasing cost of asking for one's day in court may occasion choices that are more or less "freely" made but that look increasingly coerced. These choices serve to increase the level of public cynicism about the level of real freedom citizens enjoy. Of course, settlements appear to be wholly unobjectionable, as American as apple pie. After all, they are the result of an individual's free choice and some meeting of the minds, and so they seem to track some of our basic values and institutions. Lippmann famously said that America's core values included individualism, liberty, and egalitarianism, and that the former two trumped the latter. But we understand what is meant by "an offer you can't refuse." Raising the costs of a trial—which is, after all, simply a determination of the merits of a claim or defense—so high that only a madman could insist on it makes for corrosive cynicism about basic institutions.

The death of the trial would mark the end of doing justice in *a forum where the parties are engaged face to face.* Thomas Green reminds us that the common law trial could never forget the relationship between law and justice precisely because judges, parties, witnesses, and jurors faced each other in open court. John Dewey argued that real democracy can never do without face-to-face communication. And Emmanuel Levinas has written that the irreducibly moral dimension of human life stems with true ultimacy from the experience of face-to-face contact, an experience that poses a "refutation of any totalitarian or absolutist form of economy."[49] Face-to-face encounters provide antidotes to the spirit of abstraction and forgetfulness of the human dimension of legal questions that can be lost in piles of briefs and records churned out by law factories. Face-to-face encounters can open up "a social imaginary in which an ethics of care, the soul's living response to the other may be enacted:"[50]

> Such a response points to a hidden foundation, a mythic core that is repressed by the commodified images of positive law's unreflexive, outward gaze. Behind what John Noonan once referred to as the mask of the law lies its hidden, ethical foundation: the repressed poetics of Justice. . . . The associative, affective logic of visual images help us to escape the disembodied logic of instrumental reasoning. When the flesh of the image . . . arouses and transforms the viewer's heart and soul . . . it invokes law's hidden source, which is Justice. . . . Standing face to face, the neighbor calls us. In our response to that primary ethical calling we affirm our ethical nature and give it a name. It is our own name, in recognition of the one who calls.[51]

The recent growth of summary proceedings must convince "even the most hard-hearted empiricist that some litigants in some types of cases in some courts are not receiving reasonable opportunities to present their cases."[52] Stephen Burbank, who is at least a very hard-*headed* empiricist, emphasizes the conscious modification of substantive law, such as qualified immunity doctrine in civil rights law, to render summary judgment more attractive and thus to avoid trial.[53] The aversion to trial may be affecting the substantive law in other areas as well, such as the law of scientific evidence and antitrust law. Judge Wald of the District of Columbia Court of Appeals has written eloquently of the risks of so much of federal case law being developed in the context of summary judgment.[54] There is a real danger that "the law developed through summary judgment will be arid, divorced from the full factual context that has in the past given our law life and the capacity to grow."[55]

The death of the trial would mean the end of a forum where the case is presented *orally and dramatically*. This is obviously an aspect of the trial that is irreplaceable by summary or written proceedings. The oral medium is "inherently relational," essentially a unified field of instant relationships," as McLuhan put it.[56] In order to listen to speech, "[i]n a certain sense we have become the other person; or rather, we let him become part of us for a brief second. We suspend our own identities, after which we come back to ourselves and accept or reject what he has said."[57] And, by conscious contrast, the formality of the surroundings and the physical distance between jury and witness both serve to encourage the other element, along with sympathy, of good judgment: detachment.[58]

But the trial is not only oral, it is dramatic. It involves conversations among lawyers, witnesses, and the court, all of which are performances. The performances are often adversarial and manifest the tensions among the players within the constraints of the ordinary language in which these struggles take place. At trial, as in drama, freedom encounters freedom. Some things cannot be plausibly said, and the tenor of the interpersonal relations themselves is revealing. The drama is engrossing: it forces us to dwell within the tensions among the participants.[59] It actualizes our powerful tacit powers of sensibility to grant insight "into the world's embracing horizon of meaning, within which a complex action unfolds, illuminated and judged by it."[60] It allows us to "think toward the truth 'from the middle' of our creaturely existence, and this necessarily involves a continuous activity of imaginatively constructive participation."[61] It is "in the middle"—in the unavoidable gaps among evidence and narrative and written law—that triable cases will be decided, not by deduction from first principles, but precisely by the sophisticated sensibilities that the dramatic form realizes. What Bentley says about theater is true for trials—that "the little ritual of performance, given just a modicum of competence, can lend to the events represented another dimension, a more urgent reality" that overcomes that lazy or bureaucratic indifference that is, indeed, the "rust of society."[62] It stimulates a heightened awareness of the almost infinite lines of factual and normative relations implicit in even the simplest of cases.[63]

We do live "in the middle." The most adequate representation of a human event is not one that mimics scientific objectivity, but one that evokes the range of responses appropriate to the events depicted. Those include responses of a range of human feelings that are, for us, equivalent to accurate perception.[64] The trial has *cathartic* powers. The death of the trial would deny us an opportunity for a public investigation into and explanation of a threatening event.[65] As Milner Ball has deftly summed it up, the dramatic nature of the trial allows for the communication of tacit knowledge, the redirection of aggression, the encouragement of impartiality that comes from formality and a patient movement through time, and creativity in judgment by illuminating aspects of the situation, factual and normative, that would be invisible to a more aloof consideration.[66]

The death of the trial would *reduce the level of healthy tension among our major social and political institutions*. Hannah Arendt argued that in order for different modes of social ordering to be fully reflective of the human condition, they must be kept separate and so redeem each other.[67] Some of these things—law and politics—require the maintenance of public forums where different forms of public speech take place. Assimilating these styles of thinking and acting to one another into one system can destroy the spaces of freedom that we have enjoyed. And so we must be concerned about Galanter's observation that law and management and bargaining are coming to be assimilated to one another, usually with each assuming the worst aspect of all the others:

> The vanishing trial alerts us that we can have a continuing legalization of society accompanied by the atrophy of a central and emblematic legal institution. The legal complex as a whole is flourishing. Law expands and diffuses throughout society. The culture is increasingly pervaded by images of law and of trials. *At the same time legal controls become less distinctive, less differentiated, more diverse, less public.* Within the core legal institutions, the template of adjudication is continuously elaborated and more frequently invoked, but less frequently pursued through full-blown adjudication with trial. The decomposition of adjudication into bargaining is certainly not a new thing. Its presence is marked in the institutionalization of plea bargaining and civil settlement and the long-term decline of the portion of cases that get to trial. The residue of trials remaining from this long-term attrition seems to be shrinking rapidly, so that few trials actually take place each year. (Emphasis added)[68]

Maintaining tensions among our modes of social ordering is especially important in America. Much of the adversary system as we have it evolved from relatively specific ad hoc reforms designed to counter the profound unfairness of English criminal prosecution and the paralyzing formality of civil litigation.[69] Practices that seem extreme may be defensible in light of countervailing practices. It is not only in evidence law where "an irrational advantage to one side is offset by a counterprivilege to the other" and where "reforming" only one aspect of our practice is more "likely simply to upset its present balance between adverse interests than establish a rational edifice."[70] Two wrongs may not make a right, but they can add up to less wrong than just one. This doesn't mean that all reform is impossible. It does mean that we must recall that key conservative insight—how much effort it takes to keep things from getting worse.

I need to reemphasize how the contemporary trial is already respectful of the values underlying the law of rules: stability, predictability, and central ordering. These values are well represented at the pretrial stage and also in the law of evidence and trial procedure. They are in tension with the other moral sources embedded in the narrative and dramatic practices at trial. It is that tension which gives the trial its power and discipline and allows for the integrative judgment that takes into account moral, political, and strictly legal aspects of the case. Somewhere such a judgment must be made. For us, that judgment, well-made, constitutes justice.

There is one particular set of productive tensions that the death of the trial would weaken. Social theorists often distinguish between social integration and systems integration. Social integration is "based on intentional, symbolically constituted relations, common beliefs, legitimate norms, relations of trust and identity, as well as disputes and conflicts."[71] It would be hard to describe the operative norms of the trial any more directly. System integration bypasses human intention and personal relations to function mechanically, driven by objective steering mechanisms such as finance in complex markets. System integration can be studied by objectivizing forms of social science, here economics. Within this perspective, law is seen both to enable and to limit systems integration, and the technical legal vocabulary of the law of rules may serve to normatively anchor the systems world, giving it a kind of legitimacy. But legal practices can and do exact a price for this service to the world of systems. Because legal practices, most dramatically the American trial, partake of the richer normative order of the life world, they may impose *limits on what our systems, following their own inexorable internal logic, may do*. As one author puts it:

The law serves as some kind of pivot or transmission belt between lifeworld and systems. The lifeworld is the (potential) site of a loosely connected network of non-institutionalized discourse in which collective self-reflection and self-definition take place. The law institutionalizes the channels (in the form of political and legal procedures) and provides a language or medium (in the form of binding norms) through which the results of these informal deliberative processes can become socially binding and effective—and can to a certain degree constrain and regulate the "systems."[72]

So legal procedures can hold the lifeworld and the systems world together in a way that qualifies the logic of the latter:

The modern legal and political association is not only a community of rights-bearing persons who grant each other equal rights and liberties on moral grounds. It is also a form of organized, instrumental social cooperation and to some degree also an ethical community with common values and aspirations for the life of the community as a whole. Its legitimacy accordingly has to be created by a combination of the different kinds of discourse which were mentioned above.[73]

"Lifeworld" and "system" do not identify rigidly separated social spheres so much as a distinction helpful in identifying contrasting aspects of all social spheres. All social spheres lie on a continuum, and all social spheres are steered or ordered through both human communication and systems imperatives. Thus the various operations of publicly held corporations are not only controlled by the impersonal forces of the market, but also limited by moral notions of what they may or may not do in their operations: deceive the public, for example, as to the toxicity or carcinogenicity of their products. What's necessary is a forum within which to keep the tension between moral imperatives and systems imperatives taut. The trial provides a forum within which the tension between moral imperatives and systems imperatives may be evaluated and worked out, as well as a set of languages rich enough for that to occur.

And so the death of the trial would *eliminate a source of moral and commonsense qualification of the vast systems within which we move and which are part of our identity*:

Previously, the common law system had existed to dispense justice in individual cases. One man struck another, and the offended individual struck back not

with a fist but with an assault-and-battery action in court. One individual insisted on walking through another's front yard on his way to town every morning, and the offended individual stopped him not with force but with a trespass
action in court. This adjudicatory function was critical to civilized society. Now
something else was at work as well. The Industrial Revolution saw the birth of
business enterprises with wealth and political influence previously unknown.
These enterprises mass-produced goods—but mass-produced injuries as well.
It was neither the market system nor, on its own initiative, the legislative system that forced improvements in safer work-places for railroad workers, mine
workers, and factory workers. It was the common law system. The common law
was no longer merely a system for adjudicating individual disputes; it had become a regulatory mechanism.[74]

In the main, the tort system has to speak to publicly traded corporations
in the only language we have constructed them to understand—the often crude language of monetary expenditure. Those entities are—must be,
I think, in a truly competitive market—profoundly deaf to virtually all
other languages. We have no resources other than those that are already
implicit in our practices, including our ordinary moral practices and our
economic practices and in mediating practices such as the trial.

I have shown how the discipline of the evidence at trial creates an
environment in which events are evaluated with an enormously more
searching understanding of the facts than occurs in most political debate.
I have shown as well that the common law trial is a traditional institution
drawing on ordinary morality and common sense. This mode of thought is
discontinuous with that at the heart of other major American institutions,
the private and public bureaucracies that employ, indeed are constituted
by, forms of instrumental rationality. I have argued that basic decency can
be preserved only if ordinary moral and commonsense reasoning structures the forum within which forms of instrumental rationality have to
justify themselves. That is what Arendt meant when she said that traditional American institutions and practices have saved us from the worst
excesses of "the onslaught of modernity."[75] American juries are not so naive that they do not understand the importance of thinking instrumentally
in technological and even in economic contexts.[76] Corporate cost-benefit
decisions and utilitarian reasoning in creating criminal penalties can be
justified in the language of ordinary morality only after a searching factual
review of the particular case. It is central for us that we have a forum that
consistently and carefully requires that kind of justification.

Put more broadly yet, the death of the trial would mean the end of *a particularly important way of continually refining the norms that apply to the basic structure of our society*,[77] the pattern of rules and practices within which we live our ordinary moral lives. Since the French Revolution, and, for Americans, certainly since the New Deal, it has been impossible to maintain that we have not created those rules and practices and therefore are not responsible for their shape. Unfortunately, we moderns have also inherited modes of thought that place these structures "beyond good and evil," beyond moral evaluation. In these modes of thought the basic structure can only be known scientifically, though the forms this science should take have varied quite significantly. This notion of the amorality of the basic structure of society has, in less happy lands, led to disaster and is one aspect of "the onslaught of modernity."

The trial for us is a forum within which we can carefully develop the norms that ought to apply to the basic structure of society. We can do this with adequate attention to the details of the individual case. And we can do it in a way that respects the differences that exist among the various spheres of human action and the importance of moral judgment, legal formality, and political responsibility. The trial acknowledges that most problematic situations have moral, legal, and political dimensions, and it creates a forum within which we can do exactly what we need to do: make judgments of relative importance of the norms implicit in these spheres. But we must make those judgments *only for this case*—because the next case will be different. The trial makes it possible to do practically what our best thinkers have struggled to do theoretically: determine the appropriate relationships among social spheres and modes of social ordering. Perhaps this practical acumen is part of our national genius. After all, Arendt argued that the American Revolution succeeded practically where no other modern revolution did by creating a functioning source of law and authority within which politics could flourish, but that our thinkers never really created a political theory adequate to our practical achievements.[78] Our achievement in the trial fulfills a particularly modern function without succumbing completely to modern bureaucracy. It allows us "less to create constantly new forms of life than to creatively renew actual forms by taking advantage of their internal multiplicity and their frictions with one another."[79] This is, for example, precisely what happened when American juries in the first decades of the twentieth century rejected the doctrine of contributory negligence that dominated the law of rules.

Nancy Marder has developed a "process" view of the jury which shows its relationship to the basic structure. She has noted that our actual jury practices are inconsistent with what I have called the received view of the trial. Even within the law of rules, juries actually engage in broad based interpretation well beyond what could be described as fact finding. They regularly determine what is reasonable in tort actions and make practical determinations about what constitutes reasonable doubt in criminal cases.[80] Jury determinations concerning mental states in homicide cases (which can spell the differences between acquittal, probation, and a death sentence) inevitably have a strong normative element, about which the written law gives very limited guidance.[81] Marder shows how consistent patterns of jury determinations have been significant not only in individual cases, but also in reconstituting our basic structure: "[J]uries, by declining to find contributory negligence, essentially created a regime of comparative negligence long before the legislature and judges had eliminated contributory negligence as a defense."[82] Juries have likewise changed the legal order through patterns of decisions in wrongful discharge cases and the law of product safety. Marder provides an account of the relative strengths that juries have in comparison to courts and legislatures that supplements our understanding of the ways in which the discipline of the trial elevates their commonsense judgment.[83] None of this, of course, involves a break with our traditional notions of what the jury trial is. It is fully consistent with Tocqueville's understanding of the jury trial as a political as well as a legal institution, one that is fully consistent with the original intent of the Fifth, Sixth, and Seventh Amendments.

The death of the trial would mean the loss of *a forum that offers an antidote to bureaucratic modes of social ordering.* Although the phrase is seldom used because of its negative rhetorical resonances, the critics most often attack the trial court for failing to employ what can only be called bureaucratic-formalistic modes of social ordering.[84] A bureaucratic mode of social ordering is justified as the most efficient device for achieving legislatively predetermined ends. It seeks to "exclude questions of value or preference as obviously irrelevant to the administrative task, and it would view reliance on nonreplicable, nonreviewable *judgment* or *intuition* as a singularly unattractive method for decision."[85] The dispassionate bureaucrat mechanically applying his rules regardless of context or consequences can come to be the ideal of lawfulness that leaves trial processes wanting. Bureaucratic adjudication often has, at least on the rhetorical level, a higher level of rule centeredness than do the efforts of our trial courts.

Once again, bureaucratic methods embody what White has argued is an (impoverished) understanding of legal processes as a kind of machine designed to stamp fully predetermined norms onto a fully plastic material in a wholly instrumental way.[86] For that kind of enterprise, the individual case should be known through processes that screen out life-world values and that avoid completely the more interpretive and evaluative language with which we usually describe human events. From a commonsense point of view, this will mean that only the language of power or will that is embodied in legislative or administrative rules will supply the norms for evaluating the particular case. The factual context will not be allowed to "talk back" to the rules.[87]

There is another sense of bureaucracy to which the trial stands in opposition. This sense of bureaucratic ordering rests on the notion that there exists, in one way or another, a science of society or, at least, sciences of society that exhaust the social field. In this view, we cannot know the basic structure of society using ordinary morality and common sense, but only scientifically. This science should be applied to resolving individual cases in the same way that natural science is applied to solving technical questions. Only those trained in the science can understand the arguments and make reliable judgments; a lay jury or a generalist judge cannot. Further, the jury trial itself is an intense encounter with the facts of a particular situation, understood, inevitably, in commonsense moral terms; and, however refined by the devices of the trial, those are not, in this view, appropriate for the resolution of the questions about the basic structure of society that are implicated in so many cases ("Would you want a jury to set the Federal funds discount rate?"). This perspective would suggest that the kind of society into which we are moving will inevitably (and therefore should) be administered by experts applying scientific, sometimes social-scientific, knowledge bureaucratically.[88] The jury trial could fall victim to our glacial movement toward an imperial-bureaucratic style of government. The engrossing power of the trial's languages fixes the attention of the judge and jury on the meaning of the event being tried. At trial one responds to, respects, a significance that is in a sense already there and realized only by the trial's languages. The response has pragmatic consequences, but it does not see the persons or events as a means to an end. It is a forum that limits the dynamic of instrumental thinking.

An even more bureaucratized state would make most of its decisions through what our legal system calls "informal agency action." For historical reasons, of course, cases will still find their way into court.[89] If such cases find their way to court, they should be adjudicated formalistically. (The relationship between formalism and bureaucracy is another area whose history has not yet been fully written.) The scientific principles that are embedded in a science of society can be partially embedded in detailed rules that will allow the judge to operate much like a bureaucrat. That is, he will not be distracted by the moral significance of the particular events before him. Indeed, he will be attracted by summary proceedings and demanding rules of materiality that keep him focused on the principle, discontinuous with ordinary morality, that will decide the case and so reconstitute the basic structure. He will be supported by the empty hope that the counterintuitive abstractions that have worked so well in physics will provide the sure path in law.

Though it would take us too far afield to demonstrate it in general terms,[90] the bureaucratic-formalistic project is not even fully possible. That is the weight of the argument made by legal realists of one stripe or another for a hundred years. That impossibility is a particularly contemporary reason the trial is necessary for us. It is always true that some third thing is necessary to complete the judgment between the rule and a value free account of "the facts." It will come either from the public values embedded in the languages and performances of the process by which the adjudicator is exposed to the concrete case or, in one way or another, from the decision maker's subjectivity.[91] Although the proposition is controversial, many political scientists studying appellate decision making tell us that the judge's "attitude"—a complex of very general sensibilities, political leanings, and moral commitments—"really" determines or completes the judgment in the particular case.[92] That is in sharp distinction from the characteristics of trial decision making. The law of rules provides an important framework for the trial, but the tensions arising from the counterposed narratives and arguments of the trial provide the real discipline that serves to suppress subjectivity in trial decision making. The "discipline of the evidence" is a real discipline.

And so the trial provides a form of discipline and rigor that limits the raw discretion of judges and other bureaucrats. Judges whose rejection of formalism informs their own practice can go to the opposite extreme if they believe that they don't need the trial's structure and drama to illuminate the cases before them.[93] It's then easy for them to think they can without loss decide cases in summary fashion or on a paper record. That the written law is detailed is not adequate protection: "[T]here is

THE MEANINGS OF THE TRIAL'S DEATH

a point beyond which increased complexity of law, especially in loosely ordered normative systems, objectively increases rather than decreases the decisonmaker's freedom."[94] More and more "law" does not constrain the judge; it simply gives him or her more decision points at which defensible acts of discretion can take place. What is essential is the creation of a public context that exercises power and limits arbitrariness the way logic exercises power and control over pure thought. ("He forced me to do it: he used logic on me!") But for real cases, that context cannot, of course, be formal logic. It must consist of languages and practices that realize the implicit and objective common sense of the decision maker. In the first chapter I laid out the ways in which the trial does just that.

Richard Posner has recently described his decision making in the following terms: "The way I approach a case as a judge is first to ask myself what would be a reasonable, sensible result, as a lay person would understand it and then, having answered that question, to ask whether that result is blocked by clear constitutional or statutory text, governing precedent, or any other conventional limitation on judicial discretion."[95] With regard to the constraints of text or precedent (which must, after all, be clear to prevent the exercise of discretion), Judge Posner has had this to say: "There is almost no legal outcome that a really skillful legal analyst cannot cover over with a professional varnish" at least "when the law is uncertain and emotions aroused."[96] Posner's account may seem extreme, but it is very much continuous with the accounts of others, from Chancellor Kent to Holmes to Llewellyn. The problem, of course, is that what actually decides the case in (the many) cases where the law of rules is not determinative is the apparently unstructured intuition of an elite judge about how one man in the street would see the case, an intuition that is itself likely to be based on stereotypes. Far better to provide to twelve jurors an absorbing and highly disciplined encounter with the case which realizes their own *common* sense.

One scholar argues that "after formalism" our courts are prey to the twin dangers of "fundamentalism" and "aestheticism."[97] Fundamentalism is the notion that we can achieve justice without complex mediating forms and practice, that a simple intuition of the right thing to do is all we need. Ironically, given his elite profile, Posner's statement tends in this direction. The contrasting temptation is "aestheticism," a fascination with the sheer complexity of languages. For law, "[t]he baroque labyrinth of law's institutions" are "like the bureaucratic world depicted in Kafka's writings."[98]

This labyrinth can become detached from any moral source. Formalistic rigidity and unmediated intuition can *both* deny us access to the moral sources that the trial embodies.

The death of the trial would mean the end of an important *public forum within which major questions are addressed.* Courtrooms used to provide a major source of *public* knowledge. A confidence in *public* forums where argument can take place honestly and vigorously is an important element of the popular legitimacy of the legal order.[99] Many court-annexed arbitrations are not open to the public. Most settlements can be sealed, though the states have taken the lead on limiting secrecy of settlements.[100] "As long as courts continue to be places that produce public data in volume and kinds outstripping that produced about adjudication in administrative agencies, and as long as private providers do not regularly disseminate information about or provide access to their processes, then with the declining trial rate comes a diminution of public knowledge of disputes, of the behavior of judges, and of the forging, *in public,* of normative responses to discord.[101] As I mentioned above, Bentham put it succinctly: "Publicity is the very soul of justice. . . . It keeps the judge himself, while trying, on trial."[102] Fear of this kind of publicity was one of the motivations that led business interests to undermine congressional approval of the national tobacco settlement in the 1990s. As one plaintiffs' lawyer put it: "The concept of litigation forcing legislation and public policy changes totally freaked the Chamber of Commerce and corporate America because they feared they could be next. . . . Their goal was to make sure nothing like this could ever happen again, and it hasn't happened since."[103] If the trial is allowed to die, we would also be losing a forum that meets the requirement that "justice must satisfy the appearance of justice."[104] The Supreme Court has observed that "[i]mplicit in this declaration is the notion the even the fairest and most appropriate results are likely to provoke suspicion and resistance if arrived at by means that fail to satisfy litigant and societal expectations of due process."[105] John Rawls identified "publicity," the ability of a conception of justice to be publicly stated, as a key element of justice. Social psychologists have identified those characteristics that tend to confer legitimacy on institutions and practices: "neutral, respectful, participatory procedures" with "equal access to channels of information and to mechanisms of control."[106] Note that the experience of legitimacy that trials provide extends both to parties to the trial and to those who are observers.

American justice "does not unfold legally and normally" when it "takes place behind closed doors" because "participants in secret proceedings quickly tend to lose their perspective, and the quality of the proceedings suffers as a consequence"[107]: "[P]opular justice is public justice."[108] Dwyer called the jury trial the canary in the mineshaft of our democracy. Judge Damon Keith recently reminded us that "democracy dies behind closed doors."[109]

The publicity of court proceedings can strengthen a sense of common norms. Robert Ackerman has argued from the perspective of his communitarian philosophy that "[c]ourtroom procedure becomes a common language through which a secular society honors its democratic heritage and applies its values (in particular that of fundamental fairness) to human transactions" and in which "[l]awyers and the rituals they observe, can be critical players in this process." Rather than a selfish and strident act of self-assertion, "'resort to litigation . . . involves an affirmation of community,' a willingness to subject oneself to the community's standards and procedures and 'cede a degree of autonomy in the interests of community cohesion.'" "The procedural justice literature indicates the disputants' perceptions of justice are enhanced to the extent they perceive (1) that they have had an opportunity for voice, (2) that a third party considered their views, concerns, and evidence, (3) that they were treated in a dignified, respectful manner in a dignified procedure, and (4) that the decision-maker was even-handed and attempted to be fair." "[T]he formalities of a court trial—the flag, the black robes, the ritual—remind those present that the occasion calls for the higher, 'public' values, rather than the lesser values embraced during moments of [in]formality and intimacy."[110]

Finally, it isn't just that the increased secrecy following the death of the trial would have negative consequences for the resolution of the particular case. The death of the trial would remove *an important source of public self-knowledge* stretching beyond the individual dispute. The O. J. Simpson trial and the public reaction thereafter revealed strong discontinuities in the perceptions of African Americans and whites. Landsman has noted that "[l]awsuits against the tobacco industry and gunmakers and, recently, the fast-food industry, inspire more public debate about tort law than hours of 'issues' advertisement or scholarly articles."[111] The death of the trial would also remove a source of *disciplined information about matters of public significance*: "The risks posed by asbestos, cigarettes, and a host of other items [such as lead poisoning] would not have been broadcast without the sharing of information obtained in litigation and disseminated at trial."[112] Bogus has emphasized that companies that were successful for years at keeping regulators at bay finally had to accede to the compulsory process of discovery and adverse examination of defense witnesses at trial. Our trials have posed in public and dramatic terms some of the most important issues of the day.[113] The Triangle Shirtwaist Fire trial dramatized sweatshop conditions and led to the formation of the International Ladies' Garment Workers Union.[114] The McNamara Brothers trial, the Joe Hill trial, Haymarket trial and its aftermath, and the trials of Eugene V. Debs focused publicly on issues of labor strife that were tearing the country apart.[115] Some became part of our cultural life: half a dozen major song writers have sung of Joe Hill. The Sacco-Vanzetti trial, the Alger Hiss trial, and the Angela Davis trial all had important, though quite different, political significances.[116] And on and on. It's not that each of these trials were exemplary examples of well-tried cases. Many of the earlier cases were surrounded by ballyhoo stirred up by yellow journalism. They were, however, public proceedings with public records that provided a basis for long-term and serious political debates. We would be poorer if these proceedings—or some informal substitute for them—had occurred behind closed doors. Likewise, we would be much poorer if the only public discussions of these issues were the flaccid and undisciplined forums provided by congressional hearings.

The death of the trial would be an abandonment of *an aspect of our national character*.[117] This centrality of the trial—the extent to which it is the sun, the ideological core of our system—is apparent in the reactions of many legal professionals to the vanishing trial syndrome. This notion is supported by the surprise among Americans, in whose consciousness "the place of law, lawyers, and courts . . . continues to expand," according to Galanter's findings.

> Since I began calling attention to this phenomenon a few years ago, I have encountered expressions of surprise and disbelief from citizens and students as well as from many judges and lawyers. The media's fixation on trials, fictional and otherwise, combines with myths about excessive litigation to make the decline invisible to the public and, in large measure, to legal professionals.[118]

These are some of the meanings that the death of the trial would have for us. It would eliminate a forum where equitable considerations moderate the rigor of the law of rules. It would deprive us of a distinctively American forum where a citizen can tell his own story in public and offer the evidence to make it effective. It would destroy a space where serious attention is paid to simple factual truth. It would reduce serious citizen participation in self-government and likely damage the authority of the entire judicial branch. It would roll back the hard-earned enfranchisement of women and minorities. It would transfer power to political and technical elites. It would distort the norms for settlement and have a corrosive effect on our sense of real freedom to reach compromises. It would destroy the traditional relationship between face-to-face proceedings and the notion that legal proceedings were somehow about justice. And by squeezing drama out of those proceedings, it would impoverish the range of cognitive capacities we deploy in the law. We would both feel and see less. The death of the trial would compress into a monolith the variety of and tensions among our modes of social ordering. They could not longer qualify or redeem each other. We would have less freedom to address pressing issues in different ways.

In particular, the death of the trial would render our economic systems more automatic and beyond qualification by ordinary moral norms. It would mean the end of our ability incrementally to adjust our basic structure by norms that have their homes in other parts of our social world. The death of the trial would create a more bureaucratized world. It would also create a world in which judges could exercise more raw discretion in the interstices of complex legal rules unstructured and unqualified by the objectivity of the real social norms that the trial realizes. It would mean the end of an irreplaceable *public* forum and would mean that more of the legal order would proceed behind closed doors. And it would deprive us, American citizens, of an important source of knowledge about ourselves and key issues of public concern.

# Notes

## Introduction

1. See pp. 82–111 herein for a fuller account and sources.

2. See Elizabeth Young-Bruehl, *Hannah Arendt: For Love of the World* (New Haven: Yale University Press, 1982), 136.

3. See Stuart Hampshire, *Justice Is Conflict* (Princeton: Princeton University Press, 1999).

4. Milner Ball, "A Little Mistrust Now and Then," *University of Cincinnati Law Review* 66 (1998), 887.

5. See pp. 112–13 herein.

6. Ludwig Wittgenstein, *Philosophical Investigations*, G. E. M. Anscombe trans. (New York: Macmillan, 1953), 31.

7. John Rawls, *A Theory of Justice* (Cambridge, MA: Harvard University Press, 1971), 47.

8. *New York Trust Company v. Eisner*, 256 U.S. 345, 349 (1921) (Holmes, J.)

9. William L. Dwyer, *In the Hands of the People: The Trial Jury's Origins, Triumphs, Troubles, and Future in American Democracy* (New York: Thomas Dunne Books, 2002), 36.

10. Foxes know many things, but the hedgehog knows one really important thing, or so Isaiah Berlin taught us.

11. Rawls, *A Theory of Justice*, 579.

12. Clifford Geertz, "From the Native's Point of View: On the Nature of Anthropological Understanding," in *Interpretive Social Science: A Reader*, Paul Rabinow & William M. Sullivan eds. (Berkeley: University of California Press, 1979), 239.

13. H. L. A. Hart, *The Concept of Law*, 2d ed. (Oxford: Clarendon Press, 1994), 239–41 (postscript to the 2d ed.) (describing Dworkin's jurisprudential method).

**Chapter One**

1. John Dewey, "Logical Method and the Law," *Cornell Law Quarterly* 10 (1924), 26–27.

2. Dwyer, *In the Hands of the People*, 153.

3. Jeffrey Abramson, *We, the Jury: The Jury System and the Ideal of Democracy* (New York: Basic Books, 1994), 143–76. This chapter provides a distillation and refocusing of the much longer account in Robert P. Burns, *A Theory of the Trial* (Princeton: Princeton University Press, 1999).

4. I don't dispute that more authoritarian (though not totalitarian) regimes may be more consistent with political cultures other than our own. See Robert P. Burns, "A Response to Four Readings of *A Theory of the Trial*," *Law & Social Inquiry* 28 (2003), 553–67.

5. See Hannah Arendt, "Truth and Politics," in *Between Past and Future: Eight Exercises in Political Thought* (New York: Penguin Books, 1977), 264. As the poet understood, failure at either end can lead to injustice. "Passionate intensity" can be a gift or a burden. Not only bureaucratic sloth or indifference or individual laziness or neglect, but also "energetic" fraud on the tribunal can skew the results.

6. A few witnesses are "expert" witnesses, whose testimony in the language of opinion has made their role especially controversial. See, e.g., David H. Kaye, David E. Bernstein, & Jennifer L. Mnookin, *The New Wigmore: A Treatise on Evidence; Expert Evidence* (New York: Aspen, 2003), 305–28.

7. G. K. Chesterton, *Tremendous Trifles* (London: Methuen, 1920), 65, 67–68.

8. Alan W. Scheflin, "Jury Nullification: The Right to Say No," *Southern California Law Review* 45 (1972), 213. For an illuminating account of the daily business in an American criminal trial court in Chicago as the judge's "workshop" which Chesterton would have appreciated, see Steve Bogira, *Courtroom 302: A Year Behind the Scenes in an American Criminal Courthouse* (New York: Alfred A. Knopf, 2005).

9. The trial implicitly agrees with realists such as Bernard Lonergan that experience in the sense of perception has some independence from interpretation. Bernard J. F. Lonergan, *Insight: A Study of Human Understanding* (New York: Philosophical Library, 1958). The web of belief within which we move, that provides our "life world" and conditions what we see things "as" (a threat, for example), does condition how we see things. But we can sometimes see what greatly surprises and what deeply disappoints us.

10. This is part of what Hannah Arendt means when she says that factual accuracy is the "sky above and the earth below" in the political contexts where opinion is dominant. She argues, then, that courts must be different from political assemblies if the two activities are to "redeem" each other. Arendt, "Truth and Politics," 259–64.

11. Iris Murdoch, *The Sovereignty of Good* (London: Routledge & Kegan Paul, 1970), 83.

12. Antonin Scalia, "The Rule of Law as a Law of Rules," *University of Chicago Law Review* 56 (1989), 1187.

13. The classical statement is Frederick A. Hayek, *The Road to Serfdom* (Chicago: University of Chicago Press, 1944), 72.

14. These are just the requirements of witness "competence"—that the witness had a perception, remembers that perception, and is able to communicate it with a modicum of coherence to the jury. *Federal Rules of Evidence*, Rule 602.

15. For a recent and humane defense, see Brian Z. Tamanaha, "How an Instrumental View of Law Corrodes the Rule of Law," *DePaul Law Review* 56 (2007), 469.

16. Although some evidence is "direct evidence," for example eyewitness testimony, the probative value of all evidence, dependent as it is on the credibility of witnesses, which must be assessed circumstantially, is always dependent on circumstantial evidence. See generally Keven Jon Heller, "The Cognitive Psychology of Circumstantial Evidence," *Michigan Law Review* 105 (2006), 241.

17. Peter J. Steinberger, *The Concept of Political Judgment* (Chicago: University of Chicago Press, 1993), 92.

18. Many suggestions for reform of the American jury trial are attempts to shore up this vision of the trial. For example, there have been suggestions and actual steps taken to expand the use of summary disposition, to read the jury instructions at the beginning of the trial, to rewrite the instructions so that they are more comprehensible, to limit what lawyers may say in opening statement, and to enhance the judge's "gatekeeper" function for scientific and nonscientific expert testimony. Some of these suggestions and developments are benign, but others pose a threat to deeper levels of the trial that are essential if it is to remain, as it ought to, "the central institution of law as we know it." James Boyd White, *From Expectation to Experience: Essays on Law & Legal Education* (Ann Arbor: University of Michigan Press, 1999), 108.

19. The official Comment to Section 116 of the American Law Institute's *Restatement of the Law Third: The Law Governing Lawyers* (St. Paul: American Law Institute, 2000) gives a fair sense of what this kind of active witness preparation may involve and its tension with truthfulness:

> In preparing a witness to testify, a lawyer may invite the witness to provide truthful testimony favorable to the lawyer's client. Preparation consistent with the rule of this Section may include the following: discussing the role of the witness and effective courtroom demeanor; discussing the witness's recollection and probable testimony; revealing to the witness other testimony or evidence that will be presented and asking the witness to reconsider the witness's recollection or recounting of events in that light; discussing the applicability of law to the events in issue; reviewing the factual context into which the witness's observations will fit; reviewing documents or other physical

evidence that may be introduced; and discussing probable lines of
hostile cross-examination that the witness should be prepared to
meet. Witness preparation may include rehearsal of testimony. A lawyer may suggest choice of words that might be employed to make the
witness's meaning clear. However a lawyer may not assist the witness
to testify falsely as to a material fact.

For my own consideration of the broader ethical context of this kind of witness
preparation, see Robert P. Burns, "Professional Responsibility in the Trial Court,"
*South Texas Law Review* 44 (2002), 81–110.

20. Lawyers are not ethically permitted to discourage witnesses, save relatives
and employees of the client, from speaking with the adversary. See, e.g., *ABA
Model Rules of Professional Conduct*, Rule 3.4(f). This prohibition is not, in my
opinion, universally honored.

21. We will examine some of the negative sides in the third chapter.

22. On the factual level it is analogous to Justice Frankfurter's three rules of
statutory interpretation: "Read the statute. Read the statute. Read the statute!"
Henry J. Friendly, *Benchmarks* (Chicago: University of Chicago Press, 1967), 202.

23. There are now so many exclusions from and exceptions to the hearsay rule
that the statement in the text is, I think, the fairest general statement of the rule.
*Federal Rules of Evidence*, Rules 801–807.

24. *Crawford v. Washington*, 541 U.S. 36 (2004).

25. I supply it for those whose have been spared lawyer jokes: "His lips are
moving."

26. See *American Bar Association Rules of Professional Conduct*, Rule 3.4(b).

27. This is not an accidental feature of coherent human language. As George
Steiner put it:

A sentence always means more. Even a single word, with the weave
of incommensurable connotation, can, and usually does. The inform-
ing matrix or context of even a rudimentary, literal proposition . . .
moves outward from specific utterance or notation in ever-widening
concentric and overlapping circles. . . . No formalization is of an order
adequate to the semantic mass of a culture, to the wealth of denota-
tion, connotation, implicit reference, elision and tonal register which
envelop saying what one means.

George Steiner, *Real Presences* (Chicago: University of Chicago Press, 1989), 82–83.

28. In the early nineteenth century, the judge's instructions were often understood simply as his best judgment about what the central norms controlling the
case were. Juries were understood to have the ultimate authority on the normative
as well as the factual side, to be "judges of the law." Not since the late nineteenth
century has this been consistent with prevailing doctrine, but the concrete function
of the instructions is subject to significant debate and interpretation, both "factu-

ally" and normatively. It is relatively uncontroversial to say that the jury serves an "equitable" function in "tailoring" the law to the unique facts of the case. It is a bit more controversial to say that the jury inevitably relies on a pluralism of normative sources, with the written rules providing only one of many sources. Robert P. Burns, "The Lawfulness of the American Trial," *American Criminal Law Review* 38 (Spring 2001), 205–39. Also see pp. 20–39 herein.

29. After all, the founders knew that legislatures could be "captured" and fail to express the best judgment of the citizenry. This possibility of legislative tyranny was very much on the minds of the founding generation. "Capture" of legislatures has occurred, most prominently in the Gilded Age. Unfortunately, it is now easier thanks to powerful social-scientific tools for the enterprise of gerrymandering.

30. Which is it really? The jury doesn't know until the competing interpretations of the witness's testimony have been seen in the context of all the evidence and through the critical devices of the trial.

31. Madison put it this way in *The Federalist No. 10*: "As long as the connection subsists between [man's] reason and his self-love, his opinions and his passions will have a reciprocal influence on each other; and the former will be objects to which the latter will attach themselves."

32. See Garry Wills, *A Necessary Evil: A History of American Distrust of Government* (New York: Simon & Schuster, 1999).

33. Assuming, of course, that it is indeed fair.

34. Of course, the formally valid method is only as good as the universality of the premise. No empirical propositions are inevitably universally valid.

35. Some of these methods emerged from earlier forms of "witness incompetencies," or preclusions from testifying at all, formalistically imposed by the common law, such as the rule that defendants could not testify in their own cases or that felons were unable to testify in any case. One can see here a development to a more flexible intelligence much more continuous with and respectful of the common sense of the jury and away from an aristocratic system designed to maintain control over outcomes through manipulation of the inevitably overgeneralized rules that the king's judges controlled. See Carl T. Bogus, *Why Lawsuits Are Good for America: Disciplined Democracy, Big Business, and the Common Law* (New York: New York University Press, 2001), 62–65 (the founders were eager to allow juries to exercise their common sense to approach substantive justice rather than engage in the formalistic games played by upper-class lawyers that litigation had become in England).

36. See, e.g., Francis L. Wellman, *The Art of Cross-Examination* (New York: Macmillan, 1962).

37. Thomas Hobbes, *Leviathan*, chap. 11, quoted in Arendt, "Truth and Politics," 230. Arendt goes on to argue that factual truth is far more vulnerable than the rational truths that Hobbes invokes.

38. Steven Lubet, *Modern Trial Advocacy: Analysis and Practice*, 3d ed. (South Bend, IN: National Institute for Trial Advocacy, 2004), 25 ff.

39. Jeremy Bentham, *Rationale of Judicial Evidence* (London: Hart & Clarke, 1827; New York: Garland, 1978), 1:22.

40. One could describe the trial as a device for the refinement of prejudice, if one followed Gadamer in more or less equating prejudice with common sense. Common sense itself is defined by its open-textured quality and fully realized only when engaged in concrete cases. See Lonergan, *Insight*. In this case, the trial is the institutional device for the realization of all of the powers of common sense. See Steinberger, *The Concept of Political Judgment*, 230.

41. Abramson, *We, the Jury*, 143–78; Valerie P. Hans & Neil Vedmar, *Judging the Jury* (New York: Plenum Press, 1986), 76–77. Marianne Constable, after a sophisticated review of the major book-length jury studies, concluded: "The studies claim that attempts to connect demographic states, abilities, aptitudes, temperaments, and personalities of juror to verdict had met with 'limited success' . . . and they argue that cases are decided by the evidence. . . . '[D]ifferent issues, different defendants, different contexts, different evidence should and did make for different verdicts'" (Constable, "What Books about Juries Reveal about Social Science and the Law," *Law and Social Inquiry* 16 [1991], 353–72, quoting Rita Simon, *The Jury: Its Role in American Society* [Lexington, MA: D. C. Heath, 1980], 146).

42. Harry Kalven & Hans Zeisel, *The American Jury* (Boston: Little, Brown, 1966), 91. They concluded that this finding was "flattering to the law."

43. Reid Hastie, Steven D. Penrod, & Nancy Pennington, *Inside the Jury* (Cambridge, MA: Harvard University Press, 1983), 80–81.

44. Hastie, Penrod, & Pennington, *Inside the Jury*, 230.

45. Richard Lempert, "Why Do Juries Get a Bum Rap? Reflections on the Work of Valerie Hans," *DePaul Law Review* 48 (1998), 462.

46. Dwyer, *In the Hands of the People*, 152.

47. Lonergan call these levels direct understanding and reflective understanding. Lonergan, *Insight*, 279.

48. Hannah Arendt, *Lectures on Kant's Political Philosophy* (Chicago: University of Chicago Press, 1982), 62–64.

49. John Gardner, *The Art of Fiction: Notes on Craft for Young Writers* (New York: Vintage Books, 1983), 31.

50. Alasdair MacIntyre, *After Virtue: A Study in Moral Theory*, 2d ed. (Notre Dame, IN: University of Notre Dame Press, 1984), 23–24.

51. See Jerome Bruner, *Acts of Meaning: Four Lectures on Mind and Culture* (Cambridge, MA: Harvard University Press, 1990), 44.

52. As the anthropologist Clifford Geertz put it, understanding requires "a continuous dialectical tacking between the most local or local detail and the most

global of global structures in such a way as to bring them into simultaneous view." Clifford Geertz, *Local Knowledge: Further Essays in Interpretive Anthropology* (New York: Basic Books, 1983), 69.

53. This is what Aristotle called commutative or corrective justice, the kind of justice that restores to an aggrieved person his or her rights; *Nicomachean Ethics*, Book V. The specific languages of the trial are designed to focus deliberation on corrective justice.

54. It has happened that a judge has granted a defense motion for a directed verdict after the plaintiff's opening statement, in effect saying, "If that is what even *you* say happened, then the law offers you no relief."

55. Wallace Stevens, "Connoisseur of Chaos," in *The Collected Poems of Wallace Stevens* (New York: Knopf, 1954), 275.

56. Or, as he put it with regard to historical narrative, the question about human action is always, "What type of account . . . will be both true and intelligible." MacIntyre, *After Virtue*, 213.

57. Richard Kroner, *Kant's Weltanschauung*, John E. Smith trans. (Chicago: University of Chicago Press, 1956).

58. Peirce distinguishes an "abductive" insight into a particular situation from an "inductive" insight into a generalization from a series of particular situations.

59. Rawls, *A Theory of Justice*, 579.

60. Standards such as "beyond a reasonable doubt" or "by the preponderance of the evidence" are crude attempts to turn these moral issues, for which the jury will have moral responsibility, into legal categories. For a perceptive argument, both descriptive and normative, in favor of a "variable" standard see R. Erik Lillquist, "Recasting Reasonable Doubt: Decision Theory and the Virtues of Variability," *UC Davis Law Review* 36 (2002), 85.

61. Judge Dwyer recounts the story of a sorry middle-aged nonviolent career criminal overcharged with six federal felonies for making wholly ineffectual threats to a man who had failed to return money the defendant had asked him to keep safe for him. Eleven jurors thought the case should never have been brought, but felt that under the instructions and the defendant's admissions, they were bound to convict. The foreman hung the jury after concluding that the defendant's vulgarities toward his associate were not in context "a threat at all but merely an outburst in language common to both their vocabularies." Why did he resist the considerable social pressure of the other jurors? "I had to live with myself—the one in the mirror." Dwyer, *In the Hands of the People*, 79–81.

62. The philosopher Martha Nussbaum puts it this way:

> Emotions can sometimes mislead and distort judgment; Aristotle is aware of this. But they can also . . . give us access to a truer and deeper level of ourselves, to values and commitments that have been concealed by defensive ambition or rationalization.

But even this is, so far, too Platonic a line to take: for it suggests that emotion is valuable only as an instrumental means to a purely intellectual state. We know, however, that for Aristotle appropriate responses ... can[,] like good intellectual responses, help to constitute the refined "perception" which is the best sort of human judgment.

Martha C. Nussbaum, *The Fragility of Goodness: Luck and Ethics in Greek Tragedy and Philosophy* (Cambridge: Cambridge University Press, 1986), 390.

63. If there are no doubts and uncertainties by this stage, the case almost certainly should not have gone to trial.

64. For powerful arguments that this form of argumentation is a genuine exercise of human intelligence, see Stephen Toulmin, *The Uses of Argument*, 2d ed. (Cambridge: Cambridge University Press, 2003).

65. Stuart Hampshire, "Public and Private Morality," in *Public and Private Morality*, Hampshire ed. (Cambridge: Cambridge University Press, 1978), 30.

66. John Henry Newman, *An Essay in Aid of a Grammar of Assent* (London: Longmans, Green, 1930), 288.

67. Charles Sanders Peirce, *Collected Papers of Charles Sanders Peirce*, vols. 1–6, Charles Hartshorne & Paul Weiss eds. (Cambridge, MA: Belknap Press of the Harvard University Press, 1958), 5:264.

68. In some places the instructions are read before the closing arguments, in some places after. Reforming the "legalese" in the instructions is one of the favorite goals of reformers of the trial. I wish them well, though I harbor doubts about whether the categories of the law of rules can ever be stated clearly and coherently.

69. There are no summary dispositions in criminal cases; every defendant has a legal right to a jury. (We will see shortly how the exercise of that right is taxed by the bureaucracy that controls the trial.) The trial judge may still enforce the rule of law as the law of rules by his determinations of materiality in excluding evidence and by refusing to provide instructions and verdict forms on lesser included offenses such as manslaughter in a homicide case, forcing the jury into an either-or determination of innocence or first-degree murder.

70. See chapter 5.

71. James W. McElhaney, *Trial Notebook*, 2d ed. (Chicago: American Bar Association, 1987), 499 (quoting trial lawyer Jack Liber).

72. Alexis de Tocqueville, *Democracy in America*, Henry Reeve trans. (New York: Vintage Books, 1945), 295.

73. Ludwig Wittgenstein, *Philosophical Investigations*, G. E. M. Anscombe trans. (New York: Macmillan, 1953), *129 at 50.

74. William Carlos Williams, *Paterson* (New York: New Directions, 1951), 14.

75. Newman, *An Essay*, 288.

76. Nussbaum, *The Fragility of Goodness*, 390.

77. Abramson, *We, the Jury*, 162.

78. The initial majority prevails in about 90 percent of cases. Valerie P. Hans & Neil Vidmar, "*The American Jury* at Twenty-five Years," *Law and Social Inquiry* 16 (1991), 343; Hans & Vidmar, *Judging the Jury*, 110.

79. Iris Murdoch put it this way:

> Ignorance, muddle, fear, wishful thinking, lack of tests often make us feel that moral choice is something arbitrary, a matter of personal will rather than attentive study.... The difficulty is to keep this attention fixed upon the real situation and to prevent it from returning surreptitiously to the self with consolations of self-pity, resentment, fantasy, and despair.... Realism, whether that of the artist or of the agent, is a moral achievement. This explains the central insight of Kantian ethics: "The more the separateness and differences of other people is realized, and the fact seen that another man has needs and wishes as demanding as one's own, the harder it becomes to treat a person as a thing."

Murdoch, *Sovereignty of Good*, 91, 66. My contention is that the devices of the trial seek to occasion by public methods the attention to the details of a particular situation that moral judgment requires.

80. Dennis M. Patterson, "Law's Pragmatism: Law as Practice and Narrative," *Virginia Law Review* 76 (1990), 979.

81. W. Lance Bennett & Martha S. Feldman, *Reconstructing Reality in the Courtroom: Justice and Judgment in American Culture* (New Brunswick, NJ: Rutgers University Press, 1981), 5.

82. Bruner, *Acts of Meaning*, 15.

83. David Carr, *Time, Narrative, and History* (Bloomington: Indiana University Press, 1986), 61.

84. Maria Villela Petit, "Thinking History: Methodology and Epistemology in Paul Ricoeur's Reflections on History from *History and Truth* to *Time and Narrative*," in *The Narrative Path: The Later Works of Paul Ricoeur*, T. Peter Kemp & David Ramussen eds. (Cambridge, MA: MIT Press, 1989), 35–36.

85. Hannah Arendt, *Men in Dark Times* (New York: Harcourt, Brace & World, 1968), 104.

86. "Relatively" unconstrained because it is still constrained by the anticipation of the opponent's case and the discipline of the evidence to follow, supported by the ethical rule prohibiting the lawyer from alluding to any matter of which there will not be admissible evidence.

87. As Arendt put it, "No doubt, wherever public life and its law of equality are completely victorious, wherever a civilization succeeds in eliminating or reducing to a minimum the dark background of difference, it will end in complete petrifaction, for having forgotten that man is only the master, not the creator of the

world." *The Origins of Totalitarianism* (New York: Harcourt, Brace, Jovanovich, 1951), 302.

88. Hampshire, *Public and Private Morality*, 39.

89. Melvyn A. Hill, "The Fictions of Mankind and the Stories of Men," in *Hannah Arendt: The Recovery of the Public World*, Melvin A. Hill ed. (New York: St. Martin's Press, 1979), 290.

90. Aristotle, *Nicomachean Ethics*, Book V.

91. Bennett & Feldman, *Reconstructing Reality*, 10.

92. Lonergan, *Insight*, 173–206.

93. See, e.g., Thomas A. Sebeok & Jean Umiker-Sebeok, "'You Know My Method': A Juxtaposition of Charles S. Peirce and Sherlock Holmes," in *The Sign of Three: Dupin, Holmes, and Peirce*, Umberto Eco & Thomas Sebeok eds. (Bloomington: Indiana University Press, 1983), 11–54.

94. Hayden White, "The Value of Narrativity in the Representation of Reality," in *On Narrative*, W. J. T. Mitchell ed. (Chicago: University of Chicago Press, 1981), 1. White's notion of morality is conservative or Hegelian in that he sees the morality that is invoked in narrative as embedded in social practices and institutions: "[N]arrativity, certainly in factual storytelling and probably in fictional storytelling as well, is intimately related to, if not a function of, the impulse to moralize reality, that is, to identify it with the social system that is the source of any morality that we can imagine." Id., 14.

95. T. Peter Kemp, "Toward a Narrative Ethics: A Bridge between Ethics and Narrative Reflections of Ricoeur," in *The Narrative Path: The Later Works of Paul Ricoeur*, T. Peter Kemp & David Rasmussen eds. (Cambridge, MA: MIT Press, 1989), 65.

96. Paul Ricoeur, *Time and Narrative*, Kathleen McLaughlin & David Pellauer trans. (Chicago: University of Chicago Press, 1984), 3:249.

97. Peter Kemp, "Ethics and Narrativity," in *The Philosophy of Paul Ricoeur*, Lewis E. Hahn ed. (Chicago: Open Press, 1995), 376.

98. Ronald Beiner, *Political Judgment* (Chicago: University of Chicago Press, 1983), 18.

99. Hill, "The Fictions of Mankind," 289–90.

100. Tocqueville, *Democracy in America*, 1:295.

101. Beiner, *Political Judgment*, 19.

102. Id., 24.

103. Richard Rhodes, review of Abraham Pais, *Niels Bohr's Times: In Physics, Philosophy, and Polity*, in *The New York Times Book Review*, Jan. 26, 1992.

104. *Chicago, B. & O. Ry. v. Babsock*, 204 U.S. 585, 598 (1907).

105. *United States v. Chipani*, 289 F.Supp 43 (E.D. N.Y.), *aff'd* 414 F.2d 1296 (2d Cir. 1969). For the classic, if somewhat tongue-in-cheek, expression of nonformal thinking at trial, see Joseph C. Hutcheson Jr., "The Judgment Intuitive: The Function of the 'Hunch' in Judicial Decision," *Cornell Law Quarterly* 14 (1929), 279.

106. I have tried to provide a somewhat fuller account in Burns, *A Theory of the Trial*, 183–244.

107. David Luban, *Legal Modernism: Law, Meaning, and Violence* (Ann Arbor: University of Michigan Press, 1994), 380. The trial thus meets the needs we have as modern persons who know that all of our social institutions are of our own making and thus subject to criticism.

108. David Kolb, *The Critique of Pure Modernity: Hegel, Heidegger, and After* (Chicago: University of Chicago Press, 1986), 259.

109. Hannah Arendt, *Lectures on Kant's Political Philosophy* (Chicago: University of Chicago Press, 1989), 44.

110. Arendt, "Truth and Politics," 242.

111. Nussbaum, *The Fragility of Goodness*, 69.

112. Geertz, *Local Knowledge*, 69.

113. Brian Leiter, "Heidegger and the Theory of Adjudication," *Yale Law Journal* 106 (1996), 270.

114. See generally Lillquist, "Recasting Reasonable Doubt," 85.

115. Richard J. Bernstein, *Beyond Objectivism and Relativism: Science, Hermeneutics, and Praxis* (Philadelphia: University of Pennsylvania Press, 1983), 217.

116. *American Bar Association Model Rules of Professional Conduct*, Rule 3.4.

117. Burns, *A Theory of the Trial*, 229–30.

118. Ibid., 230.

119. Charles Taylor, *Sources of the Self: The Making of the Modern Identity* (Cambridge, MA: Harvard University Press, 1989), 512.


**Chapter Two**

1. See, e.g., John H. Langbein, *The Origins of Adversary Criminal Trial* (Oxford: Oxford University Press, 2003); Thomas Andrew Green, *Verdict According to Conscience: Perspectives on the English Criminal Trial Jury, 1200–1800* (Chicago: University of Chicago Press, 1985); Robert Wyness Millar, *Civil Procedure of the Trial Court in Historical Perspective* (New York: National Conference of Judicial Councils, 1952).

2. Justice Brennan, concurring in *Teamsters Local No. 391 v. Terry*, 494 U.S. 558 (1990), warned his fellow liberal, Justice Stevens, against setting the reach of the right to a jury trial in civil cases by prevalent notions of where the jury best functions, which issues were "grist for the jury's judgment." Instead, Brennan showed himself the conservative by invoking the "language of the Seventh Amendment" to preserve "a bulwark against those who would restrict a right our forefathers held indispensable."

3. See Green, *Verdict According to Conscience*, 21; Robert P. Burns, "The History and Theory of the American Jury," *California Law Review* 83 (1995), 1477.

4. Burns, "The History and Theory of the American Jury," 1490–91.

5. See Rawls, *A Theory of Justice* (on reflective equilibrium as a cycle between particular institutions in which we have confidence and basic philosophical commitments).

6. The reader will note the congruence of this situation as the "metalevel" with that which we have seen to prevail at trial.

7. Charles Taylor, *Hegel* (Cambridge: Cambridge University Press, 1975), 218.

8. Rawls, *A Theory of Justice*, 579.

9. On the multiple nature of the functions of the jury, see Stephan Landsman, "The Civil Jury in America: Scenes from an Unappreciated History," *Hastings Law Journal* 44 (1993), 579. The very early English juries "served administrative functions" and were "bodies of citizens summoned by royal command to testify about property arrangements, local customs, and taxable resources in each neighborhood in the realm." Matthew P. Harrington, "The Law-Finding Function of the American Jury," *Wisconsin Law Review* (1999): 377, 379, quoting Landsman, "The Civil Jury in America," 583.

10. Harrington, "The Law-Finding Function of the American Jury," 381. On the jury's functions before it began to function as a case-resolution institution, see id., 386–88.

11. So-called presentiment juries determined who would be eligible for trial by ordeal. Thus some local discretion and judgment were at work even in these early forms of "adjudication."

12. The concern about eternal punishment for perjury was at least one factor in later rules that spared a criminal defendant the near occasion of mortal sin that testifying under oath would provide. Criminal defendants in England were not permitted to testify under oath until 1898. The prohibition prevailed in most American jurisdictions until after the Civil War.

13. Green, *Verdict According to Conscience*, 105. Green's description of the function of the medieval jury is thus remarkably similar to Kalven and Zeisel's account of the ways in which American criminal juries still qualify the law of rules: "The jury may consider it important that the defendant was seriously injured at the time of the crime, or that the victim is not enthusiastic about prosecuting, or that the defendant's behavior is rarely prosecuted, or would not be illegal across the river in the next state, or that the defendant was not represented by counsel. . . . More specifically, it can be important that a defendant was suffering horrendous personal tragedies during the time he (even 'knowingly') failed to file an income tax return, or that the defendant used a toy gun rather than a real gun in an armed robbery (even if the law makes the distinction irrelevant)." Burns, *A Theory of the Trial*, 147 n. 87. See Kalven & Zeisel, *The American Jury*, 270, 293, 305, 319, and 338.

14. Green, *Verdict According to Conscience*, 105.

15. Id.

16. Id., 149.

17. "Students of Tudor and early Stuart England have pointed to the fit between, on the one hand, a system of criminal justice that announced legal imperatives in definitive terms but provided abundant opportunities for bestowing mercy and, on the other, a religious ethic that portrayed all men as sinners, as subject to temptation and transgression, but preferred opportunities for redemption to all but the worst of the fallen." Green, *Verdict According to Conscience*, 376.

18. Id., 380.

19. John M. Beattie, "London Juries in the 1690s," in *Twelve Good Men and True*, J. S. Cockburn & Thomas A. Green eds. (Princeton: Princeton University Press, 1988), 214.

20. It seems anachronistic to think of this power as expressing legitimate popular *will*. As we will see in the next section, spokespersons for jury authority argued within a broadly natural-law context for the jury's superior ability to discern "true law." These arguments often relied on claims about the corruption of the judiciary or of Parliament that blinded them to fundamental law.

21. Green, *Verdict According to Conscience*, 373. It seems to me that the chief justice's intuition reached the truth that decision making in concrete cases inevitably involves processes of moral evaluation not captured in simple notions of legal categorization of value-free narrative. As Chief Justice Vaughn famously put it, "A man cannot see by another's eye, nor hear by another's ear; no more can a man conclude or infer the thing to be resolved by another's understanding or reasoning; and though the verdict be right the jury give, yet they, not being assured it is so from their understanding, are forsworn, at least *foro conscientia*. . . . [Juries] resolve both law and fact complicatively, and not the fact by itself." Chief Justice Vaughn of the Court of Common Pleas in Bushell's Case, 6 Howard St. Tr. 999, 1011, 1015.

22. Thomas Leach, a barrister and police magistrate put it this way: "In the institutions of civil government, power and right, are, and must be, convertible terms. Civil power, and civil right, are the mere creatures of the law and know no other limits, than the law imposes on them. The law speaks that language of prohibitions, not of admonition. What I permit to be done, uncensored, and firm, when it is done. It has delegated the power to do, and the exercise of that power, is of right." Green, *Verdict According to Conscience*, 338.

23. "It is also significant that mid-seventeenth century jury proponents sometimes failed to distinguish between civil and criminal trial juries. Like the Wilkites of the following century, the Levellers were concerned with private law as much— if not more—than with criminal law. Both groups sought a simpler, more accessible system of law to cover their acquisition, transfer, and protection of property." Id., 372.

24. No comparable history of actual American trial procedures in their social and political context appears to exist.

25. Langbein, *The Origins of Adversary Criminal Trial*, 52.

26. Id.

27. Id., 288. On the importance of the opening statement, see pp. 22–24 herein.

28. Id., 259.

29. John H. Langbein, "Historical Foundations of the Law of Evidence: A View from the Ryder Sources," *Columbia Law Review* 96 (1996), 1190.

30. John H. Langbein, "The Criminal Trial before the Lawyers," *University of Chicago Law Review* 45 (1978), 289.

31. Langbein, *The Origins of Adversary Criminal Trial*, 43.

32. Id., quoting a contemporary manual for justices of the peace.

33. Id.

34. Id., quoting William J. Stuntz, "The Substantive Origins of Criminal Procedure," *Yale Law Journal* 105 (1995), 417. As the nineteenth century wore on and professional police forces took over the responsibility for assembling the prosecution's case, the justice of peace's investigation began to look increasingly like our preliminary hearing, in Langbein's view.

35. Langbein, *The Origins of Adversary Criminal Trial*, 50, quoting J. M. Beattie, *Crime and the Courts in England, 1660–1800* (Princeton: Princeton University Press, 1986).

36. Id., 51.

37. Id., 16.

38. Id.

39. Id., 24.

40. Id., 25.

41. There are questions of historical causality here and questions of historical significance. Langbein recognizes that the procedural changes he recounts so meticulously connect up with larger cultural and intellectual changes. He remarks poignantly that sixteenth-century defendants falsely accused by kings seemed compliant in their own deaths in a way that suggested that a more modern sense of individual rights, including a natural right to self-defense, had not yet emerged. Id. 88–89. But the steps that led to something that looks like our adversarial criminal trial are generally explained by the relatively specific concrete needs of the trial judge.

42. See William E. Nelson, *Americanization of the Common Law: The Impact of Legal Change on Massachusetts Society, 1760–1830* (Athens: University of Georgia Press, 1994).

43. Langbein, "Historical Foundations," 1179.

44. Id. It has been suggested that one purpose of this disqualification was to encourage all commercial transactions to be in writing. Id., 1185.

45. David Lemmings, *Gentlemen and Barristers: The Inns of Court and the English Bar, 1680–1730* (Oxford: Oxford University Press, 1990).

46. Bogus, *Why Lawsuits Are Good for America*, 63. One has to conclude that a good number of the gentry and businessmen were none too eager to have their

cases decided "on the merits," if that notion even has meaning within the civil practice of the time.

47. "Without an investigative file, the American trial judge is a blind and blundering intruder." Marvin E. Frankel, "The Search for Truth: An Umpireal View," *University of Pennsylvania Law Review* 123 (1975), 1042; Stephan Landsman, "A Brief Survey of the Development of the Adversary System," *Ohio State Law Journal* 44 (1983), 733.

48. Landsman, "A Brief Survey," 734.

49. John Henry Wigmore, *A Treatise on the Anglo-American System of Evidence in Trials at Common Law*, vol. 5, James H. Chadbourn rev. (Boston: Little, Brown, 1974), 32.

50. James Alexander, *A Brief Narrative of the Case and Trial of John Peter Zenger, Printer of the New York Weekly Journal*, Stanley Nider Katz ed. (Cambridge, MA: Harvard University Press, 1963).

51. Id., quoted in Harrington, "The Law-Finding Function of the American Jury," 393. See Albert W. Alschuler & Andrew G. Deiss, "A Brief History of the Criminal Jury in the United States," *University of Chicago Law Review* 61 (1994), 904 (summarizing the deference to the jury as judge of law in the colonies).

52. Stephan Landsman, "The Civil Jury in America: Scenes from an Unappreciated History," *Hastings Law Journal* 44 (1993), 594–95.

53. Landsman, "The Civil Jury in America," 592, quoting Nelson, *Americanization of the Common Law*.

54. Bogus, *Why Lawsuits Are Good for America*, 63, citing Gordon J. Wood, *The Radicalism of the American Revolution* (New York: A. A. Knopf, 1992), 122–23. Bogus suggests that this elevated the importance of access to law and of rational procedures. Bogus, *Why Lawsuits Are Good for America*, 63.

55. Milner Ball notes how law can easily be understood using the metaphor of the bulwark if social control of the "dangerous classes" becomes its perceived central purpose. Milner S. Ball, *Lying Down Together: Law, Metaphor, and Theology* (Madison: University of Wisconsin Press, 1985), 120.

56. All quoted in Hannah Arendt, *On Revolution* (New York: Penguin Books, 1965), 67–68.

57. Id., 68.

58. Lemmings, *Gentlemen and Barristers*, cited in Bogus, *Why Lawsuits Are Good for America*, 231.

59. Langbein, *The Origins of Adversary Criminal Trial*, 31. Langbein concludes that the judiciary only gradually "retired from the political area." Id., 81.

60. Langbein refers to this colonial practice as an "anomaly, not much understood." Id., 40.

61. Zephaniah Swift, *A System of the Laws of the State of Connecticut* (Windham, CT, 1795–96), 2:398, quoted in Langbein, *The Origins of Adversary Criminal Trial*, 40.

62. Langbein, *The Origins of Adversary Criminal Trial*, 320. Such comment could be quite "directive." Langbein recounts the comment made by Judge Keble in the political trial of John Lilburn in 1649 before the defense had even offered evidence: "I hope the Jury hath seen the Evidence so plain and so fully, that it doth confirm them to do their duty, and to find the Prisoner guilty of what is charged upon him." After hearing the defense, he instructed the jury that they should "clearly find that never was the like treason hatched in England." Id., 32 n. 115. The jury rejected the judge's instruction and acquitted Lilburn. American commentators inclined to place greater trust in the fairness of the trial judge and rather less in the judgment of the jury have often lamented the American rule. See Kenneth A. Krasity, "The Role of the Judge in Jury Trials: The Elimination of Judicial Evaluation of Fact in American State Courts from 1795 to 1913," *University of Detroit Law Review* 62 (1985), 595; Renée Lettow Lerner, "The Transformation of the American Civil Trial: The Silent Judge," *William and Mary Law Review* 42 (2000), 195 (describing the greater dominance of the laissez-faire judge in the South and West); Wigmore, *A Treatise on the Anglo-American System of Evidence*, sec. 2551 at 503, citing Thayer, *Evidence* (asserting that the American trial is thus "not a trial by jury in any historic sense of the words"), 188, all cited at Langbein, *The Origins of Adversary Criminal Trial*, 323 n. 344. As recently as 1975, the United States Congress explicitly rejected a provision of the Federal Rules of Evidence that would have allowed for judicial comment. Case law is mixed as to the limits of judicial comment on some notion of inherent powers.

63. On the power of formal questioning to reveal the truth, see Burns, *A Theory of the Trial*, chap. 2. On the importance of the formality of the American trial as a vehicle for equal respect, see Milner S. Ball, *The Promise of American Law: A Theological, Humanistic View of Legal Process* (Athens: University of Georgia Press, 1981), 57, 61, 65.

64. Langbein, *The Origins of Adversary Criminal Trial*, 52–53.

65. The treatment of the defendants in the late Stuart treason trials led one commentator to remark about the behavior of the criminal court judge that he "betrayed their poor Client, to please, as they apprehended, their better client, the King." Id., 99, quoting a contemporary lawyer and commentator. I recall cross-examining a Chicago police detective about the interrogation of the defendant and drawing smiles from several jurors when the detective strongly protested that it was *he* who was protecting the young man's rights.

66. The existence of the demurrer was used by American courts to justify the much more intrusive motion for judgment notwithstanding the verdict.

67. Bogus, *Why Lawsuits Are Good for America*, 63.

68. Id., quoting C. W. Brooks, *Lawyers, Litigation and English Society since 1450* (London: Hambledon, 1998), 48–49. As is still true, before any citizen can be offered a trial, he or she must submit written "pleadings" to the trial court, which make factual claims that, in the judge's view, entitle him to relief. Depending on the

pleading regime in place, this judicial gatekeeper function can impose light burdens or nearly impossible ones. Ideally, the requirement of some pleading serves the purpose of saving the defendant from the burdens of trial in cases where the plaintiff has no legitimate claim. American courts, even those within very liberal pleading regimes, have resisted rules that would simply allow a plaintiff to announce in writing that he in effect has a vague suspicion that he may have been wronged and then seize the right to conduct lengthy and intrusive discovery to support that suspicion. But this is a very delicate matter, especially in cases where the most important information is in the hands of the defendant and the plaintiff may have only a vague suspicion of the facts that may entitle him to relief. And higher pleading requirements always do two things. First, they may be used to favor the resolution of the case on extremely abstract grounds—unconnected with the contextual picture that would emerge at trial—and they increase the authority of the trial judge to make this determination. The tensions among incommensurable values are particularly sharp here.

69. Bogus, *Why Lawsuits Are Good for America*, 64, quoting Lawrence M. Friedman, *A History of American Law* (New York: Simon & Schuster, 1973), 146.

70. Id., 146–47.

71. Nelson, *Americanization of the Common Law*, 78, quoted in Bogus, *Why Lawsuits Are Good for America*, 64.

72. Bogus, *Why Lawsuits Are Good for America*, 64–65. See Lawrence M. Friedman, *A History of American Law* (New York: Simon & Schuster, 1973), 126–30.

73. Abramson, *We, the Jury*, 88.

74. Landsman, "The Civil Jury in America," 594–95.

75. Id., 596, quoting the "Declaration of the Causes and Necessity of Taking Up Arms," in *Sources of Our Liberties: Documentary Origins of Individual Liberties in the United States Constitution and Bill of Rights*, Richard L. Perry & John C. Cooper eds. (New York: New York University Press, 1972), 288.

76. Harrington, "The Law-Finding Function of the American Jury," 395.

77. Charles Wolfram, "The Constitutional History of the Seventh Amendment," *Minnesota Law Review* 57 (1973), 655, quoting Leonard W. Levy, *Legacy of Suppression: Freedom of Press and Speech in Early American History* (Cambridge, MA: Harvard University Press, 1960), 281.

78. Hamilton was arguing against the wisdom of including a right to a jury trial in civil cases in the Constitution. The paper is a wonderful example of political rhetoric directed at what the author understood was a skeptical audience.

79. Harrington, "The Law-Finding Function of the American Jury," 391.

80. Id., 392.

81. The high-stakes nature of this device made it far less eligible than the judge-friendly methods that emerged in the nineteenth century, which we retain. For example, a defendant's motion for judgment as a matter of law need not concede irreversibly the truth of the plaintiff's proof. If the court denies that motion, the

defense is permitted to argue its case to the jury, which is still permitted to enter a verdict for the defense.

82. Harrington, "The Law-Finding Function of the American Jury," 392.

83. Id., 391.

84. It appears that colonial courts inherited English evidentiary doctrines, which were probably rooted in religious convictions about the sacredness of oaths and the moral dangers of perjury. These latter prohibited parties to civil actions from testifying and instructed jurors to presume the truth of statements made under oath, rather than weighing credibility. Id., 392. Even the nascent hearsay rule seemed to be justified more as a device to privilege statements given under oath, rather than protecting the right to cross-examination, the justification usually offered after right to counsel made cross-examination more important.

85. Morton J. Horwitz, *The Transformation of American Law, 1780–1860* (Cambridge, MA: Harvard University Press, 1977), 142, quoting *Hague v. Stratton*, 8 Va. 84, 85 (1786).

86. The Sixth Amendment added that the trial also had to occur within the "district," a limit the drafters knew would eventually make the trial more "local," as states became multidistrict. Abramson, *We, the Jury*, 22–30.

87. Wolfram, "The Constitutional History of the Seventh Amendment,"639.

88. *Federalist No. 83*.

89. Harrington, "The Law-Finding Function of the American Jury," 400. The Alien and Sedition Acts, passed by the Congress in 1798, had explicit provisions that the jury was to be the judge both of the facts and of the law in prosecutions under the Acts.

90. Wolfram, "The Constitutional History of the Seventh Amendment."

91. Gordon S. Wood, *The Creation of the American Republic, 1776–1787* (Chapel Hill: University of North Carolina Press, 1969).

92. Id.

93. Arendt, *On Revolution*.

94. *Federalist No. 51*.

95. Akhil Reed Amar, *The Bill of Rights: Creation and Reconstruction* (New Haven: Yale University Press, 1998), 96.

96. Id., 94.

97. Id., 95.

98. Amar's final conclusion on the issue of "review" is qualified: "In setting forth the strong arguments for jury review, I do not mean to suggest that I am wholly convinced. But the mere fact of their strong plausibility shows how strikingly powerful the jury might have become had post-1800 history unfolded differently." Id., 103.

99. Id., 99, describing the arguments of the great advocate William Wirt in arguing before Samuel Chase in a prosecution under the Alien and Sedition Acts.

100. Id., 104. The ambiguity that Amar describes illustrates the difficulty of precisely determining our considered judgments of justice here and the importance of arguments that seek to recover aspects of our inheritance which may have been covered over by obsolete ideological and institutional accretions. My position raises fundamental philosophical questions about the criticism of actual institutions.

101. Abramson describes an 1808 incident in which a Massachusetts lawyer was threatened with contempt for insisting on arguing the constitutionality of the Embargo Act to a Massachusetts jury. The lawyer addressed the court in the following terms:

> [I have] reflected very solemnly upon the occurrence of yesterday. . . .
> No man cherished a higher respect for the legitimate authority of [the
> court]; but he entertained no less respect for his moral obligations to
> his client. He had arrived at the clear conviction that it was his duty to
> argue the constitutional question to the jury . . . , and that he should
> proceed to do so regardless of any consequences.

Id., 77, quoting Lucius Manlius Sargent [Sigma], *Reminiscences of Samuel Dexter* (Boston: Henry W. Dutton & Son, 1857), 60–61. See *United States v. The William*, 28 Fed. Cas. 614 (case no. 16700) (D.C. Mass 1808). The lawyer was allowed to address the constitutional issue, and the jury acquitted his client.

102. Landsman, "The Civil Jury in America," 603–4.

103. Harrington, "The Law-Finding Function of the American Jury," 412.

104. *Stare decisis* denotes the obligation of a court to follow its own precedent absent distinguishing factual aspects of the immediate case or a strong reason to reformulate the preexisting rule. The principle is usually justified on grounds of formal justice over time ("Similar cases should be similarly decided") or on grounds of predictability.

105. Abramson, *We, the Jury*, 75–76.

106. Id., 76.

107. Id., 75.

108. Id., 76, quoting *State v. Croteau*, 23 Vt. 14, 19 (1849), overruled by *State v. Burpee*, 25 A. 964, 974 (Vt. 1892).

109. Abramson, *We, the Jury*, 84.

110. Id.

111. *Hilands v. Commonwealth*, 111 Pa. 1, 5 (1886), quoted in Abramson, *We, the Jury*, 425.

112. *State v. McDonnell*, 32 Vt. 491, 532 (1860), quoted in Abramson, *We, the Jury*, 427.

113. The centrality of the trial to American self-understanding should not blind us to the limitations of the trial as most of them were actually conducted in the nineteenth century. Though the trial, and the jury trial in particular, was more

important in the United States than it had been in England, the reality of what even the American trial looked like was hardly elaborate:

> Rather, it was [a] quick, slapdash proceeding. It had very little in common with what the public thinks of as a "trial." Of course, the details vary from place to place, and the research is fairly thin; but it is safe to make some generalizations about criminal "trials" before the days of plea bargaining. First of all, there was no voir dire proceeding. Twelve men were impaneled, quite quickly and with much hullabaloo; and they sat for not one but a whole series of trials. In most trials, the defendant had no lawyer at all. The trial, from start to finish, was over with[in] a day. Many trials were over within an hour. They spent very little time before reaching a verdict. There was little or no cross-examination, nobody raised objections—certainly not in the lawyerless cases—and the niceties of due process or the law of evidence were not rigorously observed. Arthur Trian, writing about felony trials in New York City in the early 20th century, noted that "in a full court day there will occur from two to four complete trials." Trials were hasty and short, in other words—quick and dirty, even slapdash.

Lawrence M. Friedman, "The Day before Trials Vanished," *Journal of Empirical Legal Studies* 1 (2004), 690. Even in the nineteenth century there were trials that that were exceptional in the attention they received, but they were just that—exceptions: "The system has always lacked the time, the resources, and the will to give the full treatment to mine-run cases." Id., 693.

114. Id., 696. Friedman makes the point that very few of these more frequent encounters with the legal order involved what we would consider "trials."

115. Id., 397.

116. *Trial of Samuel Chase, An Associate Justice of the United States, Impeached by the House of Representatives for High Crimes and Misdemeanors before the Senate of the United States*, Samuel H. Smith & Thomas Lloyd eds. (1805), 5, as quoted in Harrington, "The Law-Finding Function of the American Jury," 414.

117. Harrington, "The Law-Finding Function of the American Jury," 414.

118. Id., 416.

119. *Liebart v. The Emperor*, 15 Fed. Cas. 508, 509 (Adm. Ct. Pa. 1785), quoted in Harrington, "The Law-Finding Function of the American Jury," 416.

120. Harrington, "The Law-Finding Function of the American Jury," 377 n. 2.

121. Id., 416, quoting Alexander Addison, "Charges to Grand Juries of the Fifth Circuit in the State of Pennsylvania" (1883), 53–59.

122. *Bartholomew v. Clark*, 1 Conn. 472, 482 (1816), quoted in Harrington, "The Law-Finding Function of the American Jury," 421.

123. Horwitz, *The Transformation of American Law*, 142.

124. Friedman, "The Day before Trials Vanished," 697.

125. See chapter 4.

126. Harrington, "The Law-Finding Function of the American Jury," 418.

127. It is fair to say that before the nineteenth century, the bodies of law that we now call contract and tort law did not exist. Rather, lawyers thought more formalistically of the writs that might be available to remedy a perceived injury.

128. A. W. B. Simpson, "The Horwitz Thesis and the History of Contracts," *University of Chicago Law Review* 46 (1979), 600, quoted in Langbein, *The Origins of Adversary Criminal Trial,* 216.

129. J. H. Baker, review of Patrick Atiyah, *The Rise and Fall of Freedom of Contract, Modern Law Review* 43 (1980), 469.

130. Harrington, "The Law-Finding Function of the American Jury," 429–32.

131. 156 U.S. 51 (1895).

132. Dwyer, *In the Hands of the People,* 81.

133. Landsman, "The Civil Jury in America," 605, quoting Wex Malone's history of the doctrine, "The Formative Era of Contributory Negligence," *Illinois Law Review* 41 (1946), 151.

134. *Haring v. New York and Erie Railroad,* 13 Barb. 2 (N.Y. Sup. Ct. 1852), quoted in Landsman, "The Civil Jury in America," 607.

135. Landsman, "The Civil Jury in America," 609. Landsman cited John T. Noonan Jr., *Persons and Masks of the Law: Cardozo, Holmes, Jefferson, and Wythe as Makers of the Masks* (New York: Farrar, Straus, & Giroux, 1976).

136. Landsman, "The Civil Jury in America," 609, quoting Seymour Thompson, *Commentaries on the Law of Negligence,* vol. 1 (Indianapolis: Bowon-Merrill, 1901), 168–69.

137. Landsman, "The Civil Jury in America," 606, quoting Fleming James Jr., "Last Clear Chance: A Transitional Doctrine," *Yale Law Journal* 47 (1938), 704–5.

138. See Steven A. Hetcher, *Norms in a Wired World* (Cambridge: Cambridge University Press, 2004), 215–25, on the continued vitality of juror commonsense norms in tort law.

139. Landsman, "The Civil Jury in America," 610, quoting Charles E. Wyzanski Jr., "A Trial Judge's Freedom and Responsibility," *Harvard Law Review* 65 (1952), 1286.

140. Nancy S. Marder, "The Myth of the Nullifying Jury," *Northwestern University Law Review* 93 (1999), 910. This effect of the cumulative momentum of hundreds of jury determinations on legal doctrine was nothing new. The imposition of royal jurisdiction in homicide cases in the twelfth century turned many homicides that had been treated as lesser offenses into capital crimes and removed self-defense in a range of situations where it had traditionally been thought to apply. Green provides an account of the effect of "merciful" jury determinations and the reform of the law of homicide to provide for a more robust manslaughter

category and make the law of self-defense more consistent with moral intuitions. *Verdict According to Conscience*, 50–51. The "merciful" character of jury decisions in opposition to the law of rules came to be an accepted feature of English justice and so integrated into the practices of the English criminal courts.

141. Suja A. Thomas, "Why Summary Judgment Is Unconstitutional," *Virginia Law Review* 93 (2007), 139.

142. This development was far less well established in the criminal context where the concerns about oppression of the citizen by the state prevailed, though even here the application of the rules of evidence gave the judge the power to constrict the evidentiary basis of the trial in ways that deprived the jury of the wherewithal intelligently to make a commonsense determination based on ordinary morality.

143. The Seventh Amendment to the United States Constitution is as follows: "In suits at common law, where the value in controversy shall exceed twenty dollars, the right of trial by jury shall be preserved, *and no fact tried by a jury, shall be otherwise re-examined in any Court of the United States, than according to the rules of the common law.*" (emphasis added). The Seventh Amendment remains one of the few provisions of the Bill of Rights not to be imposed on the states by "selective incorporation" into the due process clause of the Fourteenth Amendment; the latter prohibits states from depriving persons of life, liberty, or property without due process of law. See *Duncan v. Louisiana*, 391 U.S. 145 (1968). On the other hand, all states have their own versions of the Seventh Amendment, which provide similar rights.

144. 319 U.S. 372 (1943).

145. *Greenleaf v. Birth*, 9 Pet. 292, 299 (1835).

146. *Galloway*, 402, quoting *Parks v. Ross*, 11 How. 362, 374 (1850).

147. *Galloway*, 404, quoting *Schuykill and Dauphin Improvement Co. v. Munson*, 14 Wall. 442, 447, 448 (1871).

148. Thomas, "Why Summary Judgment Is Unconstitutional."

149. *Sparf and Hansen v. United States*, 156 U.S. 51 (1895).

150. There is a little polemic surrounding the question of whether judges should weigh evidence when engaging in these summary proceedings. Regardless of the doctrine, some weighing seems to be inevitable.

151. Abramson, *We, the Jury*, 77–79 (discussing the case of *United States v. Battiste*, 24 Fed. Cas. 1042 [C.C.D. Mass. 1835] [case no. 14,545]).

152. Reva B. Siegel, "Constitutional Culture, Social Movement Conflict and Constitutional Change: The Case of the de facto ERA," *California Law Review* 94 (2006), 1353 (citing William Lloyd Garrison's famous phrase).

153. J. G. A. Pocock, *The Ancient Constitution and the Feudal Law: A Study of English Historical Thought in the Seventeenth Century* (Cambridge: Cambridge University Press, 1987), 35. Coke also lent authority to the closely related notion

that the common law envisioned a sharp distinction between fact and law, over which the jury and the judge respectively had exclusive authority.

154. Edson R. Sunderland, "The Inefficiency of the American Jury," *Michigan Law Review* 13 (1915), 302.

155. Stephen B. Burbank, "Vanishing Trials and Summary Judgment in Federal Civil Cases: Drifting toward Bethlehem or Gomorrah?" *Journal of Empirical Legal Studies* 1 (2004), 597.

156. Id., 600.

157. Id., 601, citing Proceedings of Meeting of Advisory Committee on Rules for Civil Procedure of the Supreme Court of the United States. This "no real difference" standard is probably much stricter than the one actually employed by the courts under the "no genuine issue as to any material fact" language actually in the rule.

158. Burbank, "Vanishing Trials and Summary Judgment in Federal Civil Cases," 601.

159. Id., 602.

160. *Crawford v. Washington*, 541 U.S. 36 (2004).

161. Paul Butler has suggested provocatively that the death of the trial parallels "white flight." As the number of black jurors has increased, the number of trials has fallen as parties seek to avoid their proximity. Butler, "The Case for Trials: Considering the Intangibles," *Journal of Empirical Legal Studies* 1 (2004), 627.

162. Compare *Eldridge v. Matthews*, 424 U.S. 319 (1976), with *Goldberg v. Kelly*, 397 U.S. 254 (1970).

163. See *Teamsters Local No. 391 v. Terry*, 494 U.S. 558 (1990). In *Terry*, Justice Brennan invoked the text and history of the Constitution to expand the right to trial by jury in a civil case. He rejected a more functionalist mode of thought that would have focused solely on contemporary judgments about the contexts within which we might think that the jury is likely to function well. See Arendt, *The Origins of Totalitarianism*, 299. Arendt argues for the relative vitality in the twentieth century of historically based "rights of Englishmen" compared to claims of transcultural "natural rights."

## Chapter Three

1. Geertz, "From the Native's Point of View," 239.

2. In the modern age, these general moral principles will almost invariably be principles of equal respect for rational individuals. Taylor, *Sources of the Self*.

3. Walter Jost, "Sweating the Little Things in Sidney Lumet's *12 Angry Men*," in *The* Ethos *of Rhetoric*, Michael J. Hyde ed. (Columbia: University of South Carolina Press, 2004).

4. *Detroit Free Press v. Ashcroft*, 303 F.3d 681, 683 (6th Cir. 2002).

5. Continental systems have far weaker discovery regimes.

6. On publicity as a condition for a viable concept of justice, *see* Rawls, *A Theory of Justice*, 177–82.

7. The comedy of errors surrounding the identity of the true decision maker(s) in the Department of Justice and the White House on the firing of eight United States Attorneys in November 2006 provided a recent example. A number of high-profile prosecutions of top corporate officials have (usually) rejected their claims of ignorance of the corrupt goings-on within their companies.

8. See David Luban, *Lawyers and Justice: An Ethical Study* (Princeton: Princeton University Press, 1988), xix–xxi.

9. Green, *Verdict According to Conscience*, 149.

10. Dwyer, *In the Hands of the People*, 71. For a very recent invocation of analogous notions to argue against the aggressive use of the law of evidence, see Todd E. Pettys, "The Immoral Application of Exclusionary Rules," http://papers.ssrn.com/sol3/papers.cfm?abstract_1102565.

11. *Federalist No. 10*.

12. *Federalist No. 83*.

13. Not always. Some radical partisans of the jury right have argued that the judge's view of the law was entitled to no deference at all.

14. The Levellers were divided on the weight to be given the judge's view of the law. Green, *Verdict According to Conscience*, 197–98.

15. Id., 154.

16. Lonergan, *Insight*, 213–14.

17. Paul Carrington, "Of Time and the River," *Journal of Legal Education* 34 (1984), 222.

18. Brian Leiter, "Rethinking Legal Realism: Toward a Naturalized Jurisprudence," *Texas Law Review* 76 (1997), 276, quoting Jerome Frank, *Law and the Modern Mind* (New York: Tudor, 1930).

19. H. L. A. Hart, *Punishment and Responsibility: Essays in the Philosophy of Law* (New York: Oxford University Press, 1968). In the nineteenth century the United States Supreme Court prohibited prosecution of common-law crimes. In earlier times, there was less discomfort with the notion of criminal punishment being visited on an individual for violation of an incompletely determined moral obligation that did not yet have a clear definition in the language of rules.

20. That was, once again, the emphasis of Benjamin Butler, a delegate to the Massachusetts Constitutional Convention of 1853, during debate of an amendment to the state constitution that would have restored to the jury the authority to "find law": "Which is the best tribunal to try [a]case. This man who sits upon the bench, and who ... has nothing in common with the people; who has hardly seen a common man in twenty years. ... Is he the better man to try the case than they

who have the same stake in community, with their wives, and children, and their fortunes depending on the integrity of the verdicts they shall render." Quoted in Abramson, *We, the Jury*, 84, from *Official Report of the Debates and Proceedings in the State Convention to Revise and Amend the Constitution* (Boston: White & Potter, Printers to the Convention, 1853).

21. There is a further ambiguity about the extent to which legal reasons are equivalent to the reasons that can be derived solely from the meanings of legal rules.

22. This is my summary of Brian Leiter's understanding of the formalist creed. Brian Leiter, "Positivism, Formalism, Realism," *Columbia Law Review* 99 (1999), 1145–46.

23. Kalven & Zeisel, *The American Jury*, 91.

24. Plato articulated a related objection to writing as necessarily overgeneralized compared to oral conversation. A wise man can be infinitely more refined in his accommodation of the concrete needs of his conversation partner than could any written communication. Of course, this relates to a notion of philosophy that was quite different from the source of true doctrine.

25. This is precisely what the evidentiary doctrine of materiality is designed to accomplish. Once again, under common law landlord-tenant rules, the tenant was required to pay his rent regardless of the condition of his apartment. Thus the tenant was not permitted to admit evidence of even criminally negligent maintenance by the landlord.

26. Dwyer, *In the Hands of the People*, xiii.

27. MacIntyre, *After Virtue*, 212–13.

28. In the technical language of evidence law, "relevant" details, broadly, those that common sense finds to be pertinent to the plausibility of the story.

29. Dewey, "Logical Method and the Law."

30. Theodore J. Lowi, *The End of Liberalism: Ideology, Policy, and the Crisis of Public Authority* (New York: Norton, 1969).

31. Nussbaum, *The Fragility of Goodness*.

32. Green, *Verdict According to Conscience*, 163.

33. Arendt, *The Origins of Totalitarianism*, 299.

34. Green, *Verdict According to Conscience*, 171.

35. Id., 186.

36. Dwyer, *In the Hands of the People*, 70.

37. These notions are not of merely antiquarian interest. For contemporary arguments that "natural law" and "ordinary morality" largely coincide see Alan Donagan, *The Theory of Morality* (Chicago: University of Chicago Press, 1977); Edward B. McLean ed., *Common Truths: New Perspectives on Natural Law* (Wilmington: ISI Books, 2000).

38. Green, *Verdict According to Conscience*, 180.

39. Murdoch, *The Sovereignty of Good*, 66.

40. James Boyd White, *From Expectation to Experience: Essays on Law and Legal Education* (Ann Arbor: University of Michigan Press, 1999), 20.

41. Put historically, the closer the trial actually approaches a Socratic dialogue, of course, the less likely it will be allowed to exercise power in the political world.

### Chapter Four

1. Marc Galanter, "The Vanishing Trial: An Examination of Trials and Related Matters in Federal and State Courts," *Journal of Empirical Legal Studies* 1 (2004), 459. In 1938 about 18 percent of federal civil cases were resolved at trial. Marc Galanter, "A World without Trials?" *Journal of Dispute Resolution* (2006), 12.

2. Galanter, "The Vanishing Trial," 460.

3. "Dispositions" include all the means by which a case ends: summary disposition, settlement, and trial. For purposes of the research, a "trial" was defined as "a contested proceeding at which evidence is introduced." Such a proceeding includes hearings leading to final orders, but also hearings on injunctions that were "temporary" or "preliminary," merely maintaining the status quo. The numbers also include as "trials" cases where the parties settle before judgment is entered on a verdict at trial, so they tend to overstate the number of trials. In 1988 almost a quarter of cases that reached trial ended "during" trial; in 2002, after the percentage of cases going to trial had decreased dramatically, the percentage of cases that ended during trial had declined to just under 20 percent. Galanter, "The Vanishing Trial," 461.

4. It is interesting to note that the decline in the percentage of bench trials has been even more dramatic than that of jury trials. One can only speculate on the reasons. It may be that judges so clearly signal their view of the case that lawyers come to think a trial is "unnecessary." Given that the judge can only have an impressionistic view of the case before trial, this would not be a happy turn of events.

5. The decline in absolute numbers has not been consistent: the number of trials reached its apex in 1985 and has declined dramatically since then. Id., 464, table 1.

6. Id., 463–64. The legal historian Lawrence Friedman has noted that trials "have become more complex over the years, though it is not easy to document this rigorously and historically." Friedman, "The Day before Trials Vanished," 697.

7. Galanter, "The Vanishing Trial," 464.

8. Wayne V. McIntosh, *The Appeal of Civil Law: A Political-Economic Analysis of Litigation* (Champaign: University of Illinois Press, 1990), 124, 126–28. Lawrence M. Friedman & Robert V. Percival, "A Tale of Two Courts: Litigation in Alameda and San Benito Counties," *Law & Society Review* 10 (1976), 267, quoted in Galanter, "The Vanishing Trial," 464–65.

9. Galanter, "The Vanishing Trial," 466–68.

10. Id., 468 n. 15.

11. Id., 468.

12. Id., 470–72.

13. Magistrate judges are not lifetime appointees to the federal bench, as are federal district court judges. They perform a range of important supervisory functions during the pretrial process in both civil and criminal cases and may preside over jury trials with the consent of the parties.

14. Id., 480, citing Thomas H. Cohen & Steven K. Smith, "Civil Trial Cases and Verdicts in Large Counties, 2001," *Bureau of Justice Statistics Bulletin*, April 2004.

15. Galanter, "The Vanishing Trial," 478.

16. Id., 480.

17. Id., 479.

18. Id., 480.

19. Id., 484.

20. Three Supreme Court cases decided in 1986 appeared to liberalize the doctrine surrounding the summary judgment device and gave the green light to district courts to grant summary judgment more often. See Arthur Miller, "The Pretrial Rush to Judgment: Are the 'Litigation Explosion,' 'Liability Crisis' and Efficiency Clichés Eroding Our Day in Court and Jury Trial Commitments?" *New York University Law Review* 78 (2003). Stephen Burbank has concluded, based on empirical evidence surrounding the time of the increase in summary judgments, that there appears to be no causal relationship between the liberalization of Supreme Court doctrine and the increase in summary judgment. Stephen Burbank, "Vanishing Trials and Summary Judgment in Federal Civil Cases,"620; both cited in Galanter, "The Vanishing Trial," 484–85.

21. Galanter, "The Vanishing Trial," 484.

22. Id.

23. Id., 485.

24. Id., 492–93.

25. Id., 495.

26. Id., 494, figure 24.

27. Galanter, "A World without Trials?" 9.

28. Galanter, "The Vanishing Trial," 507–8.

29. Id., 510.

30. Id., 512, table 7.

31. Id., 513, table 8.

32. Judith Resnik, "Whither and Whether Adjudication?" *Boston University Law Review* 86 (2006), 1122, 1126. Of course, if the Boston federal district court had experienced the same kind of decline that we have seen nationally, the numbers would by now be dramatically lower.

33. Galanter, "The Vanishing Trial," 521. He argues that these figures actually overstate the number of completed trials.

34. Id., 522–23.

35. Galanter, "A World without Trials?" 12.

36. Galanter, "The Vanishing Trial," 506.

37. White, *From Expectation to Experience*, 108.

38. Galanter, "The Vanishing Trial," 460.

39. Galanter, "A World without Trials?" 19.

40. For a general comparison of common law and civil law "trials," see Mirjan R. Damaska, *The Faces of Justice and State Authority: A Comparative Approach to the Legal Process* (New Haven: Yale University Press, 1986).

41. Galanter, "The Vanishing Trial," 525. Some of these documentary submissions are byzantine. To survive summary judgment under the permissible local rules in one district where I have practiced, a lawyer must submit a draft of a "Final Pretrial Order" to the defendant and then undertake a series of negotiations as to its contents. It will contain, inter alia, an "Agreed Statement of Undisputed Facts," "An Agreed Statement of Disputed Facts," "A Disputed Statement of Undisputed Facts," and "A Disputed Statement of Disputed Facts." It must likewise contain similar statements as to the law. The underlying rule of civil procedure requires sworn written statements to support each of the facts of which each party claims there is evidence. The latter can be in support either of a claim that there is no evidence to the contrary of the sworn fact, thus making the granting of summary judgment appropriate, or of a claim that there is such a dispute, rendering the summary judgment inappropriate. These documents are drafted by attorneys, not presented orally to the court by witnesses. This requires significant time and effort and often results in an artificial "carving" of the factual material in the case.

42. Id., 525–26.

43. Id., 526–27. Several sociologists found a similar pattern in child-support litigation.

44. The Social Security Disability System, which is probably the largest system of adjudication of any kind in the country, does not employ fully adversary proceedings. The federal government is not represented in opposition to the claimant, though it may be that this perversely leads some administrative law judges to take up the government's cause. See Jerry L. Mashaw, *Bureaucratic Justice: Managing Social Security Disability Claims* (New Haven: Yale University Press, 1983).

45. Galanter offers a provocative analogy to the fate of Rust Belt cities:

> Our displacement scenario suggests a picture of the legal system that resembles the familiar landscape of the older American city, with its declining core and its sprawl of flourishing suburbs. Taken as a whole, the metropolitan area grows, but the central city shrinks even though it is marked by ever grander towers. The central core is increasingly devoted to corporate and governmental use; its imposing towers are surrounded by decay and depopulation. Except for a remnant trapped by race or poverty, the inhabitants have fled to the periph-

ery, where they occupy an array of comfortable, but pedestrian tract
houses and undistinguished high-rises, with commerce dominated by
enclosed shopping malls, occupied by chain stores, and laced together
by freeways. The sprawl, fragmentation and dearth of public space
that characterize this urban prospect are matched by the legal landscape. In their imposing public structures, the core legal institutions
house big-time litigation and celebrity trials, but routine legal business thrives in the sprawling suburbs or private institutions and the
convenient malls of ADR. Linking all of these is a layer of media
representation of the legal, a rich stew of fictional and newsworthy
parties, lawyers, and courts, in which trials remain the central event.
There is the elaborated celebrity trial, the reassuring fiction of *Law
and Order*, and the capsulized version of Judge Judy. The thrust of this
media coverage is "a strong ideological message about law's ability to
achieve justice in our society.

Galanter, "A World without Trials?" 26–27. See Naomi Mezey & Mark C. Niles,
"Screening the Law: Ideology and Law in American Popular Culture," *Columbia
Journal of Law & the Arts* 28 (2005), 91; Jessica Silbey, "Patterns of Courtroom
Justice," *Journal of Law & Society* 28 (2001), 97.

46. Galanter, "The Vanishing Trial," 514.

47. Id., 515.

48. Id.

49. Id.

50. Stephan Landsman, "So What? Possible Implications of the Vanishing Trial
Phenomenon," *Journal of Empirical Legal Studies* 1 (2004), 980.

51. Judith Resnik, "Migrating, Morphing, and Vanishing: The Empirical and
Normative Puzzles of Declining Trial Rates in Courts," *Journal of Empirical Legal
Studies* 1 (2004), 814.

52. Id., 814. *Dean Witter Reynold, Inc. v. Byrd*, 470 U.S. 213 (1985).

53. Id., 815. Resnik describes cases that show how far the federal courts' deference has gone. In one the Eighth Circuit reversed a trial court determination refusing to honor an arbitration agreement in an unpaid overtime case. The agreement
shortened the statute of limitations, required employees to bear half the arbitration
costs and to conduct the arbitration in California regardless of where the employees
worked, and prohibited class-type relief. Id. Another court honored an employment
contract that provided that "biblically based mediation" was the "sole remedy" for
disputes. The Fifth Circuit ruled in another case that the inability of the employees
to read the arbitration contract didn't affect its enforceability. Id., 815–16.

54. It is roughly equivalent to the "displacement thesis" described above.

55. Resnik, "Migrating, Morphing, and Vanishing," 785.

56. Id., 791–804.

57. Galanter, "A World without Trials?" 27.

58. Id.

59. Johan Huizinga, *Homo Ludens: A Study in the Play Element in Culture* (Boston: Beacon Press, 1950), 10.

60. Restrictive rules on interlocutory (immediate) appellate review often make the judge's determination all but unreviewable. See, e.g., *Digital Equipment Corporation v. Desktop Direct, Inc.*, 511 U.S. 863 (1994).

61. Robert P. Burns, "The Enforceability of Mediated Agreements: An Essay on Legitimation and Process Integrity," *Ohio State Journal of Dispute Resolution* 2 (1986), 93.

62. Galanter, "A World without Trials?" 30.

63. Id., quoting Wolf Heydebrand, "Process Rationality as Legal Governance: A Comparative Perspective," *International Sociology* (2003), 325.

64. Galanter, "A World without Trials?" 31.

65. Id. See Rex Perschbacher & Debra Lyn Bassett, "The End of Law," *Boston University Law Review* 84 (2004), 60.

66. Galanter, "A World without Trials?" 31.

67. Id.

68. In the legal literature, it is associated with Carrie Menkel-Meadow. See Carrie Menkel-Meadow, "Is the Adversary System Really Dead? Dilemmas of Legal Ethics as Legal Institutions and Roles Evolve," in *Current Legal Problems*, vol. 57, Jane Holder, Colm O'Cinneide, & Michael D. A. Freeman eds. (Oxford: Oxford University Press, 2004), 85.

69. Id., 112.

70. Galanter, "A World without Trials?" 32.

71. Galanter, "The Vanishing Trial," 516.

72. Id. On the rationality of risk aversion on important matters see Rawls, *A Theory of Justice*, 154–56. Most individuals would consider all criminal charges, however "minor" to be "important" in this sense.

73. Milton I. Shadur, "Trials and Tribulations (Rule 56 Style)," *Litigation* 29 (2003), 5 (summary judgment can easily cost more than trial).

74. Landsman, "So What? Possible Implications," 980.

75. See Marc Galanter, "Reading the Landscape of Disputes: What We Know and Don't Know (and Think We Know) about Our Allegedly Contentious and Litigious Society," *UCLA Law Review* 31 (1983), 4; Galanter notes that as trials become fewer and more costly, it makes sense that the smaller cases are pushed out. See Gillian K. Hadfield, "The Price of Law: How the Market for Lawyers Distorts the Justice System," *Michigan Law Review* 98 (2000), 953; William Haltom & Michael McCann, *Distorting the Law: Politics, Media, and the Litigation Crisis* (Chicago: University of Chicago Press, 2004).

76. Galanter, "The Vanishing Trial," 518. See John Lande, "Failing Faith in Litigation? A Survey of Business Lawyers' and Executives' Opinions," *Harvard Negotiation Law Review* 3 (1998), 1. These beliefs may actually be held, though

they may serve simply to rationalize business-friendly policies in relation to the legal system. See Michael Orey, "How Business Trounced the Trial Lawyers," *Business Week*, Jan. 8, 2007, 44.

77. Galanter, "The Vanishing Trial," 518 n. 106.

78. Id.

79. Id., 518 n. 108.

80. It is true that most of those resources in the federal courts have gone not to increase the number of judges (which has doubled since 1962), but to other personnel, who could fairly be called administrative or even bureaucratic.

81. Id., 519.

82. Steven C. Yeazell, "The Misunderstood Consequences of Modern Civil Process," *Wisconsin Law Review* (1994), quoted in Galanter, "The Vanishing Trial," 519.

83. Galanter, "The Vanishing Trial," 519, quoting Gregory Kellam Scott, "Judge-Made Law: Constitutional Duties and Obligations under the Separation of Powers Doctrine," *DePaul Law Review* 49 (1999), 517. Galanter recounts the canonical version of this attitude in the trial courts, manifest in the following dialogue in a Kansas City lower court in the late nineteenth century:

> "Your Honor, you are overruling the Supreme Court," said the lawyer.
> "I do that every day, my friend; sit down," replied the justice, and his decision was recorded.

"The Vanishing Trial," 519, quoting "Facitiae," *Green Bag* 11 (1899), 599. This view is entrenched in legal lore around the country. I have heard it attributed to a state court judge in one of the branch courts in the southern suburbs of Chicago. For an example of a trial judge (who had been reversed on his initial ruling dismissing a slander action against Diana Ross) making a number of discretionary determinations on discovery issues that could well have doomed the case, see *Davis v. Ross*, 107 F.R.D. 326 (S.D.N.Y. 1985).

84. Galanter, "The Vanishing Trial," 5.

85. Resnik, "Migrating, Morphing, and Vanishing," 831 n. 234.

86. Id., 811.

87. Hubert L. Will, Robert R. Merhige, Jr., & Alvin B. Rubin, "The Role of the Judge in the Settlement Process," 75 F.R.D. 203, 203 (1978).

88. See pp. 101–8 herein.

89. Galanter, "A World without Trials?" 20–21.

90. Galanter, "The Vanishing Trial," 522. These days the National Institute for Trial Advocacy often finds it easier to fill its deposition practice programs than its trial advocacy programs.

91. AO Judicial Business Report 2002, 23–24, cited in Resnik, "Migrating, Morphing, and Vanishing," 834.

92. In the system, jury commissioners followed the recommendations of locally

influential "key men" in identifying potential jurors "of recognized intelligence and probity."

93. See MacIntyre, *After Virtue* (discussing the contrast between traditional moral evaluation and modern expertise, often based on applied social science, whose natural home is in bureaucratic organizations).

94. See M. David Ermann & Richard J. Lundman eds., *Corporate and Governmental Deviance: Problems of Organizational Behavior in Contemporary Society*, 6th ed. (Oxford: Oxford University Press, 2002).

95. Stephan Landsman, "Appellate Courts and Civil Juries," *University of Cinncinnati Law Review* 70 (2000), 881.

96. See Galanter's analogy of the structure of contemporary litigation to an American Rust Belt city in n. 45 above.

97. Galanter, "The Vanishing Trial," 501.

98. Id.

99. Id.

100. Id., 487.

101. Id., 488–91. The JPML was created to address the administration of over 2,000 antitrust actions filed against heavy electric equipment manufacturers in the early 1960s. Of those cases, only nine went to trial and only five to judgment. Id., 488–89.

102. George Fisher, *Plea Bargaining's Triumph: A History of Plea Bargaining in America* (Stanford: Stanford University Press, 2003).

103. Id., 90.

104. Id., 114 ff. Foster rejects Langbein's suggestion that plea bargaining flourished because trials were becoming unsupportively complex and expensive.

105. Id., 123.

106. Id., 129.

107. Id., 133. "There can be little doubt that the plea-withdrawal rule has contributed to the extraordinary dominance of plea bargaining in the modern American courtrooms, where the guilty plea rates above ninety or even ninety-five percent are common." Id., 134.

108. Id., 153.

109. Id., 175.

110. Id., 176.

111. Id., 194. When indeterminate sentencing (and so the judge's inability to reliably promise a given term) threatened plea bargaining, ingenious methods were found first to evade those consequences and then to eliminate indeterminate sentencing.

112. Id., 202.

113. In 2005 the Supreme Court held, in a badly split decision, that its own constitutional jurisprudence on the role of the jury in sentencing mandated that the

sentencing guidelines could only be guidelines and could not absolutely bind the sentencing judge. It seems that most judges continue to follow them fairly closely. *United States v. Booker*, 543 U.S. 220 (2005).

114. Id., 225.

115. Id., 230.

116. I argue for the lawfulness of the trial in Robert P. Burns, "The Lawfulness of the American Trial," *American Criminal Law Review* 38 (2001), 205, and Burns, "The Rule of Law in the Trial Court," *DePaul Law Review* 56 (2007), 307.

117. Some such distinction seems inevitable for us. The philosophers John Dewey and Alasdair MacIntyre, otherwise quite different, employ a distinction between healthy practices from which we can derive vital ideals, and the more or less corrupt institutions within which they are embedded.

118. Dwyer, *In the Hands of the People*, 112. Dwyer finds them analogous to six of the seven deadly sins, which may, as he notes, mean that they can never fully be avoided.

119. Id., 115.

120. Id.

121. The "adversary" trial is not just a single thing. The contemporary trial, for example, is balanced with a number of nonadversary features, such as the ethical obligations on lawyers not knowingly to present plausible but false testimony and various levels of obligation to share information through the discovery process. For an argument from a scholar who has a high regard for adversary proceedings that such nonadversary methods are growing in the criminal trial, see Darryl K. Brown, "The Decline of Defense Counsel and the Rise of Accuracy in Criminal Adjudication," *California Law Review* 93 (2005), 1585.

122. See D. Michael Risinger, "Unsafe Verdicts: The Need for Reformed Standards for the Trial and Review of Factual Innocence Claims," *Houston Law Review* 41 (2001), 1281 (stressing the special importance of this range of cases).

123. It is not, I believe, accidental, that we have inadequate discovery in criminal cases and often overblown discovery in civil cases. As Stephen Yeazell has pointed out, we have effectively socialized criminal prosecution and defense while we have privatized civil practice. We effectively starve the public sector, while allowing the market to prevail in the civil context to the benefit of the clients who can pay for civil legal services. On the connection between liberal discovery and the advent of the ubiquitous billable hour, see George B. Shepherd & Morgan Cloud, "Time and Money: Discovery Leads to Hourly Billing," *University of Illinois Law Review* (1999), 91.

124. Quoted in Samuel R. Gross & Barbara O'Brien, "Frequency and Predictors of False Conviction: Why We Know So Little, and New Data on Capital Cases," University of Michigan Public Law Working Paper No. 93 (2007), http://SSRN .com/abstract=1018458.

125. Death penalty cases tend to receive very high levels of post-conviction scrutiny, and rape cases often have the benefit of DNA evidence.

126. Gross & O'Brien, 13–15.

127. Brian Forst, *Errors of Justice: Nature, Sources, and Remedies* (Cambridge: Cambridge University Press, 2004), 89. The problem is intensified by the lack of any kind of deposition practice in most criminal cases in which the witness could be asked about the procedures employed. See Robert P. Burns, "A Wistful Retrospective on Wigmore and his Prescriptions for Illinois Evidence Law," *Northwestern University Law Review* 100 (2007), 141–43.

128. Most glaringly, "[i]n the past decade several systematic programs of police perjury have been uncovered, which ultimately led to exonerations of at least 135 innocent defendants who had been framed for illegal possession of drugs or guns in Los Angeles, in Dallas, and in Tulia, Texas." Forst, *Errors of Justice*, 4.

129. Id., 17.

130. Steven A. Drizin & Richard A. Leo, "The Problem of False Confessions in the Post-DNA World," *North Carolina Law Review* 82 (2004), 891.

131. Forst, *Errors of Justice*, 199.

132. Dwyer describes a libel case in which plaintiff's counsel had not rested his case after four months of trial, leading to a juror "rebellion" and the declaration of a mistrial. *In the Hands of the People*, 120–21.

133. Shari Seidman Diamond, "Jury Room Ruminations on Forbidden Topics," *Virginia Law Review* 87 (2001), 1857 (withholding information can lead to jury speculation that is often wrong).

134. Such time limits are again far more effective and democratic devices for the focusing of trials than the "micromanaging" of evidence through exclusionary rules.

135. Dwyer, *In the Hands of the People*, 125.

136. Reznick, "Migrating, Morphing, and Vanishing," 786.

137. Langbein, *The Origins of Adversary Criminal Trial*, 332–33.

138. Id., 333.

139. Continental systems do not really have "trials" in the American sense— once-and-for-all presentations of all the evidence on each side of a case. Rather, the judge has the authority to adjourn the formal proceedings and conduct further investigations. It is a *Prozess*, to use the title of Kafka's often mistranslated classic.

140. Ball, *Lying Down Together*, 132. Ball is at pains to reject "battle" metaphors for litigation.

141. See, e.g., Kuo-Chang Huang, *Introducing Discovery into Civil Law* (Durham: Caroline Academic Press, 2003) ("alleging that civil law regimes typically under-investigate claims because judges, who control the investigatory phase, lack incentives to probe deeply"), quoted in Stephen C. Yeazell, "Socializing

Law, Privatizing Law, Monopolizing Law, Accessing Law," *Loyola Law Review* 39 (2006), 701. Yeazell argues that allowing parties to conduct discovery directly "allows litigants to probe facts and uncover uncomfortable truths that state officials might be reluctant to dirty their hands with." Id. For an account of situations where litigation has unearthed sometimes lethal wrongdoing that was effectively concealed from government regulators, see Bogus, *Why Lawsuits Are Good for America*, 138–72.

142. Charles Taylor, "Interpretation and the Sciences of Man," *Review of Metaphysics* 25 (1971), 27.

143. See, e.g., David L. Hull, *Science and Selection: Essays on Biological Evolution and the Philosophy of Science* (Cambridge: Cambridge University Press, 2001) (employing metaphors of natural selection to explain scientific progress); Dewey noted the differences in "Logical Method and the Law."

144. American Bar Association, *Principles for Juries and Jury Trials*, Stephan Landsman, reporter ([St. Paul, MN]: Thomson West, 2005). The U.S. Court of Appeals for the Seventh Circuit has initiated a pilot project to test some of the committee's recommendations.

145. Judge Dwyer offers this example from Nevada's attempted murder instruction:

> It is not essential that the willful intent, premeditation or deliberation, shall exist in the mind of the defendant for any considerable length of time before the actual perpetration of the crime. It is sufficient if there was a fixed design or determination to maliciously kill distinctly framed in the mind of the defendant before the shots were fired.

He suggests that what this amounts to is:

> The state does not have to prove that the defendant planned for a long time to kill the other person. It is enough if he intended to kill him and fired the shots for that purpose.

No one can object to the Standards' insistence that the trial court provide instructions to the jury "in plain and understandable language." So it may seem mere cavil to wonder whether they may manifest an undue optimism about what is possible in this regard and whether that optimism overestimates the role of the "law of rules" in the American jury trial. On the question of possibility, for example, consider Standard 6 C. 1. It mandates that the court give preliminary instructions "that explain the jury's role, the trial procedures including note-taking and questioning by jurors, the nature of evidence and its evaluation, the issues to be addressed, and the basic relevant legal principles, including the elements of the charges and claims and definitions of unfamiliar legal terms." For some cases, I have a hard time imagining instructions that answer all those questions in plain language that is fair to the law. I am not sure whether such a disquisition at the beginning of the trial will really improve the level of trial decision making. Recall Louis Nizer's views:

Although jurors are extraordinarily right in their conclusion, it is usually based upon common sense "instincts" about right and wrong, and
not on sophisticated evaluations of complicated testimony. On the
other hand, a Judge trying a case without a jury, may believe that
his decision is based on refined weighing of the evidence; but ... he,
too, has an over-all, almost compulsive "feeling" about who is right
and who is wrong and then supports his conclusion with legal technology. Because Judges, sometimes, consciously reject this layman's
approach of who is right or wrong and restrict themselves to precise
legal weights, they come out wrong more often than the juries.

Nizer's view, supported in some ways by some good social-scientific investigation,
should make us wary of encouraging juries to attempt to make "legal technology"
too central a part of their decision making. (Of course, the law of rules has and
should have an important place in the jury trial; the issue concerns the appropriate
balance of that law with other "moral sources.")

146. Others have gone further and recommended the end of the peremptory
challenge.

147. Abramson, *We, the Jury*, 247–50.

148. This is a very difficult question, and one must wonder whether it is too
difficult to resolve at the national level. I give only the briefest summary of the
debate here. The ABA Standards provide a very broad range of situations where
challenges for cause should be permitted: "At a minimum, a challenge for cause to
a juror should be sustained if the juror has an interest in the outcome of the case,
may be biased for or against one of the parties, is not qualified by law to serve on a
jury, has a familial relation to a participant in the trial, or may be unwilling to hear
the subject case fairly and impartially." They provide as well that there should be
no limit to challenges for cause and that a juror should be removed even if there
is "reasonable doubt" that the juror may be fair and impartial. With such robust
provisions for challenges for cause, why do they need to be supplemented by peremptory challenges? The answer that has prevailed in all American jurisdictions
and is very well articulated in the Comments to the Standards, is that they allow
for strikes when it is difficult to articulate an intuited basis for the strike, allow
the elimination of outlying levels of partiality, and protect against judicial error
especially where voir dire is conducted in a very compressed manner. Generally,
the peremptory is a protection against a judge who does not rule on challenges for
cause in a fair-minded way. No liberalization of challenges for cause can circum-
vent the judge's crucial role in ruling on them. Peremptory challenges have been
under fire because of the perception by jurors successfully challenged, and those
who have "survived," that this part of the trial expresses an excessively adversary
culture (striking the most knowledgeable jurors, for example) and because of the
practices occasioned by *Batson* and its progeny. The Standards deal with the *Bat-*

*son* issue in a manner consistent with existing law. (This includes the unhelpful burden-shifting language, in my view.) Under *Batson*, lawyers exercising peremptories to strike jurors in suspect classes are required to articulate a "nondiscriminatory basis" for the challenge. To reject the challenge, the court must find the tendered reason "pretextual." Put bluntly, the court must find that the lawyer, who is ethically bound not to make any misrepresentation of fact to the court, has lied about his motive in making the strike. When this occurs the strike is not allowed (and the lawyer is never, as far as I know, referred for disciplinary action). Some believe that the practice of some law offices is systematically to flout this system by a usually successful hunt for pretextual grounds for discriminatory strikes and that judges, for a variety of reasons, are unable or unwilling to find that lawyers who often practice before them are lying. This has led some commentators to suggest that we are better off without the peremptory in the post-*Batson* world. (Of course, one may wonder whether the same issues may resurface in the context of rulings for cause, but there the inquiry is focused on the likelihood of bias by the juror rather than the motivations of a partisan advocate for making the peremptory strike.)

149. Robert P. Burns, "Notes on the Future of Evidence Law," *Temple Law Review* 74 (2001), 69.

150. *United States v. Shonubi*, 895 F. Supp. 460, 493 (E.D.N.Y. 1995) (Weinstein, J.). See also Peter W. Murphy, "Some Reflections on Evidence and Proof," *South Texas Law Review* 40 (1999), 327.

151. *Michelson v. United States*, 335 U.S. 469, 485–86 (1948).

## Chapter Five

1. Friedman, "The Day before Trials Vanished," 697.

2. See, e.g., Marc Galanter, "The Turn against Law: The Recoil against Expanding Accountability," *Texas Law Review* 81 (2002), 285.

3. Kalven & Zeisel, *The American Jury*, 270, 293, 305, 319, 338. Burns, *A Theory of the Trial*, 147 n. 87.

4. See p. 11 herein.

5. This injection of "equitable" considerations usually happens in an extremely contextual, case-by-case manner. But sometimes the equitable reconsideration of the law of rules turns out to be more systematic. An end to the trial would mean the end to this integration of commonsense norms into the legal structure, as in the case of our experience with the contributory negligence doctrine described herein at pp. 60–62.

6. Paul Butler, "The Case for Trials: Considering the Intangibles," *Journal of Empirical Legal Studies* 1 (2004), 634.

7. The philosopher Stuart Hampshire discusses how important Hart's attitude was to his own philosophy in *Justice Is Conflict*, 8–9, 79–98. In Terence Anderson & William Twining, *Analysis of Evidence: How to Do Things with Facts Based on Wigmore's "Science of Judicial Proof"* (Boston: Little, Brown, 1991), 41–44, the authors offer a delightful hypothetical murder investigation that demonstrates how just one additional fact can completely change the meaning of all the prior evidence.

8. My arguments with the law of evidence are set out in Robert P. Burns, "Notes on the Principles of Evidence Law," *Temple Law Review* 74 (2001), 69.

9. I say "American" skepticism, but, of course, this is a conviction with roots deep in the same Western tradition of which the founders were very much aware. Gordon Wood, *The Creation of the American Republic, 1776–1787* (Chapel Hill: University of North Carolina Press, 1969). Recall Plato's argument that the skills of gaining power and those of ruling wisely were discontinuous, and Augustine's sharp divide between the cities built by charity and those built by the *libido dominandi*, that is, all earthly cities, even the best.

10. Arendt, "Truth and Politics," 236.

11. Carr, *Time, Narrative, and History*, 50, 61.

12. Arendt, *Men in Dark Times*, 22.

13. David Luban, "Explaining Dark Times: Hannah Arendt's Theory of Theory," in *Hannah Arendt: Critical Essays*, Lewis P. Hinchman & Sandra K. Hinchman eds. (Albany: State University of New York Press, 1994), 97.

14. Milner Ball, *Called by Stories* (Durham: Duke University Press, 2000). By "apperception," Ball means "the uniquely human capacity to know something without knowing how one has come to know it, and to bring what one knows in this way to what one knows in other ways, and in so doing, to discern what is humanly true or false." Id., 3.

15. Id.

16. Milner S. Ball, *The Word and the Law* (Chicago: University of Chicago Press, 1993), 207 n. 42.

17. Robert A. Kagan criticizes this approach in favor of authority and *in*formality in *Adversarial Legalism: The American Way of Law* (Cambridge, MA: Harvard University Press, 2001). For precisely the opposing view, one with which I obviously have much more sympathy, stressing the importance of autonomy and formality, see Ball, *The Promise of American Law* (the importance of protecting the individual through formality and "the masks of the law" from state power). William T. Pizzi analogizes the American combination of autonomy and formality with American football in *Trials without Truth: Why Our System of Criminal Trials Has Become an Expensive Failure and What We Need to Do to Rebuild It* (New York: New York University Press, 1999), 5–24.

18. See pp. 116–17 herein. I attempted to address the philosophical question of how such comparative judgments could be made at all in Burns, "A Response to Four Readings," 565–66.

19. Peter Bal, "Discourse Ethics and Human Rights in Criminal Procedure," in *Habermas, Modernity and Law*, Mathieu Deflem ed. (London: Sage, 1996), 81. His conclusion that continental procedure can be coercive is the result of his own empirical investigation of transcripts in criminal cases. Peter Bal, *Dwangkommunikatie in de Rechtzaal* (Arnhem: Gouda Quint, 1988).

20. See *Republican Party of Minnesota v. White*, 536 U.S. 765 (2002).

21. See, e.g., Akhil R. Amar, *The Bill of Rights: Creation and Reconstruction* (New Haven: Yale University Press, 1998), 98–104; Bogus, *Why Lawsuits Are Good for America*; Wolfram, "The Constitutional History of the Seventh Amendment"; Marder, "The Myth of the Nullifying Jury"; Landsman, "The Civil Jury in America"; Burns, "The History and Theory of the American Jury"; Harrington, "The Law–Finding Function of the American Jury."

22. Hampshire, *Justice Is Conflict*.

23. Damaška, *The Faces of Justice and State Authority*.

24. It is true that there is no one "adversary system." Although the American system is generally the most adversarial, that does not mean that we have not incorporated various aspects of inquisitorial systems within our practice, nor that we should not. As I note above, it simply counsels caution. For an interesting set of proposals to increase accuracy in criminal adjudication by a scholar who appreciates the power of adversary presentation, see Darryl K. Brown, "The Decline of Defense Counsel and the Rise of Accuracy in Criminal Adjudication," *California Law Review* 93 (2005).

25. See, e.g., Robert M. Cover, *Justice Accused: Antislavery and the Judicial Process* (New Haven: Yale University Press, 1975); Horwitz, *The Transformation of American Law*; William Nelson, *Americanization of the Common Law: The Impact of Legal Change on Massachusetts Society, 1760–1830* (Athens: University of Georgia Press, 1994). For a fine jurisprudential reflection on the limits of the law of rules' claim to be "law," see Marianne Constable, "Laying Aside the Law: The Silences of Presumptive Positivism," in *Essays in Honor of Frederick Schauer*, Linda Meyer ed. (Oxford: Hart, 1999), 61–78.

26. Lon L. Fuller, "The Forms and Limits of Adjudication," *Harvard Law Review* 92 (1978), 353.

27. This is a point that James Boyd White has consistently and eloquently made; see White, *From Expectation to Experience*. It also means that criticism of the trial, especially the jury trial, for producing inconsistent results will often be hard to evaluate. Usually that criticism vastly underestimates the significance and the importance of variations in the factual contexts from case to case and overestimates the ease with which we can have one size fit all.

28. Richard K. Sherwin, "Law, Metaphysics, and the New Iconoclasm," http://ssrn.com/sol3/papers.cfm?abstract_id=1004361.

29. Stephan Landsman, "Appellate Courts and Civil Juries," *University of Cincinnati Law Review* 70 (2002), 875.

30. Abramson, *We, the Jury*, 2.

31. Landsman, "So What? Possible Implications," 974.

32. Id.

33. Abramson has emphasized the importance of the distinction between diversity of perspective and diversity of interest. *We, the Jury*, 115–27. It is still true that few juries hang, a fact that suggests that our level of fragmentation decreases when we carefully consider specific facts rather than clichés and abstractions. Id., 198.

34. *Federalist No. 83*.

35. Landsman, "So What? Possible Implications," 975.

36. Id., 983.

37. Tocqueville, *Democracy in America*, 1:295.

38. Butler, "The Case for Trials," 622–24.

39. He takes a self-consciously Weberian position that these determinations are "irrational" because they cannot be "reduced to a formula, a proposition, and algorithm" and certainly cannot be "predicted or accounted or logically or deducted [*sic*: deduced] from legal principles." Friedman, "The Day before Trials Vanished," 698. The deeper question is whether "right answers" are reducible to the methods that Friedman identifies.

40. Id.

41. Id., 699.

42. Landsman, "So What? Possible Implications," 974.

43. Id., quoting Tocqueville, *Democracy in America*, 1:293.

44. *U.S. v. Shonubi*, 895 F. Supp 460, 493 (1995) (Weinstein, J.) (on the sophistication of American juries and the reduced need for paternalistic expedients); Murphy, "Some Reflections on Evidence and Proof," *South Texas Law Review* 40 (1999), 328 (faith in the "maturity and reasoning powers" of juries is well justified).

45. William Blackstone, *Commentaries on the Laws of England* (1768; Chicago: University of Chicago Press, 1979), 3:379.

46. Landsman, "So What? Possible Implications," 980. A bad judge can refuse to see the significance of the details that the trial reveals, but trial makes it harder for him to do that.

47. Id.

48. See pp. 123–26 herein.

49. Adriaan T. Peperzak, preface to *Emmanuel Levinas: Basic Philosophical Writings*, Adriaan T. Peperzak, Simon Critchley, & Robert Bernasconi eds. (Bloomington: Indiana University Press, 1996).

50. Sherwin, "Law, Metaphysics, and the New Iconoclasm," 21.

51. Id., 11.

52. Burbank, "Vanishing Trials and Summary Judgment in Federal Civil Cases," 622.

53. Qualified immunity is the defense to a civil rights claim that asserts that the

plaintiff's right, though legally valid, was not "clearly established" at the time of the claimed injury, and so the defendant is not liable for damages. The Supreme Court has taken two important steps to reduce the percentage of such cases that go to trial. First, the Court made the question an "objective" question of law and determined that the defendant's sincerity or motivation was irrelevant. Second, the Court made the defense one of the very few from an adverse ruling on which the defendant could successfully seek an "interlocutory appeal," that is, an appeal before a final judgment after trial. *See Nixon v. Fitzgerald,* 457 U.S. 731 (1982); *Mitchell v. Forsyth,* 472 U.S. 511 (1985).

54. "Federal jurisprudence is largely the product of summary judgment in civil cases." Patricia M. Wald, "Summary Judgment at Sixty," *Texas Law Review* 76 (1998), 1897.

55. Burbank, "Vanishing Trials and Summary Judgment in Federal Civil Cases," 626.

56. Marshall McLuhan, *Understanding Media: The Extensions of Man* (New York: McGraw-Hill, 1964), 241.

57. Bernard Hibbitts, "Making Sense of Metaphors: Visuality, Aurality, and the Reconfiguration of American Legal Discourse," *Cardozo Law Review* 16 (1994), 344, quoting Julian Jaynes, *The Origin of Consciousness in the Breakdown of the Bicameral Mind* (Boston: Houghton Mifflin, 1976), 96.

58. Beiner, *Political Judgment,* 102.

59. Michael Polanyi, *Personal Knowledge: Towards a Post-Critical Philosophy* (Chicago: University of Chicago Press, 1974).

60. D. C. Schindler, *Hans Urs von Balthasar and the Dramatic Structure of Truth: A Philosophical Investigation* (New York: Fordham University Press, 2004), 17.

61. Id., 22.

62. Eric Bentley, *The Theatre of Commitment, and Other Essays on Drama in Our Society* (New York: Atheneum, 1967), 207, quoted in Ball, *The Promise of American Law,* 58.

63. See Robert P. Burns, "The Distinctiveness of Trial Narrative," in *The Trial on Trial: Truth and Due Process* (Oxford: Hart, 2004), 167–69.

64. Nussbaum, *The Fragility of Goodness,* 390.

65. Butler, "The Case for Trials," 629.

66. Ball, *The Promise of American Law,* 58–62.

67. Arendt, "Truth and Politics," 259–64.

68. Galanter, "A World without Trials?" 33.

69. Langbein, *The Origins of Adversary Criminal Trial,* 253–55.

70. *Michelson v. United States,* 335 U.S. 469, 485–86 (1948) (discussing evidentiary rules).

71. Bernhard Peters, "On Reconstructive Legal and Political Theory," in Deflem ed., *Habermas, Modernity, and Law,* 121.

72. Id., 122.

73. Id., 111.

74. Bogus, *Why Lawsuits Are Good for America*, 135.

75. Arendt, *On Revolution*, 196.

76. See Haltom & McCann, *Distorting the Law*.

77. Rawls, *A Theory of Justice*, 7. The basic structure is "the way in which the major social institutions distribute fundamental rights and duties and determine the division of social cooperation."

78. Arendt, *On Revolution*, 194.

79. Kolb, *Critique of Pure Modernity*, 259.

80. Lillquist, "Recasting Reasonable Doubt," 85.

81. Andrew E. Taslitz, "Temporal Adversarialism, Criminal Justice, and the Rehnquist Court: The Sluggish Life of Political Factfinding," *Georgetown Law Journal* 94 (2006), 1603–6.

82. Marder, "The Myth of the Nullifying Jury," 910.

83. Id., 918.

84. Roberto Unger notes that the combination of bureaucratic and formalistic understandings of law was a product of the nineteenth century, and that combination produced what we know as a "legal system." Formalism added the ideals of generality and consistency to older bureaucratic methods. Roberto Mangabeira Unger, *Law in Modern Society: Toward a Criticism of Social Theory* (New York: Free Press, 1976): 45–55. On formal justice, see Rawls, *A Theory of Justice*, 235–43.

85. Mashaw, *Bureaucratic Justice*, 26. Rules enable a ruler to communicate abstract features of his will to an army of enforcers, but the rule of law can then take on a momentum of its own because of its internal ideals.

86. White, *From Between Expectation and Experience*, 88.

87. It is no accident then that Hannah Arendt classically described bureaucratic modes of social ordering as "rule by nobody." Our selves are constituted by the moral judgments we make. Taylor, *Sources of the Self*, 25–52. Concretely, in avoiding the description of the case before him in any languages other than that supplied by the rules, and in particular avoiding simple everyday language, the bureaucrat is bracketing his moral self. At an extreme, he will find himself speaking in Orwellian terms with Kafkaesque results.

88. Weber was shocked by precisely this vision of modernity: "[N]umbing bureaucracy administering a society regulated only by considerations of performance and efficiency, the domination of capital, and the conversion of all human relations and culture into commodities, a world of enforced conformity and superficial variety." Kolb, *Critique of Pure Modernity*, 258.

89. There is a long history of argument, fought out in legal doctrine, about what kinds of issues can be addressed administratively, either through informal action

or agency adjudication, and which must be adjudicated in a civil court and, if the latter, by jury trial. Both the natural rights and the republican traditions are in play in this argument as a limitation on instrumental rationality. See, e.g., *NLRB v. Jones and Laughlin Steel Corp.*, 301 U.S. 1 (1937); *Atlas Roofing Co., Inc. v. OSHA*, 430 U.S. 442 (1977).

90. I make a start at Robert P. Burns, "The Distinctiveness of Trial Narrative," in *The Trial on Trial: Truth and Due Process*, Antony Duff et al. eds. (Oxford: Hart, 2004), 167–69.

91. On the notion of norms actually embedded in social practices, see Taylor, "Interpretation and the Sciences of Man."

92. See, e.g., Jeffrey A. Segal & Harold J. Spaeth, *The Supreme Court and the Attitudinal Model Revisited* (Cambridge: Cambridge University Press, 2002); Theodore W. Ruger et al., "The Supreme Court Forecasting Project: Legal and Political Science Approaches to Predicting Supreme Court Decisionmaking," *Columbia Law Review* 104 (2004), 1150.

93. These are many, many judges ("We are all realists now."). Many of them read Karl Llewellyn's *The Bramble Bush* in law school. The book celebrated the plasticity of legal materials in the hands of a really intelligent judge, Posner's "really skillful legal analyst." *The Bramble Bush: On Our Law and Its Study* (New York: Oceana Publications, 1981).

94. Mirjan Damaška, "Structures of Authority and Comparative Criminal Procedure," *Yale Law Journal* 84 (1975), 528.

95. Richard Posner & Philip B. Heyman, "A TNR Online Debate: Tap Dancing." *New Republic* Online, Jan. 31, 2006, http://ssl.tnr.com/p/docsub.mhtml?i=w06013 08&s=hymannposner013106, quoted in Brian Tamanaha, "How an Instrumental View of Law Corrodes the Rule of Law," *DePaul Law Review* 56 (2007).

96. Richard A. Posner, "Foreword: A Political Court," *Harvard Law Review* 119 (2005), 52, 48.

97. Sherwin, "Law, Metaphysics, and the New Iconoclasm," 10.

98. Id.

99. Morgan Cloud, "Yugoslavia," *Green Bag* (1999), 351 (the close relationship between illegitimacy and the absence of public institutions in which there is confidence).

100. Resnik, "Migrating, Morphing, and Vanishing," 830.

101. Id., 831. See Judith Resnik, "Due Process: A Public Dimension," *University of Florida Law Review* 39 (1987), 405.

102. Resnik, "Migrating, Morphing, and Vanishing," 831 n. 234.

103. Mark Curriden, "Up in Smoke: How Greed, Hubris and High-Stakes Lobbying Laid Waste to the $246 Billion Tobacco Settlement," *ABA Journal* (March 2007), 29. Curriden notes that "obscene" amounts of money were recovered by the plaintiffs' bar in the tobacco cases.

104. *Offut v. United* States, 348 U.S. 11, 14 (1954); cited in Landsman, "So What? Possible Implications," 976.

105. *Offut v. United* States, 348 U.S. 11, 14 (1954).

106. Landsman, "So What? Possible Implications," 976, quoting the classic study on perceptions of legitimacy, John W. Thibaut & Laurens Walker, *Procedural Justice: A Psychological Analysis* (Hillsdale, NJ: Erlbaum, 1975).

107. *Oxnard Publishing Co. v. Superior Court,* 68 Cal Rptr. 83, 95 (2nd Dist. 1968), quoted in Ball, *The Promise of American Law*, 46.

108. Id.

109. *Detroit Free Press v. Ashcroft*, 303 F.3d 681, 683 (6th Cir. 2002).

110. Robert M. Ackerman, "Vanishing Trial, Vanishing Community? The Potential Effect of the Vanishing Trial on America's Social Capital," *Journal of Dispute Resolution* (2006), 166–69.

111. Id., 630.

112. Landsman, "So What? Possible Implications," 976. Landsman emphasizes the importance of simple factual truth in, ironically, one of the tort reformers' favorite canards: the multimillion dollar award for burns a woman suffered from a cup of McDonald's coffee. The record disclosed that the plaintiff's "injury was just one of several hundred coffee-related injuries suffered by McDonald's patrons, and that Mrs. Liebeck had to spend seven days in the hospital, that she had multiple skin grafts, and that McDonalds's coffee was served at least 20 degrees hotter than anyone else's in the food industry." Id.

113. Edward W. Knappman, Stephen G. Christianson, & Lisa Olson Paddock, eds., *Great American Trials: From Salem Witchcraft to Rodney King* (Detroit: Visible Ink Press, 1994).

114. Id., 255.

115. Id., 251, 273, 194, 209.

116. Id., 288, 441, 612.

117. Id., 635.

118. Galanter, "A World without Trials?" 12.

# Index